WITH THE WITNESSES

With the Witnesses

Poetry, Compassion, and Claimed Experience

DALE TRACY

McGill-Queen's University Press

Montreal & Kingston • London • Chicago

ISBN 978-0-7735-5027-8 (cloth)
ISBN 978-0-7735-5028-5 (paper)
ISBN 978-0-7735-5029-2 (ePDF)
ISBN 978-0-7735-5030-8 (ePUB)

Legal deposit second quarter 2017
Bibliothèque nationale du Québec

Printed in Canada on acid-free paper that is 100% ancient forest
free (100% post-consumer recycled), processed chlorine free

This book has been published with the help of a grant from the
Royal Military College of Canada. Funding was also received from the Queen's
University Fund for Scholarly Research and Creative Work and Professional
Development (Adjuncts).

McGill-Queen's University Press acknowledges the support of the
Canada Council for the Arts for our publishing program. We also
acknowledge the financial support of the Government of Canada
through the Canada Book Fund for our publishing activities.

Library and Archives Canada Cataloguing in Publication

Tracy, Dale, 1984–, author
With the witnesses : poetry, compassion, and claimed experience / Dale Tracy.

Includes bibliographical references and index.
Issued in print and electronic formats.
ISBN 978-0-7735-5027-8 (cloth). – ISBN 978-0-7735-5028-5 (paper). –
ISBN 978-0-7735-5029-2 (ePDF). – ISBN 978-0-7735-5030-8 (ePUB)

1. Poetry – 20th century – History and criticism. 2. Memory in literature.
3. Witnesses in literature. 4. Suffering in literature. 5. Psychic trauma in literature.
6. Self-disclosure in literature. I. Title.

PN1083.M4T73 2017   809.1'9353   C2017-900946-X
C2017-900947-8

This book was typeset in Sabon.

Contents

Acknowledgments

I first encountered the idea of witness in a course that I took at Carleton University for my master's degree. Brenda Vellino's "The Proxy Witness in Twentieth-Century Human Rights Poetry" challenged me; it introduced me to poems that initially I did not want to think about again once the course was over. I had found engaging with histories of injustice through the kind of reading that poetry requires – closely holding each word, lingering over the sounds and rhythms of, here, accounts of suffering – particularly difficult. I read these poems in as much isolation from the rest of my life as I could manage, and, when the course ended, I boxed up the books and put them in a closet until the expected scenario occurred: the thing put in some inconvenient, shut-off space will be needed again. This rule seems to work as much for mental spaces as for physical ones. I found myself returning to the box and ideas often enough that I moved the poetry onto its own bookshelf, then onto a shelf at a more convenient height, and finally onto my desk. I returned to the texts because they upset me, and what prolonged study has taught me is that whatever is most genuinely upsetting to me is the project I'll need, eventually, to take on. If self-reflection is the foundation to any scholarly work I can do, and I think it is, I can't do responsible scholarly work while avoiding what strikes me deeply.

So I would like to thank Dr Vellino for introducing me to some of the poems I study in this book. In her course I became acquainted with Peter Balakian's writing as witness poetry. Although in this book I do not consider their collections within the framework of proxy witness, I also came to a few of Seamus Heaney's poems, Dionne Brand's *Inventory*, Rachel Tzvia Back's *On Ruins and Return*, and Adrienne Rich's *An Atlas of the Difficult World* in this course.

My gratitude goes to Michael Snediker and Sylvia Söderlind for their sensitive and careful guidance as my supervisory team when this book began in my dissertation. Early in the project, Sylvia's comments helped me learn about how my own mind works. This insight has had many effects, but, most tangibly, I was able to affirm a less dominating relationship with the semicolon. In her role as my external examiner, Leslie Sanders provided supportive and intellectually stimulating comments that kept serving me throughout my revision process.

Thank you to Asha Varadharajan for her help with the process of preparing a manuscript. Her advice was valuable and her care was fortifying. Thanks as well to Holly McIndoe and Jeffrey Weingarten for offering clear-sighted comments as readers of some early materials.

I am grateful to McGill-Queen's University Press for the support and attention during this process, and my special thanks go to Mark Abley for his perceptiveness and patience. This book is stronger thanks to its anonymous reviewers, and I appreciate their thoughtful reading and the time it took them.

I would like to acknowledge the support of the Fund for Scholarly Research and Creative Work and Professional Development (Adjuncts) from Queen's University and of the Department of English at the Royal Military College of Canada. I would also like to thank my colleagues in the Department of English at RMC for creating the heartwarmingly supportive environment I have spent much of my time in as I worked on this book. My doctoral work was supported by Ontario Graduate Scholarships, William C. Leggett Graduate Fellowships, Queen's Graduate Awards, and the Social Sciences and Humanities Research Council. Some of my work for this book has appeared in *MaComère: Journal of the Association of Caribbean Women Writers and Scholars* 14.1–2 (2013–14): 170–86 as "Reading Metonymically in Dionne Brand's *Inventory*."

information to include in future reprints. Seamus Heaney's poem "Basket of Chestnuts" originally appeared in the following publications:

Heaney, Seamus. "Basket of Chestnuts." *Seeing Things*. London: Faber and Faber, 1991. 25–6.
Heaney, Seamus. "Basket of Chestnuts." *Seeing Things*. New York: Farrar, Straus and Giroux, 1991. 26–7.

Thanks to my parents, Jim Tracy and Sharon Yuill-Tracy, for their enthusiastic support. Thanks to Crystal Frappier for phone calls that are always easy. A special thank you to Kris Singh who has been a constant interlocutor and supporter in all things.

WITH THE WITNESSES

Introduction

With the Witnesses proposes a theory of compassion developed through twentieth- and twenty-first-century witness poetry, a genre that I define as poetry responding to social suffering and atrocity. This body of poems offers strategies for responding to suffering. Central to these strategies and the resulting theory of compassion is the recognition of distance in response. Metonymy is the key trope signalling this distance in witness poetry. As a trope that defers meaning contiguously, metonymy evokes witness as engagement with suffering that comes across various distances and compassion as response to suffering that involves feeling with (rather than as) another. As an investigation into a theory of compassion that emerges through witness poetry, this book is not a biographical investigation of poets' corpuses. Instead, *With the Witnesses* privileges the contiguities among global Anglophone witness poems. These poems respond to diverse atrocities and conflicts, as well as national and transnational contexts of marginalization.

Despite the prevalence of this compassionate witness across contexts, dominant modes for reading witness poetry do not make space for this poetry's strategies. In this book, I argue that a currently common understanding of art's relationship to the suffering it represents forecloses compassion. I explore this problem through witness poetry. There are several interrelated issues leading to what I see as a limiting approach to witness poetry and thus to the models we have to respond to suffering – the models we have as scholars in the humanities but also the models we include in the social narratives we produce for our students and other publics, not to mention use in our own lives. Each of these interrelated issues involves a form of identification. The four troubling forms of identification I see involved in readings of witness poetry include (1) the emphasis on identification in approaches to literature; (2) the assumption that readers of lyric poetry take the position of the speaking "I"; (3) the emphasis on empathy in responses to suffering; and (4) trauma theory's dominant sense of trauma as contagious.

To begin with identification, I will consider empathy as a value many scholars, teachers, and laypeople believe reading delivers. As Martha Nussbaum influentially explains it, "literary works typically invite readers to put themselves in the place of people of many different kinds and to take on their experiences" (*Poetic Justice: The Literary Imagination and Public Life* 5). Literature typically, in this view, helps people know what it is like to be someone else; it expands their capacities to imagine other lives. I believe this approach to literature is misguided. Literature does not help one to know what it is to be another. Rather, literature helps one to know what it is to encounter another. Reading, much like living, does not give the experience of another person's experiences (even if they have been described exceedingly well). Literature is about meeting new people, not being them. Yet I've never taught a class in which my literature students did not declare admiration, frustration, boredom, or disdain based on whether or not they could relate to the characters under study. I do not see in this identification much possibility for expanded compassionate response. Students' identificatory responses to literature seem to suggest that literature might help them to identify with those they already have the capacity to identify with, those who are most like themselves. It is the work done after the initial moment of identification (or lack of identification) that allows the expanded capacity to engage with others' experiences.[1]

I am not alone in my reservations about the relationship between empathy and literature. Suzanne Keen "explores the implications for literary studies of the widely promulgated 'empathy-altruism' hypothesis" (*Empathy and the Novel* vii). She argues that there is much less proof for this hypothesis than is generally acknowledged, insofar as reading cannot be shown to lead to an empathy that, in turn, leads to positive effects like altruistic action. The concept of empathy more broadly has recently garnered attention in popular forums. Articles like "The Trouble with Empathy" (*Guernica*, 2016), "Empathy: Overrated?" (*The Atlantic*, 2015), and "Welcome to the Empathy Wars" (*openDemocracy*, 2015) question whether empathy ought to be considered an emotion of moral guidance. My position on empathy can be situated within this wider cultural conversation.

Even in the discourse surrounding compassion rather than empathy, I find an inclination to privilege identification. Nussbaum devotes a section of *Upheavals of Thought: The Intelligence of Emotions* to compassion. Drawing on arguments from the philosophical tradition, Nussbaum suggests that, for compassion, "we need to turn to works of art" to "mak[e] people capable of inhabiting, for a time, the world of a different person, and seeing the meaning of events in that world from the outsider's viewpoint" (431). Rather than "inhabiting" another's position, I understand feeling compassion as inhabiting relationship. To imagine ourselves in the place of another is always still to imagine that other from our own viewpoint, not theirs. I see the most value, then, in attending to one's own position from the perspective of its connection to that of another.

The history of lyric poetry contributes to the emphasis on identification in witness poetry. There is a long tradition that suggests that readers adopt the speaker's position when reading lyric poetry – thus, in this context, becoming the witness. Helen Vendler's influential scholarship on lyric poetry offers a particularly strong example of this focus on readerly inhabitation of the lyric "I": "A lyric poem is a script for performance by its reader. It is, then, the most universal of genres ... because it presumes that the reader resembles the writer enough to step into the writer's shoes and speak the lines the writer has written as though they were the reader's own" (xl–xli). In *I Made You to Find Me: The Coming of Age of the Woman Poet and the Politics of Poetic Address*, Jane Hedley discusses the options for approaching the lyric "I," listing "three different ways of conceiving of the lyric" (4). Nevertheless, I will show that all three options allow for a similar identificatory approach. The first option is the one proposed by Vendler (4). The second option for understanding the lyric is that "poems are 'overheard' by their readers" (4). While the first option obviously asks readers to occupy the speaker's position, Hedley describes overhearing in similar terms: "each reader is in a condition of solitude that corresponds to the condition of solitary self-communion in which the poem was 'uttered' in the first place. As Virginia Jackson explains ... 'this structure is one ... in which the poet's solitude stands in for the solitude of the individual reader – a self-address so absolute that every self can identify it as his own'" (7). However, Hedley notes W.R. Johnson's disagreement with this position. For Johnson, Hedley explains, "this way of understanding lyric utterance misrepresents its origins in Greek and Roman poetry" in which the speaker was understood as a social being addressing a social being (8). The third option Hedley lists for understanding the lyric, the option to which Johnson adheres, is the belief that "hypothetical readers are always implicated" in a poem's "structure of address" (10). This position is also my own. Yet Johnson's is not currently the most popular approach to the lyric. Indeed, Hedley, who makes clear that she thinks "none of these ways of describing the lyric is mistaken" (9), wrangles Johnson's position back into one much more like Vendler's. She argues, "Johnson's approach also helps to explain what is going on when" the "you" is a "rhetorical device for generalizing from the speaker's feelings and experiences to others who are, or can imagine being, comparably situated": this "you" "actively constructs the possibility of stepping into another person's shoes" (10).

These assumptions about reading lyric poetry, paired with a cultural emphasis on the ethical value of "putting yourself in another's shoes" or assuming that "I feel your pain," create conditions in which readers may take the space of the speaker as a gesture of empathy.[2] Yet, if the speaker is closely connected to the poet (as it is in witness poetry where the poet's relation to suffering is under scrutiny) while the speaker position is also held open for the reader, there is a tension in the assumption that the reader will (or should) engage through identification. In this book, I focus closely on what positions poems legitimately suggest and what positions readers might valuably take.

I propose my understanding of compassionate engagement as a mode of reading, relating, and thinking that more precisely attends to the positions poetry provides while also allowing for a reaction more grounded in each reader's particular self. From this contiguous position, this position of with-ness, a reader is able to respond with feelings that may or may not be those that are expressed in the poem but that occur in reaction to those feelings. Lyric, in my reading, is still a quintessential mode for the expression of individual emotion. The poems I discuss use the lyric form for self-reflective response and expression of suffering together with another (feeling one's own suffering in response to another's suffering).

Before explaining my fourth issue with contemporary response to suffering (the issue of trauma studies' dominant notions of contagiousness in response to suffering), I will expand on my idea of compassionate relationship, its role in witness poetry, and the alternative it presents to approaches based in identification.[3] Compassion cannot be other than self-reflective. That is the lesson I take from witness poetry. I find in poetry that witnesses lives attended by war, atrocity, and injustice a model for engagement that privileges the space of relationship between the self and the suffering other. This poetry does not accept the collapse of that relationship through an identificatory, empathic leap into another's shoes. The firm confidence in leaving wide the space between witness and experience, between caring and knowing, suggests an optimism for a human capacity to be with each other. Such a capacity is defied in any rush to understand, to feel what the other feels; it is defied as soon as one denies one's own feelings to try to know another's.[4]

I conceptualize compassion not as a well-defined feeling, but as underpinning the various emotions that can come out of engagement with suffering. According to the OED, compassion is "suffering together with another" or "the feeling or emotion, when a person is moved by the suffering or distress of another, and by the desire to relieve it" (np). The distinction between feeling in response to another – suffering together with – and actually feeling the same feelings as another is foundational to my project. I thus chose the term compassion in contrast to both empathy – "the power of projecting one's personality into (and so fully comprehending) the object of contemplation" (OED) – and sympathy – "the fact or capacity of entering into or sharing the feelings of another or others" (OED). The terms "empathy" and "sympathy" suggest moving into the other person or that person's feelings; "compassion," in contrast, maintains a distance that allows one's feelings to be one's own.

Compassionate witnessing is about finding a distance from which one can offer one's attention, thought, and emotion. I propose a distance from which one does not presume to know what another's pain feels like, but does offer one's own emotion as a part of intellectual rigour and dedicated consideration. Though my rereading of witness poetry is formulated as an intervention in current critical practices concerning the genre, this intervention is only one aspect of my wider aim to think through affective and attentive reading methods. Witness poetry uniquely models this reading strategy. Yet I believe that this kind of interpretive skill would be analytically and ethically productive whether one is reading a poem, an event, or another person.

To be clear, I do not consider identification to be an improper route of engagement; rather, I think it is quite often the first way that we engage with another. I am proposing, instead, that there are other possible modes of attentive connection, modes which might require conscious thought to enact. These modes beyond identification are important for cases in which widely divergent experience makes identification difficult, as well as for preventing over-confidence in one's knowledge of another or another's experience. Rather than reaching for the stasis of this accomplished knowing, I suggest thinking of compassion as an attitude in which we must continually enact engagement through ongoing relationship.[5]

To turn to my final complaint about identification, my argument – that witness poetry calls for waiting in relation to another without knowing another's suffering – contrasts discussions of witness poetry that suggest a transmission of trauma from speaker to reader. The idea in trauma theory that trauma is transferrable through literature, when paired with typical ways of reading lyric poetry specifically and literature more generally, results in a treatment of witness poetry that is strongly identificatory. While identification – the search for points of agreement, of shared experience, of similar understanding – seems a reasonable first response to a text, I would not wish for response to end at this point. I explore here another mode of engagement which witness poetry – a poetry with an interest in compassion – suggests for itself.

The fallacy of identification[6] in reading witness poetry is connected to the impulse to understand the poem as indexical and to understand trauma as contagious. Many critics position a poem as direct evidence of a trauma it holds and passes on. The resulting suppression of the relationship between reader and poem (poem as poem rather than indexical sign of suffering) certainly shapes how these critics might understand a poem. The issue here is twofold: the distance which I will explore has to do with the relationship between depiction and experience as well as with emotional and cognitive responses to another's trauma and suffering. Witness poetry mobilizes compassion as an engagement that does not pretend to dissolve the distance involved in poetic mediation. Additionally, witness poetry emphasizes the compassionate ability to imagine, not pain one did not feel, but a relation to others feeling pain.

My purpose is not to dismiss the study of trauma. On the contrary, I believe further interdisciplinary work on trauma is imperative. Rather, I suggest that trauma studies' dominance in the humanities has led to a strategy of reading for trauma that silences other strategies for reading trauma, for representing trauma, and also for reading and representing other forms of suffering that may not fit trauma's definition. Further, trauma theory, when applied to texts in the way that has become orthodox in the humanities, courts specific kinds of misreadings. Without discounting the value of approaching literature from the perspective of trauma theory, I argue that particular investments in trauma theory, as with investments in any theory, can come with blindspots. While I will be critical of the texts in which investment in trauma theory gets in the way of textual analysis, it is important to state that my approach is in some important ways aligned with the approach of scholars such as Dori Laub, Geoffrey Hartman, and Dominick LaCapra. Moreover, I recognize that the scholars I disagree with here would not have such a strong following and extensive impact on contemporary thought if they were not saying something significant. The following pages will consist of an extended critique of arguments close to the heart and thought of many individuals concerned with responses to suffering. Since I am pursuing an alternative approach to understanding suffering represented in art, my aim with trauma studies is to offer the corrective of alternative tools and methods.

Trauma studies have had decades of prominence, and though several critics have (sometimes vociferously) pointed out issues with the initial foundation laid in seminal 1990s texts by Cathy Caruth, Shoshana Felman, and Dori Laub, in 2007 Susannah Radstone can still argue that "the political and cultural contexts within which this theory has risen to prominence have remained largely unexamined" ("Trauma Theory: Context, Politics, Ethics" 9).[7] Despite an existing critical conversation that questions trauma theory and its usage, I, like Radstone, do not see trauma theory changing to meet these or other criticisms to its grounding theories. Indeed, in 2013 Caruth published *Literature in the Ashes of History*; though this book extends her theories to new literary texts, it does not address the criticisms her earlier book garnered.[8] By critiquing this book and Felman's earlier seminal contributions in my first chapter, I suggest issues with both the close reading and the conclusions resulting from a discourse whose popularity and subject matter seem to insulate its central tenets and practices from decades of ongoing criticism.

Trauma Studies

In trauma studies, psychoanalytic concepts help theorists to attend to the testimony of those who have undergone trauma as well as to consider the relationship between that trauma and a listener or witness to testimony. Given these concerns, trauma studies play a large role in the development of theories of witnessing and testimony. In the humanities, trauma theory has become the dominant discourse for the consideration of suffering. Although suffering is a broader category into which the traumatic experience falls, the dominance of trauma theory has resulted in a lack of differentiation in discourse surrounding representations of suffering, creating a monologue for a diversity of experiences. Suffering that may not be traumatic, or that is not identified by others as traumatic, lacks models for response. Further, in order to respond according to trauma studies' models, one must first decide if another's suffering counts as trauma. Radstone asserts that "trauma criticism arguably constructs and polices the boundary of what can be recognised as trauma" (24). However, the "questions of firstly, who it is that gets claimed by trauma theory, and who ignored, and secondly, which events get labelled 'trauma' and which do not have been omitted, entirely, from critical commentary" (24). In this book, my move from trauma to compassion (a focus on response rather than on the degree or kind of suffering) as a critical lens is in part an attempt to avoid labelling another's suffering.

Founded in psychoanalytic and deconstructivist ideas, trauma theory's premise is that an individual does not truly experience the initial traumatic event and later compulsively relives the traumatic experience. As Dominick LaCapra explains in *Writing History, Writing Trauma*, "At least in Freud's widely shared view, the trauma as experience is 'in' the repetition of an early event in a later event – an early event for which one was not prepared to feel anxiety and a later event that somehow recalls the early one and triggers a traumatic response" (81–2). Since the initial event was not truly experienced, that experience is "unclaimed" (to use Caruth's word). For many scholars, trauma – because it is unclaimed and unconsciously performed in language – can erupt as literal trace in language to move contagiously to those who bear witness to it through literature.

That is, the task many scholars using trauma theory take on is to find traces of trauma in texts, becoming traumatized "in turn" (to use a phrase that saturates Felman's contributions to *Testimony* and that is connected to the idea of traumatic contagion). LaCapra "question[s] the desire to identify fully with, and relive the experience of, the victim in however vicarious a fashion" (WH 98) and argues that "the focus on trauma and the use of concepts derived from psychoanalysis should not obscure the difference between victims of traumatic historical events and others not directly experiencing them" (ix). Yet LaCapra notes a broad reach to this conflation in trauma studies: "Trauma has been a prevalent preoccupation in recent theory and criticism. At times it has even become an obsession or an occasion for rash amalgamations or conflations (for example, in the idea that contemporary culture, or even all history, is essentially traumatic or that everyone in the post-Holocaust còntext is a survivor)" (x). Similarly, in "Memorizing Memory," Amy Hungerford explains, "the implications of that deconstructive shift from language as representation to language as performance" means that concern for the actual traumatic events, the actual historical violence, "may be unnecessary to trauma theory at its most abstract level," the abstract level that allows trauma theory to suggest "that the experience of trauma is what defines not only the survivor, but all persons" (80).

The consistent core of LaCapra's argument throughout his many contributions to trauma studies is that total identification with sufferers should not be the goal; critics and historians have an obligation to attempt working-through the trauma they engage in their scholarship rather than acting-out through vicarious victimization or a generalized sense of history as trauma. He argues, "One danger of identification with the victim is that it seems to make one a surrogate victim and a survivor, hence to justify an approach to life, including politics, that is not justified for someone who has in fact not undergone truly incapacitating experiences in relation to which survival may itself be more than enough" (WH 145–6). In critical scholarship, it can likewise seem as though witnessing the represented suffering is more than enough, without raising questions about what the consequences of that particular approach to witnessing might be.

Identifying appropriate positions and responsibilities for scholars as witnesses is no simple task. In *Testimony*, Laub argues, "Bearing witness to a trauma is, in fact, a process that includes the listener. For the testimonial process to take place, there needs to be a bonding, the intimate and total presence of an *other* – in the position of one who hears" (70). Clearly, intimate bonding may not be what occurs for scholars applying trauma theory to historical, cultural, and artistic texts. As LaCapra states, "the academic (as academic) is not – and is not entitled simply to identify with – a therapist working in intimate contact with survivors or other traumatized people" (WH 98). Yet evidenced in Felman's contributions to *Testimony* is the overwrought emotional response that Laub lists as one of the defensive moves individuals who ought to provide total presence demonstrate when hearing testimony. He calls this response the "hyperemotionally [*sic*] which superficially looks like compassion and caring. The testifier is flooded, drowned and lost in the listener's defensive affectivity" (Laub 73). LaCapra, discussing hyperbole in writing about trauma more generally, argues, "hyperbole need not, and in my judgment should not, be the unmodulated response to all problems, especially when it takes the form of an all-or-nothing philosophy, typically linked to mimetic emulation of one or another variant of critical theory reduced to an all-purpose methodology or stylistic passe-partout" (*WH* xii–xiii). A response to suffering "becomes questionable when it is routinized in a methodology or style that enacts compulsive repetition, including the compulsively repetitive turn to the aporia, paradox, or impasse" (47). Troublingly, in this questionably routine methodology, the critic can claim the unspeakable trauma passed on by one who suffered a traumatic event, but at the same time can speak authoritatively about that trauma, even while emulating the aporia, paradox, and impasse of trauma's confusions.

In reaction to the spirit of reading in which "I feel your pain" because I read your trauma, I turn to compassion as an alternative possibility of response. LaCapra's use of the term "empathy" is similar to my use of "compassion" as he contrasts empathy with the "unchecked identification" that "implies a confusion of self and other" (28). Nevertheless, LaCapra considers empathy in terms of imagining what it is like to be the other. While, he writes, empathy "does not entail this identity [of victim]," it instead "involves a kind of virtual experience through which one puts oneself in the other's position while recognizing the difference of that position and hence not taking the other's place" (78). Compassionate response, in contrast, does not depend on this virtual component. Readers of witness poetry need not imagine what it is like to be the speaker in order to respond. The poetry I study here does not ask readers to have a virtual experience but instead puts readers into actual relationship with a poem's speaker, asking them to reflect on a real position in relation to another.

To whatever degree of force one ascribes it, this privileging of virtual experience is a commitment to identification. As LaCapra states in "Lanzmann's 'Shoah': 'Here There Is No Why,'" "the goal should not be full empathy in the sense of an attempt to relive the trauma of the other but rather the registering of muted trauma and the transmission of it to the reader or viewer" (267). Where LaCapra argues for a more moderate version of the same approach, I consider engagements with suffering in which the idea of transmitted trauma (muted or not) may not be the most appropriate idea to guide response.[9] LaCapra comes closer to this position as he continues, "If one objected to the notion of a muted trauma and maintained that the very term *trauma* should be reserved for limit-cases that pass a certain threshold, it would be more cogent to argue that the secondary witness should reactivate and transmit not trauma but an unsettlement ... that manifests empathy (but not full identification) with the victim and is at most an index of trauma" (267). As his idea of empathy is a more moderate version of identification, his idea of response is a more moderate version of the contagious theory of trauma. Still present is the idea of direct cause and effect: the suffering transmits response to the secondary witness. Unsettlement is an index of trauma like smoke is an index of fire; the one produces the other. My approach considers a more dynamic interaction between suffering and witness in which the first does not certainly cause a specific response as fire certainly causes smoke. I believe the "with-ness" asked for in some witness poetry's strategies positions readers for forms of interaction that are often explicitly open to the individual roles and experiences a reader brings to a readerly position.

Witness Poetry

Trauma studies have largely been applied to poetry without any tailoring of the approach to the particular context, leading to a discourse peculiarly inattentive to some aspects of poetry itself. Poet and human rights advocate Carolyn Forché's *Against Forgetting: Twentieth-Century Poetry of Witness* names and defines "poetry of witness." Since Forché has provided the defining comments for this genre, my project responds to her stance. While Forché articulates a poetry of witness, I articulate a poetry of with-ness. In her seminal anthology, Forché collects poems that "bear the trace of extremity within them, and are, as such, evidence of what occurred" along with "biographical notes to illuminate the experience of extremity for each poet" (30). This genre is particularly reliant on biographical interpretation.[10] Critical attention has followed Forché's emphasis on biography to focus on the witness poem's relationship to its poet's experience, often considering how a poet's trauma emerges in a poem. In his article included in *Witness and Memory: The Discourse of Trauma*, literary scholar Thomas A. Vogler critiques the tendency to read witness poems as though they formally manifest authors' trauma, providing "raw *facts* of existence rather than *effects* produced by rhetorical technique" (174). For Vogler, "It would seem that only a willful blindness to how poetry and language work could lead so many critics to make so many claims for traumatic traces in the poems they discuss" (191) since "the 'breaking of form' is not evidence of a loss of control, but of an *exercise* of control designed to produce particular effects" (196). This mistake – reading the poem as though the poet's suffering resides within it – contributes to two problems I have already mentioned: the conflation of speaker and author and the idea that readers experience the suffering they read.

Vogler focuses his critique in part on Forché's defining remarks about the genre. In her introduction to *Against Forgetting*, Forché argues that poetry of witness takes as its subject matter "situation[s] of extremity" (31). Later, in her opening remarks to a roundtable discussion collected in William H. Gass and Lorin Cuoco's *The Writer in Politics*, Forché explains, "Regardless of apparent 'subject matter,' these poems bear the trace of extremity within them, and they are, as such, evidence of what occurred. They are also poems as much about poetry as are poems that have no subject other than poetry itself" ("The Poetry of Witness" 139). Though Forché here recognizes poetry's place as art, her claim that this poetry serves as "evidence of what occurred" raises difficult issues regarding artistic depiction.

Critiquing Forché, Vogler explains that for her "the *form* of the poem is an indexical sign of the poet's mental state, and the 'broken' state of the poet's mind is a sign of the real 'conditions of extremity,' responding to a force outside itself" (195).[11] He suggests that "in order to be sure that we have a poem of witness in this sense, we must have an authentic poet of witness, and we are back to the biographical and contextual materials needed to establish that fact, and the poet's identity or biography are of equal or greater importance than the poem" (190). Forché begins to address this issue of the poem's relation to the event:

> To talk about a poem as the sole trace of an event, to see it in purely evidentiary terms, is perhaps to believe our own figures of speech too rigorously. If, as Benjamin indicates, a poem is *itself* an event, a trauma that changes both a common language and an individual psyche, it is a specific kind of event, a specific kind of trauma. It is an experience entered into voluntarily. Unlike an aerial attack, a poem does not come at one unexpectedly. One has to read or listen, one has to be willing to accept the trauma. So, if a poem is an event and the trace of an event, it has, by definition, to belong to a different order of being from the trauma that marked its language in the first place. (*Against Forgetting* 33)

I quote Forché at length to give an idea of the progression of ideas in this passage. Her critique of her own use of the poem as evidence ends up confirming the use of the poem as evidence. Though she makes clear that reading the poem should not be considered a traumatic event of the same kind of which the poem is a trace, she does not suggest at all that the poem as trace is any less evidentiary. That is, her argument shifts partway through this paragraph such that we might still go on "believ[ing] our own figures of speech too rigorously." In her account, the poem is still "the trace of an event" and to read this trace is "to accept the trauma" it carries, even as reading the poem is a new event with its own trauma of a different order.

This argument's complications seem to arise from a grounding conception of a witness poem's evidentiary status. It is not surprising that the truth of the connection to the event would be foregrounded in a poetry representing experiences of atrocity, and the witness genre is particularly reliant on biographical interpretation.[12] In *Against Forgetting*, Forché includes "biographical notes to illuminate the experience of extremity for each poet" (30). Elsewhere, she directly addresses this issue of the poem's relation to lived experience:

> A poem that calls on us from the other side of a situation of extremity cannot be judged by simplistic notions of "accuracy" or "truth to life." It will have to be judged, as Ludwig Wittgenstein said of confessions, by its consequences, not on our ability to verify its truth. In fact, the poem might be our only evidence that an event has occurred: it exists for us as the sole trace of an occurrence. As such, there will be nothing for us to base the poem on, no independent account that will tell us whether or not we can see a given text as being "objectively" true. Poem as trace, poem as evidence. ("The Poetry of Witness" 142–3)

Again, this line of argument is complex: Forché notes that the poem's truth is not what is at issue and that it may be impossible to judge. At the same time, however, she suggests that the poem is in fact its own evidence, the "trace of an occurrence"; that is, the poem is not a depiction, but holds "vestiges or marks remaining and indicating the former presence, existence, or action of something" ("trace," OED). Forché moves into the framework of "truth to life" even as she disavows that framework. Though the tension between an inability to judge a poem's accuracy and the poem's serving as evidence nonetheless may not be simply resolved, this tension itself warrants attention.

Moreover, the idea of poem as evidence unites strangely with the idea that readers take on the speaker's trauma. While we are asked to associate the speaker with the poet and his or her authentic experience, we are also asked to take the space of the speaker as our own. Yet, if, as the expression goes, "I feel your pain," what I am actually feeling is my own pain in response to the pain that I imagine you feel. Indeed, in a poem whose speaker witnesses another's pain, this situation is modelled. The speaker is voicing an engagement with and understanding of that pain that is based on the available signs of suffering. Within the world of the poem, the speaker's feelings are not the same feelings as those of the sufferer but, rather, are feelings in response to those feelings, just as the reader's feelings are likewise a response to the compassion that is in response to the pain. That is, the reader's relationship to the suffering which the poem represents is filtered through the witness's compassionate engagement. The reader is not (or not exclusively and directly) in a witnessing relationship to the suffering other, but in a relationship to the witnessing "I."

Witness poems have speakers; readers, accordingly, might understand themselves as listeners. If readers are listening to a speaker's witness, then they are not occupying the same role as that witnessing speaker. Within this relationship, there is space for a reader's listening response to differ from that speaker's witnessing response. Readers need not assume that the emotion depicted in the poem is that which they must feel. Reading with an idea of this relationship and range of response in mind mitigates the tendency for response to suffering to involve silent awe or respectful passivity. Though respect for suffering may make attention to one's own feelings seem self-centred, these feelings are actually essential because witness poetry is invested in readerly response. Readers can only find this response in themselves, as that response is shaped by the poem. A reading position is already implicated in the poem's telling of suffering, and the mode of that telling shapes a request for a mode of listening.

Witness as With-ness

This listening involves interpretation, and interpretation necessarily involves some form of waiting. Waiting has an indexical quality because it is in actual relationship to the passage of time, insofar as waiting is the experience of ongoing temporality. The interpretation involved in compassionate response, then, involves the anticipatory temporality of waiting and the retrospective temporality of reflection. I attend to the distance from which I as a particular reader and critic read these poems. This attention comes through waiting in relation to signs of suffering and reflection on that relation.

Compassionate witness is living, however briefly, in connection to another's signs, and striving to interpret them as best as one can through this lingering in relation. In compassion, my feelings become contiguous with yours; my feelings do not stand in for your feelings but stand with them. Our feelings can be in association, such that what I feel gains significance through being in relationship with your feelings. Witness does not involve only attending to another, but also attending to how one comes into association with that other. As I find it in the poetry through which it centrally operates, witness is a process of waiting through the intimacy of allowing oneself to be – and to be attentive to being – in relationship. As an ongoing process of relation, witness is not completed in an action or feeling. In this focus on self-reflection, my idea of witness is compatible with Kelly Oliver's philosophical approach to witness in *Witnessing: Beyond Recognition*. She argues, "Self-reflection is not a turn inward but a turn toward otherness. It is not a return but a detour" (219). I characterize self-reflection not as a return or as a detour, but as a tour. With its obsolete sense of a "manner or mode of being" and "the course or compass of anything; what it amounts to; range, scope" (OED), the tour of self-reflection is the course of compassionate living, living in relationship to others, in the range between oneself and others, in the scope of conscious relationship. Since compassion is about feeling in response to another's expression of feeling, it is as much about the self as it is about the other.

Correspondingly, my argument focuses on changing one's modes of response to another's suffering. I do not consider direct methods for altering the conditions under which another lives. However, I examine how one might prepare oneself to be in conversation with another who suffers. Attention to the self is not narcissistic but necessary. Genuine response to another requires self-awareness. I think carefully about how my argument positions people in relation to each other because this book proposes not only reading differently, but living differently. Compassionate witness is a way of organizing and living relationships, actual or potential. Compassion, as a mode of being, is a foundation to feeling and action. In any activism or humanitarian intervention, the doing is essential for change, but the quality of these actions is shaped by the mental and emotional standpoint from which action grows. Thus, I argue that witness requires particular attention to the self-in-relationship and a willingness to wait in a space of return and reflection. I maintain that whether or not compassion leads to action is a separate issue outside of compassion proper.

Witness requires the response of listeners. Witness poetry's metonymic strategies are an invitation for listeners' compassionate responses. A central claim of this book is that metonymy is compassion's formal representation. The prevalence of metonymy in the corpus I study demonstrates a commitment to contiguity. Through multiple lateral progressions, I develop my theory of compassionate response through its operation in poems working in idiosyncratically contiguous ways to address different historical events and positions of engagement. I am guided by the poetry into a theory generated by and for that poetry. To interpret any communication as much as possible on its own terms is an ethical challenge pertinent to reading in general as much as to witness and compassion.

Forms of association such as index and metonymy involve a pre-established relationship between their terms. The index is a semiotic term for the causal relationship between a sign and referent. Metonymy is a rhetorical term for a relationship between signs. In both cases, the relationship is pre-existing. As a relation, compassion is indexical and, when articulated literarily, takes the form of metonymy. Indexical and metonymic relations, as well as the other kinds of contiguities and juxtapositions that I will discuss in this project, have in common this actual proximity – whether spatial (metonymy) or temporal (index) – which suggests an experience of connections as they exist. Such relationships must take into account the existing complexity of detail.

I find with-ness, metonymy, and contiguity so fruitful as approaches to suffering because they assume some degree of distance in response. Response is arguably most important when experiences are so dissimilar that imagination fails. My study considers poetry that represents what it means to enter into a relationship with another and what, aside from understanding, might emerge from such engagement. Since these poems represent afflicting events through various forms of distance, it makes sense that the representation and response emphasize mediation, that these poets explore the relative intimacy and distance involved in various positionings of readers, speakers, and poets in relation to each other and to contexts of suffering.

Though I privilege metonymy in this study, my analyses also involve metaphor. I do not set up a strict dichotomy between metonymy and metaphor because, while the two can be usefully distinguished, they cannot be fully separated. In "Articulation and the Limits of Metaphor," Ernesto Laclau considers the relationship between metaphor and metonymy both through Gerard Genette's analysis of their co-functioning in Proust's work and through Roman Jakobson's well-known distinction between the two axes of language.[13] Jakobson finds that signs can operate through combination or through substitution (Laclau 58) and that "this distinction corresponds to the two axes of language identified by Saussure: the syntagmatic and the paradigmatic" (59). Laclau explains, "From these two axes of language – the paradigmatic and the syntagmatic, substitution and combination – Jakobson moves to the rhetorical field: metonymy would correspond to combination, and metaphor to substitution" (59). With Genette's analysis, however, Laclau adds that "contiguity and analogy are not essentially different from each other, but the two poles of a continuum" (62). In this book, I privilege metonymy as the pole that shows its work. As Laclau notes, "The only distinction it is possible to establish between these figures is that, in the case of metonymy, the transgression of the structural locations that define the relations of combination is fully visible, while in metaphor, analogy entirely ignores those structural differentiations" (62). In witness poetry, I see metonymy as showing the "with" of feeling along with another while metaphor shows the final substitution; thus, I associate metonymy with compassion and metaphor with identification. Yet, because metonymy and metaphor are not essentially opposed but rather essentially connected as the ends of a continuum, I consider the various ways this relationship plays out in witness poetry. Similarly, compassion and identification are not opposed reactions, but points on a continuum of response. Laclau notes that "there are several possibilities as to how to conceive the interaction between these two dimensions" (56), and, in the pages ahead, I will attend to the interactions between combination and substitution that poetry uses in witnessing and that appear as continuums between a variety of related terms like metonymy and metaphor, carrying and holding, index and icon, beside and inside, and heuristic and hermeneutic.

What Follows

This book is divided into three parts: Trauma and Compassion (chapter 1), Compassion and Representation (chapters 2 and 3), and Witness in Social and Artistic Structures (chapters 4 and 5). Through these chapters, I examine poetry by Frank Chipasula (introduction); Peter Balakian, Joy Harjo, and Seamus Heaney (chapter 1); Harjo, Adrienne Rich, Walt Whitman, Hart Crane, and Elizabeth Bishop (chapter 2); Rich, Harjo, Whitman, Lee Maracle, and Rachel Tzvia Back (chapter 3); Les Murray and Dionne Brand (chapter 4); Heaney, Brand, Antjie Krog, and Derek Walcott (chapter 5), and Harjo, Krog, and Jack Mapanje (conclusion). Poets appear across multiple chapters because my purpose is to attend to the contiguities among contemporary poems compassionately responding to suffering, not to the contiguities among a poet's collections over time. Thus, a structure considering the connections and divergences among poems is important to my exploration of how witness poetry theorizes and models compassion, and a structure that moves individually through each poet's corpus would work against my purpose. While I will provide enough information from each poet's life and body of work to ground the poems in their contexts, my attention will be fixed on individual poems. I believe each poem is a unique philosophical endeavour; a poem might defy the expectations the poet's corpus and public statements lead readers to bring to it. As a theory of experience, a poem also has something to say that cannot be reduced to the poet's personal experience. While this point may seem obvious, poetry is easily overwritten by summaries of experience, particularly experience of extremity.

Since I respond to reading strategies that substitute the poet for the speaker and a reading of a poet's life for a reading of a poem, I am concerned that an understanding of a poet's corpus does not take the place of hearing what a particular poem has to say.[14] In *The Particulars of Rapture: An Aesthetics of the Affects*, Charles Altieri argues that "most 'ethical' readings tend to produce abstract substitutes for the text and so end up sharing with socio-political historicism a tendency to overread for 'meaning' while underreading the specific modes of affective engagement presented by works of art" (1–2). Witness poetry suffers particularly from such abstract substitutes. In her study of the Eastern European influence on Seamus Heaney's poetic explorations of ethics, Magdalena Kay notes that close reading "may be deemed old-fashioned or even critically naïve, exposing our unconsciousness of better, more theoretically or technologically sophisticated methodologies" (6–7). Heaney has himself, Kay records, expressed "irate impatience" with this concept of sophistication in the scholarly imaginary (204n2). In her engagement with Heaney's poetic grappling with abstract terms like "witness" and "justice," Kay claims that, without close reading, "a poem becomes yet another historical document, and there are more straightforward historical documents than poems. Poetry will not give us reliable images of history. It will also not be reliably historical" (8). In the context of witness poetry, this statement is actually quite provocative. However, in recognizing what poetry might reliably give us, we stand to meet poetry halfway to receive the most from what it offers. Witness poetry gives us, not straightforward historical accounts, but relational structures of witness identifiable through close reading. Meeting a poem halfway means reading it as a poem (responding to its imaginative strategies) rather than as something else (a straightforward historical document). In this way, we could receive an understanding of the poem's approach to witness, an understanding we may not receive if we look primarily for factual statements about history. There are many more direct forms in which people could choose to convey witness, but witness poetry offers its own strength in evoking the relational structures involved in telling and hearing suffering.

Thus, my focus is not on poets, their biographies, and their larger collections but, instead, on connections among poems as seen through the lens of my concerns. Metonymy functions as the force demanding,

to some extent, the selectivity that allows me to follow chains of connection among the poems I read. As though with the "pairing knife" we
will find in Brand's *Inventory*, I am interested in bringing these poems
together through, in some ways, extraction from other contexts. From
within this book, one of these poems might say, along with Rich in "An
Atlas of the Difficult World," "These are not the roads / you knew me
by" (I.75–6) but "this is where I live now" (I.60). This paring/pairing
is the opening of new roads to compassionate engagement. Thus, my
project is more about metonymy than it is about a poet's corpus; I am
making an argument about witness poetry and how it is read.

I use the term "witness poetry" because my selected poems do not
all meet Forché's criteria for the genre she calls "poetry of witness."
This study works from the premise that there exist different kinds of
suffering requiring corresponding discourses and practices. I deliberately include both poets who have experienced extremity personally
and those who witness with more distance. This choice reflects my
discomfort with deciding who is close enough to extremity to be an
authentic witness. It also reflects my interest in the ways poems examine their various distances as part of their witness. Witness poetry, then,
is a broad and undefined category including various relationships with
extremity. Since the parameters of my study are undefined in this way,
my selection may seem arbitrary. However, the category's broadness is
essential because I aim to show that these compassionate strategies are
widespread, not only taking place in response to some particular atrocities or forms of suffering and not only arising from particular national
literary traditions. A totally representative selection is impossible with
regard to all contemporary poetry written in English.[15] Nevertheless,
I have aimed for coverage of poets writing in multiple contexts to
demonstrate that compassionate strategies based in a principle of contiguity are happening in enough poetry that this contiguous witness is
significant and deserves consideration. I study largely established poets
to show that the experience of speakable suffering, though apparently
unknown to scholarship, is well known in poetry.

If my selection of poems seems to lack an organizing principle,
this is because I am seeking to be guided by witness as with-ness
rather than by an existing framework for selection. My project

works against trauma theory as such a framework since I believe the approach that this organizing principle suggests gets in the way of the approach these poems offer. If I selected these poems by some other single existing structure of literary criticism (postcolonial, Trans-Atlantic, diasporic, etc.), I would risk supplanting one set of assumptions with another. And if my selection of poets seemed obvious – if these poets immediately seemed the natural choices to look at together – this obviousness might betray a problem in my approach.

I meet these poems on their own terms. In my analyses of these poems' theoretical efforts, I replicate this poetry's contiguous movements. Witness poems provide the models through which I work out my understanding of compassion and witness, and I insist on their strategies. That compassion is a strategy across borders is the essential point underlying both my structure and my selection of poetry. These border-crossings and contiguous connections may well be dizzying. Poetry is, at its core, dizzying. Poems can place disparate components beside each other, holding in connection what does not necessarily belong together through poetic work. I consider poetry to be a safeguard of what falls out of thought dominated by linear argument. I must be aware that, as I search this poetry in the service of a linear argument, I may break contiguous connections and lose life-enhancing offerings that are uniquely possible in the poetic form. My book's structure and strategy represent my attempt to lose less.

"Manifesto on Ars Poetica"

By way of example, I provide a reading of Frank Chipasula's "Manifesto on Ars Poetica" from his collection *Whispers in the Wings* (1991). Chipasula's poem is particularly suited to illustrating my approach because it explicitly takes as its subject its own relationship to witness.[16] Chipasula's poem also sets up concerns that will reappear across this book's chapters (namely, relationships between land and body, community and nation, and art and artist). As its name suggests, "Manifesto on Ars Poetica" is a manifesto on the art of poetry, and, as its topic will make clear, the manifesto is about witness poetry particularly.

Chipasula is a Malawian poet who writes in response to Hastings Kamuzu Banda's oppressive regime (1961–94). In an article considering Chipasula's poems as efforts against truths lost in censorship, Reuben Makayiko Chirambo explains, "As a single-party dictator, Banda saw Malawi as a personal fiefdom, consistently referring to its people as *my* people, in the manner of a grand patriarch that brooded no opposition; he authorized detention without trial, political persecution, forced exile, torture, and even murder of those opposed to him" ("A Monument to a Tyrant" 4). According to James Gibbs, in 1973, Chipasula, after publishing a collection of poetry, "cut short his undergraduate career and, apparently convinced that he faced imminent detention, went into exile" (20). As Chirambo writes in "Dissident Writing: Home and Exile in Frank Chipasula's *Whispers in the Wings*," "exile meant living in perpetual fear of being killed by agents of Banda, a fact that Chipasula acknowledges in his poems" (4). In "Manifesto on Ars Poetica," Chipasula examines art's role in witnessing such violence and fear.

Chipasula explicitly works through what it means to use poetry to speak truth. The poem begins, "My poetry is exacting a confession"; it ends, "Today, my poetry has exacted a confession from me." In between these lines, then, is the confession. "Confession" must be understood here in the sense of "recognizing or acknowledging (of a person or thing) as having a certain character or certain claims; declaration of belief in or adhesion to; acknowledgement, profession, avowal when asked" (OED). By asserting that the poem has exacted a confession rather than testimony, Chipasula differentiates between the declaration of avowed truth (confession) and the declaration of what one has experienced (testimony). What we know of the speaker's personal experience is limited to how he will declare his avowed truth through this poem. Indeed, Chipasula positions his speaker as someone who knows the truth, but not exactly as the witness in this poem. Rather, the speaker asks that the poem will be the witness through his adhesion to the truth: "I will ask only that the poem watch the world closely; / I will ask only that the image put a lamp on the dark / ceiling in the dark sky of my land and light the dirt" (23–5). The speaker does not put a lamp on the ceiling: the image does. The speaker's repeated future-tensed "I will" indicates what he will have done by the shift to past tense in the poem's final line. What he will have done is use his avowed truth to create images and metaphors that can work together to "watch the world closely" (the world of "my land" rendered an image of home through the domestic imagery of the lamp and ceiling).

The poem "exacts" in two senses: it compels a confession and also perfects it. The confession is transformed by the poem. The opening lines explain this commitment to truth as art professes it: "I will not keep the truth from my song. / I will not bar the voice undressed by the bees / from entering the gourd of my bow-harp" (2–4). Later, the speaker says he will "undress our raped land and expose her wounds" in this confession (14). First, though, the land – in the synecdoche of bees and gourd – will undress his voice. That is, he uncovers the land's wounds, but first the land undecorates his voice so that it can speak the truth of those wounds. In the process of speaking through song, he redecorates the land, its wounds, and his own voice. Confessing truth in poetry, Chipasula's manifesto indicates, does not provide readers with direct access to a poet's truth; we get the truth as the bow-harp speaks it.

Making the song truthful means not barring the voice undressed by bees. These bees collect a metaphorical pollen from the voice, undressing it in the sense they might undress a flower of its pollen, leaving it bare. Bees take the ingredient for sweetness from the words; the sweetener is the part that is not the truth, and it is the sweet untruth the bees remove. The speaker allows the undressed voice, with the sweetness taken away, to enter the bare, hollowed-out vessel of the instrument (made of a gourd, a vessel hollowed out from fruit, and thus also made bare for the truth). The voice that is stripped away to the truth enters that which will make it into song. Interestingly, though, the song on the bow-harp, as art, will have its own sweetness; to turn the truth into song dresses it up again. The undressed truth will presumably be transformed in some way on this bow-harp. The speaker will put bare truth into the poem, but the poem will dress it with its music. In this way, Chipasula's poem clearly asks us not to read the witness it creates as simply Chipasula's experience. The poem transforms his experience into a witness song that speaks a truth dressed differently from the truth he knows because he chooses to confess that truth through song. The song's sweetness, or the poem's aesthetics, creates its own witness.

The poem can keep compelling confessions – in the sense of acknowledgement of its claims – from readers. Thus, the role of readers is to confess their own witness of the poem, not to imagine they know the speaker's experience of suffering. Indeed, the poem is addressed primarily to others who suffered under the tyrant in Malawi. The speaker "serve[s]" his words "to our people" (19). The "people" who are "pounded to pulp" (17) are not only those whose suffering the poem witnesses but also those whom the speaker serves. Readers not being served these words are positioned to consider how they, by reading, serve as tertiary participants in the network of relationships the poem creates. I contend that such a reader's role is not to imagine that he or she understands how it might feel to be "pounded to pulp" nor to imagine that he or she now witnesses alongside this speaker-as-poet. Rather, this poem asks the readers it does not directly serve to note how – through its poetic strategies – it serves as witness for Malawians. For the non-Malawian reader, the confession might be precisely the acknowledgement of the poem's witnessing power: I confess this poem does "distil life into the horrible adjectives" (10).

Thus, though the dominant approach to witness poetry today involves looking for fragmentation as a sign of unspeakable suffering, such an approach here would defy the reading the poem demands. Stylistically, "Manifesto on Ars Poetica" is not fragmented but explicitly based on "[t]he run-on line" (8). An anaphoric "I will" unifies the poem, as do the many semicolons that strongly link pairs of lines (twelve of the poem's twenty-seven lines are connected by semicolons). As its title indicates, the poem creates the united statement of a manifesto. As for gaps or ellipses, there is only the emptiness of the line that holds the single, right-aligned word "metaphors" (17): "I will pierce the silence around our land with sharp / metaphors" (16–17).[17] The silence clouds the land, but metaphors can pierce silence to bring clarity. The empty space in the poem suggests the hole the speaker has pierced in the silence with the metaphor's sharpness. To read this gap as silence, as a traumatic eruption, or as unspeakable suffering would be to ignore the specific power the poem attributes to this collaboration between the speaker's confession and the poem's witness.

Accordingly, Chipasula's poem and its speaker work together as two victims of tyranny's violence:

> I will not wash the blood off the image;
> I will let it flow from the gullet
> slit by the assassin's dagger through
> the run-on line until it rages in the verbs of terror (5–8)

The speaker allows the blood *on* the image to rage *as* the poem's blood. The blood first let in violence is this poem's lifeblood. When the poem is itself attacked, the assassin's cut to the run-on line does not fragment it, but infuses the poem with life. Thus, this poem is not rendered unable to speak by violence; as poetic witness, it exists through and because of that violence, and it speaks that existence clearly. The blood rages in the verbs of terror, verbs of which "to rage" is one. Likewise, "horrible" is an adjective signifying horror. The poem is what it says; it refers to its own internal consistency. Later, verbs reappear as "volatile verbs that burn the lies" (22). These verbs, then, rage like fire, not like an angry person. As the poem proceeds, the verbs move from holding the speaker's rage to holding their own volatility. This poem is about its own powerful living witness.

This shifting verb-work also illustrates the contiguous strategy I find in witness poetry more broadly, a strategy prominent in Chipasula's poem. Consider truth's movement: "I will not keep the truth from my heartstringed guitar; / I will thread the voice from the broken lips / through my volatile verbs that burn the lies" (20–2). The truth would move across the guitar's strings, which are also the heart's strings. Then, the thread becomes the speaker's voice that can move from his mouth to string together verbs that might explode to burn the lies. The speaker strings together his truth such that the speaking and ownership of the truth become dispersed across several agents, instruments, and locations. These include his instrument for telling the truth, which is partly himself, his own heartstrings, and partly a separate object, a guitar; the suffering that he generalizes with the definite pronoun – "the broken lips" – suggesting the connection of his heartstrings to a broader suffering related to the national silence, the "silence around our land"; and the poem that witnesses that suffering and pierces that silence. The effect of "Manifesto on Ars Poetica" is to emphasize how art shapes witness, to remove that witness from the literal without hazarding its truth.

What the poem makes explicit is that readers do not feel the speaker's rage, let alone the poet's. Rather, we feel the verb's raging that reflects Chipasula's rage while belonging to the poem. A reader's role is to feel something in relation to the raging verbs. This feeling-together with the poem is the strategy for compassion I find in witness poetry. Chipasula demonstrates in this manifesto the importance of art's mediating factor in compassionate response to witness poetry.

Part One

Trauma and Compassion

A Contagious Notion of Trauma

With the Witnesses intervenes in how trauma theory has been applied to art. Though this book's main purpose is to engage contemporary Anglophone witness poetry's compassionate strategies, this chapter first makes clear the dominant approach to witness poetry – demonstrated in Cathy Caruth's *Literature in the Ashes of History* and Shoshana Felman and Dori Laub's *Testimony: Crisis of Witnessing in Literature, Psychoanalysis, and History* – which my book sets itself against. Not only are Caruth and Felman the field's much-cited foundational thinkers, but their own mutual citation also shows that they participate in a shared conversation. Through selected chapters from *Testimony* and from *Literature in the Ashes of History*, I critique the popular trauma studies model these two key thinkers have shaped. At the end of the chapter, I read Peter Balakian's "The Oriental Rug" in contrast to the reading it has received on this model in Walter Kalaidjian's *The Edge of Modernism: American Poetry and the Traumatic Past*. To situate Balakian's poem in my approach, I also read it in comparison with witness poetry by Joy Harjo and Seamus Heaney.

My argument in this chapter is that, while trauma theory is valuable, the form it has taken in the humanities – with its special emphasis on inaccessible histories, unspeakable suffering, and unconscious witnessing – is predisposed to a reading that denies power and agency in witnesses by rhetorically transferring that power, through an idea of contagious trauma, to those engaging witness through art. I do not find unclaimed experience in the poetry I read here. Clearly, positing the ability and responsibility to respond to representations of suffering is essential so that those receiving testimony have the power to answer its call. However, the tactic is troubling insofar as it gives listeners power by disempowering those witnesses appearing in or witnessing through artistic texts.

Caruth's *Unclaimed Experience* has faced harsh critique along these lines. In *Trauma*, Ruth Leys is "unsympathetic to the way in which [Caruth] tends to dilute and generalize the notion of trauma: in her account the experience (or nonexperience) of trauma is characterized as something that can be shared by victims and nonvictims alike, and the unbearable sufferings of the survivor as a pathos that can and must be appropriated by others" (305). Leys notes that these "ideas about trauma are today much in vogue in the humanities" because Caruth's "work epitomizes the contemporary literary-critical fascination with the allegedly unrepresentable and unspeakable nature of trauma" (16). Not fascinated herself, Leys expresses an "impatience with the sloppiness of her theoretical arguments," contending that "in the name of close reading," Caruth "produces interpretations that are so arbitrary, willful, and tendentious as to forfeit all claim to believability" (305). While Caruth's theoretical arguments seem grounded in psychiatrist Bessel van der Kolk's work, Leys notes that the two thinkers draw on each other's work to validate their shared ideas in circular fashion, thus shoring up their mutual "relishing" of this "currently modish idea" about trauma (304). While Van der Kolk believes that trauma is literally not available to the brain's ordinary memory processes, Leys shows "that such a literalist view of trauma is not only theoretically incoherent but also poorly supported by the scientific evidence" (16). Nevertheless, these "ideas have helped solidify a powerful trend in the humanities to recognize in the experience of trauma, especially the trauma of the Holocaust, a fundamental crisis for historical representation (and at the limit, for representation as such)" (16).[1]

LaCapra points out "two questionable consequences" to the idea of trauma's unrepresentability, "even if one does not go to the hyperbolic point of identifying that excess with the 'real' or with the idea that, in traumatic memory, the event is repeated in its incomprehensible, unreadable literality" (WH 92). One, this emphasis "may divert attention from what may indeed be represented" (92). Two, it may "prompt a foreclosure, denigration, or inadequate account not only of representation but of the difficult issue of ethically responsible agency" (93). Both issues are central to the reading and writing of witness poetry. Caruth's position does not allow one to recognize the suffering represented in such poetry or to respond responsibly to it. Witness poetry represents suffering that may be called "unspeakable." Yet these poems do speak that suffering. Suffering often finds practical articulation. Without, perhaps, being able to explain fully or even satisfiably how suffering feels, one can represent or communicate suffering to some useful degree such that others might respond to it. This point does not reduce suffering's importance; rather, the acknowledgement of diverse experiences of suffering prevents an approach that must ignore what it cannot account for. Some experiences of suffering, rather than transcending human experience, are accessible and integrated parts of both daily life and life narratives.

Since Caruth's engagement with artistic texts in *Unclaimed Experience* has already been addressed,[2] I focus on her newest text. In my engagement with *Literature in the Ashes of History*, I will address points where Caruth's literary analyses remove agency from witnessing characters. In her second chapter, Caruth considers Honoré de Balzac's *Colonel Chabert*. Here, her problematic conflation of disfigurement with "literal" dehumanization (25) and her larger idea of the character's degree of powerlessness is related to her investment in reading this novel's witnessing as "peculiar," "strange," "haunting," "remarkable," "singular," "surprising," "odd," and "enigmatic." Her reading depends on making the witness into "a figure of inhumanity" (25) (she also confuses the inhuman and the dehumanized) so that the strangeness of witness can more emphatically remain outside of structures of representation. Similarly, in her fourth chapter, Caruth consistently depends on a merging of desire, ease, and ability in Ariel Dorfman's *Death and the Maiden* to claim a disappearance of Paulina's torture that the play does not suggest (indeed, Caruth must omit evidence that contradicts her argument). Caruth reads Paulina's acute discomfort with hearing the music that accompanied her torture as an inability to listen that becomes a generalized condition. Thus, Caruth relies on a model of contagion that dilutes the meaning of trauma. This strategy is most obvious in her comments on the play's conclusion where she turns the possibility for audience self-reflection into a conflation of audience with victims.

To begin with Balzac's *Colonel Chabert*, here the titular character is believed to have died in battle when he returns to Paris – poverty-stricken, sickly, and disfigured – to regain his identity. In Caruth's words, Chabert becomes "the man mutilated and barely recognizable as human" (25). Caruth takes for granted that disfigurement is dehumanizing, though the story does not evidence such a reading. Since the social repercussions of conflating dehumanization with representations of disfigurement or disability can only be harmful, this misreading is all the more significant. It is not possible to read Chabert, as Caruth insists we do, as "a figure of inhumanity" (25); he does not return "as a cry for humanity emanating from someone not yet recognized as human" (25). In fact, the story is largely made up of Chabert encountering others who recognize his need and help him regain his health. Some of these people accept him as Chabert, though most do not. In the story, the mutilation is important because it makes him unrecognizable as himself, not because it makes him unrecognizable as human. In fact, the mutilation makes it difficult for him to claim his identity, but does not make him completely unrecognizable; his wife recognizes him immediately (74). Further, each time his claim to his identity is ridiculed, his poverty, not his mutilation, causes disbelief. The story clearly situates poverty as a condition that leads to unjust treatment and prejudice. The only time Chabert is dehumanized is when he is called "that old greatcoat" by Simonnin the clerk, who is immediately reprimanded with: "No matter how poor a client is, he's still a man, damn it!" (1). This opening scene in which Chabert rhetorically becomes his poor wardrobe, the outward sign of his poverty, sets up the story's concern with poverty as a force shaping perceived identity.

Thus, while the story critiques the mistreatment of the poor, and offers this moment of corrected dehumanization to illuminate this mistreatment, it never suggests that Chabert's disfigurement renders him inhuman. In a footnote, Caruth observes "the difference" between the lawyer Derville's first encounter with Chabert and his last: "Chabert's face is now described as noble, rather than as ghastly or ghostly. The emphasis on Chabert's disfigured face, in this story, has intriguing implications ... for the ethical dimension implicit in the address of the unrecognizable other" (106n27). Yet Chabert's face changes for Derville as soon as Derville gives him the bit of money that extricates Chabert from total poverty: "He no more resembled the Chabert of the old greatcoat than an old sou resembles a newly minted forty-franc gold piece. Looking at him, anyone could easily have recognized one of the noble remnants of our former army" (69). Caruth omits this much earlier recognized nobility and its relationship to material means. This earlier passage describing Chabert's nobility matches in length[3] what Caruth argues to be the "extended and lengthy development" of his original "ghastly and ghostly" appearance (106n27) while also indicating the transitory and inessential nature of a ghostly appearance that can be dissipated by a loan.

Indeed, Caruth's emphasis on Chabert's disfigured face has "intriguing implications for the ethical dimension implicit" in her need for him to be a figure for a ghostly history that repeats itself as an unrecognizable other. Though he has a "cadaverous physiognomy" (that is, death-like, not inhuman), still "an observer, especially an attorney, would have found signs of the poverty that had stricken this face" (17). His disfigurement is hidden under a wig (18) and when he accidently shows his scar, the clerk Boucard thinks, "If he isn't Colonel Chabert, he must be some other brave trooper!" (18). By this disfigurement, the clerk recognizes Chabert not only as human but as either Chabert or someone like himself, and as someone deserving of his respect. Though Caruth dehumanizes Chabert for her argument, the text does not support her reading.

Literature in the Ashes of History's fourth chapter, "Disappearing History: Scenes of Trauma in the Theater of Human Rights," similarly disempowers a suffering character by providing her with an inability she does not have. Caruth argues that Paulina from Dorfman's *Death and the Maiden* suffers from an inability to listen that results from her torture. According to Caruth's reading, this inability to listen is bound up with Paulina's inability to tell her story. To provide some context, *Death and the Maiden* takes place in a country that is moving from a dictatorship to democracy. Before the play begins, and before this political transition, Paulina was tortured and raped. Now her husband, Gerardo, works for a new commission that will investigate human rights violations. Paulina's story cannot be heard since the investigations are limited to violations causing death. When Roberto, a stranger who had helped Gerardo with a flat tire earlier, arrives with a spare tire, Paulina believes she recognizes his voice as that of her torturer. She captures Roberto and creates her own commission, forcing him to confess to her and Gerardo. She believes Roberto is guilty, and the play ends without the audience knowing if she follows through on her threat to kill him. Caruth's argument more generally in *Literature in the Ashes of History* is that there is "a new kind of history, one that is made up of events that seem to undo, rather than produce, their own remembrance" (back cover). In her reading of Dorfman's play, she is invested in showing Paulina caught up in such a history. While Paulina is indeed caught up in a history of disappeared people and a commission that will not hear her story of suffering, the disappearance for Paulina of her own history is not validated by the play.

Caruth claims that "the play's unspecified setting extends its significance beyond any particular political limitation" (56). But, Dorfman specifies a very particular political context. As Caruth herself cites from the play, the setting "could be any country that has just departed from a dictatorship" (54). This emergence from dictatorship is the particular political limitation to the play's significance. Thus, it is a problem that Caruth proceeds as though the play is about History rather than about the specified historical context the play explicitly works within. She argues, "There appears to be a more fundamental problem, in other words, at the heart of Paulina's return – in the figure of Paulina and in the action of the rest of the play" (56). The more fundamental problem is the problem of the "new kind of history" Caruth traces throughout her book. Paulina becomes a "figure" of this "legal, societal, cultural and psychological" problem (110n8) rather than an individual living through and past dictatorship. Turning characters (representations of people) into figures (representations of ideas – particularly here the ideas the critic has before reading the text at hand) is the repeated issue I am tracing through Caruth's and Felman's work.

Paulina as figure must show the forgetting Caruth posits for her new history. Paulina's torturer played Schubert's "Death and the Maiden" as a soundtrack to her torture; Caruth argues that Paulina's "torture has created an *inability to listen*, a physiological repugnance whenever the music is played. And this inability to listen is not limited to Paulina's inability to listen to the music used during her torture. It seems to spread to others, to be bound up, indeed, with the inability of her husband to listen to her speak" (63). It may seem a small exaggeration to move from Paulina's feeling "extremely ill" (Dorfman 21) when she hears the music that played while she was tortured to her "*inability to listen*" to it. Informally, people often use "unable" to mean actually able but not without negative consequences. This inaccurate conflation, though, is the foundation for Caruth's argument. Not only does Caruth claim that Paulina's inability to listen spreads to others, but she also uses it as evidence of Paulina's inability to know and testify to her torture, as evidence of her torture's disappearance.

Though Caruth argues for the "inability" of Gerardo to listen to Paulina speak, Gerardo is not, in fact, unable to listen to Paulina's story. Caruth writes, "If for Paulina the inability to listen to the Schubert is the return of the experience of torture, the referent that is absolutely real for her, for Gerardo, on the other hand, Paulina's mode of responding to music only produces a desire not to listen to Paulina and a disbelief in the veracity of her words" (63). Gerardo never doubts that Paulina was raped and tortured, so Caruth's comments about the music calling up this "referent that is absolutely real for her" in contrast to Gerardo's disbelief "on the other hand" are misleading. Gerardo's inability to listen quickly changes, in Caruth's own words, into "a desire not to listen." The proof Caruth gives for this desire not to listen is Gerardo's "Don't go on, Paulina" (63). Yet this statement does not come in reaction to Paulina trying to tell her story of torture. Rather, Gerardo responds to Paulina's explanation of her former hope to attain revenge by having Gerardo rape her torturer. Thus, Gerardo does not exhibit a "disbelief in the veracity of her words" but an unwillingness to have her narrate a revenge fantasy with himself as its agent. Further, we find later that the reason Gerardo does not know the details of Paulina's torture is not necessarily or primarily because he does not want to know but because when Paulina initially began to tell him, she was interrupted by the evidence of Gerardo's infidelity (53). Indeed, Gerardo in this scene is asking Paulina for her story. Though he needs the story to give it to Roberto so that Roberto might satisfy Paulina with his testimony, this request and the reason for Paulina's previous silence at the very least complicate Caruth's account of Gerardo's desire not to listen and his infection by a contagious inability to listen.

Caruth herself notes that when Gerardo asks for Paulina's story he is "finally professing a desire to listen to Paulina" (64). She does not, though, explain what this sudden desire means in relation to her foregoing argument nor does she contextualize his desire with his plan to relay it to Roberto so that he might construct a convincing testimony. In fact, Caruth must leave out this aspect of the play to make her argument about Paulina's ultimate disempowerment, which is how she characterizes the moment near the end of the play when Paulina's voice, telling the story of her torture, is supplanted by Roberto's voice. As the stage directions explain, first we hear "*Paulina's voice*" and then "*we hear Roberto's voice overlapping with Paulina's*" (Dorfman 58). Caruth argues

> the continuity between Paulina's words, which begin the story, and Roberto's words, which continue it, appear to provide a convincing account of Paulina's rape and torture. But this narrative continuity, notably, takes place in a sequence in which Paulina's words break off, and Roberto's words take over, drowning out Paulina's voice at the very moment that she describes the beginning of Roberto's actions in the past. The fading away of Paulina's narrative occurs, moreover, just as she refers to the first time she heard, during her captivity, the music of Schubert. (65)

Yet, significantly, the breaking off of Paulina's words to be carried on by Roberto takes place at the level of the play, not within its plot. It is Dorfman who drowns out Paulina's voice here, not Roberto. Moreover, read with an awareness of the plot, this staging decision needs to be understood otherwise: Paulina has arranged this moment where Roberto takes her words as his own. Caruth writes, "The breaking off of Paulina's narrative in the dark and the transition to the words of Roberto, as the music comes up over the scene, also *reenacts* the events that are being told, and does so in the disappearance of Paulina's words behind the voice of Roberto" (65). This analysis does not account for the fact that this is a conscious and deliberate re-enactment that Paulina herself orchestrates. Paulina has given false details in her testimony to Gerardo because she knows he plans to pass the story on to Roberto. If he gives the accurate details rather than these false ones in his story, he shows to Paulina that he was her torturer (Dorfman 64).

This trick takes a form similar to the one the torturer, "playing the role of the good guy," uses when he plays the music to win Paulina's trust only to use that same music as a soundtrack to her torture and rape (Dorfman 58). Caruth argues, "The music will thus lose its power to evoke and refer to Paulina's own will and desire and, from that point on, evoke and refer itself only to the desire and power of Roberto, and to the missed moment of her inscription in his game. Paulina's very words *about* the music, in her scene of testimony, will likewise elicit and become lost in the narration by Roberto" (66). Again, Caruth leaves out the way that Roberto's narration comes from Paulina's false details that Gerardo gives him as the "good guy" in Paulina's trick, details that make Roberto feel he might be saved but that actually refer to the "will and desire" of Paulina. Paulina clearly brings Roberto into the story in a way that mimics how he (or her torturer) brought her into the music. Yes, Roberto's words take over, but only to show how he has been tricked: she has spoken to give him the words that, when he speaks them, make him lose the game. As Paulina says, "I'm the one who came out on top in this game" (Dorfman 64).

Thus, Caruth's conclusion is not at all in keeping with the play's plot: "Although Paulina keeps speaking, her words cannot be heard –

we are unable to listen to them – just as she describes how the music
to which she originally listened with pleasure is turned into a tool for
her torture" (65). The audience, though, is not unable to listen to Paulina's words; rather, the audience hears her words told in a way that
implicates and traps Roberto just as she meant them to. Further, it
is important to note that her words are not inaccessible to us "just
as" torture made the music inaccessible to her. Clearly, the audience's
literal inability to hear words not spoken on a stage is not "just as" a
torture victim's illness at hearing music associated with her torture.
Caruth too easily posits a contagious notion of the inability to hear.
She misreads the play and the audience's relationship to it because (1)
she disempowers Paulina in ways that the narrative and its staging
do not allow and (2) she gives Paulina's experience to the audience
in ways that the play does not allow. Audiences following Caruth's
reading cannot respond to Paulina compassionately, as I understand
compassion, because they must ignore much of what Paulina says and
does. To catch this contagious inability to listen, they must not listen to
Paulina bear witness to her own story.

But, for Caruth, Paulina is unable to tell her story. She argues that
because Paulina was inscribed into the music against her will, "the
capacity to hear now becomes the site of a reenactment of the torture.
Thus losing the capacity to *listen* on her own terms, Paulina loses listening as a possible form of singular testimony, as a way in which she
might remember and tell others of what has happened and thus be able
to bear witness to her disappearing past" (67). Not being able to listen
on one's own terms is not the same thing as not being able to listen at
all. If an experience of coercion, an experience not on one's own terms,
becomes a disappearing past that one cannot bear witness to because
remembering cannot occur outside of that coercion, then there would
be no possibility of witness and testimony. Thus, aside from the faulty
proof Caruth bases this point on, I find the point itself troubling. A
more useable approach might be to consider all testimony to tell of
a past coercion such that the very occurrence of testimony bespeaks
the ways that coercive experience cannot be left in the past but must
be part of its telling. I see no value in approaching those testifying as
though such coercive experiences have made them utterly powerless.

Moreover, Caruth's argument is troubled by the fact that Paulina does in fact both remember and tell. Her past does not disappear from her or from the play. Her comments to Roberto show that she knows the details of her torture: "Isn't this bizarre, that I should be telling you all this as if you were my confessor, when there are things I've never told Gerardo, or my sister, certainly not my mother. She'd die if she knew what I've really got in my head. Whereas I can tell you exactly what I feel, what I felt when they let me go" (29). While the difficulty of finding an adequate witness is apparent here, so is Paulina's ability to know and tell her past. Yet Caruth argues, "Her inscription in Roberto's performance – too soon for her to realize, too late for her later to undo – returns in her later life as a constant reenactment of what she can no longer simply hear or tell. The past thus disappears in this *betrayal of listening*, a betrayal that appears, on the level of the play itself, to infect all forms of hearing" (67). There is a new issue here in Caruth's notion of betrayal. If Paulina had been betrayed, but never realized that she had been, and continued on with her initial misconception, then Caruth's account of a corrupted ability to hear or tell that experience might be accurate. But, Paulina understands that her initial misconception was a misconception; she understands what happened accurately. Of course she experiences the betrayal before she realizes and after it happens. A betrayal can be experienced in no other way. If a betrayal happens after one already knows it will happen, it is not properly a betrayal, since there must be trust to be betrayed. Caruth suggests that no experience involving betrayal can be adequately heard or told.

As Caruth posits Paulina's inabilities, she does so within a power dynamic that favours the audience. She argues, "This moment when Paulina loses her ability to listen to Schubert is itself enacted as something not fully grasped by Paulina, as the very break in the sentence as she describes her act of listening: 'There is no way of describing what it means to hear [*escuchar*, to listen to] that wonderful music in the darkness'" (66). Yet Paulina says there is no way of *describing* what it means to her, not no way of grasping it. Paulina understands; it is communicating that understanding to others that is not possible. When Caruth disempowers Paulina by saying she does not grasp her own

experience of listening, she relies on the contagious notion of suffering
that suggests that we – as audience or onlookers who also experience
"an inability to listen that makes the evidence of the torture inaccessible as a mode of truth" (64) – can nevertheless access Paulina's suffering and know how it feels and means for her. While Paulina says there
is no way to make another understand her experience, Caruth reverses
the situation: Caruth takes the understanding from Paulina for herself.
Caruth's approach is invested in taking away the witness's abilities, not
out of malicious intent, but to prove an idea about history as catastrophe through the impossibility of witnessing, the inaccessibility of truth,
and the unrespresentability of trauma.

Of course, whatever understanding the audience has must ultimately
be folded back into the new kind of history of disappearance that is
Caruth's ultimate point. Significantly, Caruth turns the play's moment
for audience self-reflection into one of identification. At the end of the
final act's first scene, "*Paulina and Roberto are covered from view by
a giant mirror which descends, forcing the members of the audience
to look at themselves. For a few minutes, the Mozart quartet is heard,
while the spectators watch themselves in the mirror. Selected slowly
moving spots flicker over the audience, picking out two or three at a
time, up and down rows*" (66). By forcing audience members to view
themselves as watchers of this play, Dorfman positions them as active
witnesses to what they have just seen. They, as real individuals in the
world, have received this story, and Paulina's fictional life enters their
non-fictional realities. Caruth, though, claims that "we might think
of the faces in the mirror coming before the audience and actors as,
perhaps, giving us the faces of the disappeared, as the placards of the
Mothers of the Plaza de Mayo did – hence faces that are also prosopo-
poeic figures of absence or death as much as representation of living,
present people" (116–17). There is simply no suggestion in the play
that audience members might see themselves as the disappeared, and
Caruth does not attempt to provide any evidence for why we might
"perhaps" understand appearances in the mirror to function in this
way. In conflating the audience with the disappeared, Caruth seems to
strengthen her position that the audience could not have heard Paulina's story, that stories of torture and death are absent, and that their

presence in this play only further signals that absence. Yet it is difficult to believe that audience members, seeing their own faces, would imagine themselves as disappeared. Moreover, there is significant value in the self-reflection invited in the audience's spotlit faces that is lost in Caruth's reading. It is my aim in this book to demonstrate the loss, in identificatory strategies, of such opportunities to consider the unique and individual nature of one's position in relation to specific suffering.

Shoshana Felman brings such identificatory strategies to *Testimony*. In her first chapter, she describes her class's response to videos of testimony from Holocaust survivors. After her students react with what she characterizes as a traumatic crisis, she tells them that their experience of listening to this testimony is one through which they can identify with Celan's experience in the Holocaust, "this loss that we have all been somehow made to live" (50), such that "you can now, perhaps, relate to this loss more immediately, more viscerally, when you hear the poet say that *language was 'all that remained'*" (50). While many scholars have criticized this characterization of her class's experience as a loss akin to the loss experienced by Holocaust survivors,[4] the pedagogical strand of Felman's argument is also a problem. She presents "the trauma they had gone through" as a model of learning in general, arguing that the crisis has "the validity of a generic pedagogical event and thus of a generic lesson. I would venture to propose, today, that teaching in itself, teaching as such, takes place precisely only through a crisis" (52). Either she dilutes the meaning of trauma in suggesting that the difficult change of learning (anything) is traumatic, or she negates her claim that her class was traumatized to conclude that they had instead only genuinely learned something (from the testimony). Despite Felman's celebration of the situation as a paradigm of learning, LaCapra notes that "the extreme traumatization of a class through a process of unchecked identification with victims would obviously not be a criterion of success in the use of survivor videos" (*WH* 102). Yet Felman's conflation of learning and trauma leaves open only one plausible ethical position to those encountering another's suffering: a position of identification in which individuals learn the other's suffering by taking it as their own. The relationship in which learning and response might take place disappears if the unique position of the responder is denied so that the position of sufferer can be claimed, even when, as LaCapra puts it, "it is blatantly obvious that there is a major difference between the experience of camp inmates or Holocaust survivors and that of the viewer of testimony videos" (102–3). Felman's idea that her class now has a "visceral" idea of the trauma of the Holocaust disavows and forecloses whatever actual feelings and ideas her students might have had in response to a trauma they do not know.

I find striking the frequency with which LaCapra must note, as he does in both above quotations, what is "obviously" wrong with Felman's argument. Since the problems are indeed obvious, I imagine that her perspective has been so taken up by scholars for decades because of what comes across as her genuine emotion about a subject matter that easily demonstrates the inherent value in being studied. Felman's work is compelling insofar as it shows a person committed to what she is writing. However, scholarship is not the spontaneous expression of powerful feeling. While response to suffering is not entirely voluntaristic, as LaCapra notes ("Lanzmann's 'Shoah'" 267), the writing of analytic response to art can (and should) involve a great deal of self-reflection, re-engagement, and revision. Moreover, though Felman's critical work ostensibly expresses an emotion that she cannot contain, trauma studies maintains a strange tension between the contagion of trauma and the ability of the scholar or teacher to make meaning from that trauma. Felman intervenes in her students' crisis by assigning them tasks that will let them, she explains in her chapter, reclaim their knowledge and understand their suffering as important. Thus, Felman creates a model for responding to trauma in which scholars and students experience another's trauma but, unlike the original traumatized individual, can emerge from the trauma with greater knowledge and a new self-importance.

Felman's analysis of Claude Lanzmann's *Shoah* in her final chapter for *Testimony* betrays the same urge to empower those engaging with art at the expense of a traumatized individual. LaCapra notes that Lanzmann's similar urge is prominent in *Shoah* as well. In his article

"Lanzmann's 'Shoah': 'Here There Is No Why,'" LaCapra critiques Lanzmann's aim to provoke and relive the trauma suffered by others. LaCapra argues that, in *Shoah*, Lanzmann makes harmful choices (harmful to the survivors and to the representation the film creates) to serve his desire "to put himself in exactly the same position as the traumatized victim who relives what has not been lived" (255). In Felman's chapter, which LaCapra calls "perhaps the most famous and influential" reading of the film (245), LaCapra likewise finds the "unmediated transition from the status of the witness to that of the shattered, traumatized victim" combined with a "routinization of hyperbole or excess" (246). In what LaCapra calls Felman's "marked overinterpretation of the scene in front of the church" (249), I argue that Felman dehumanizes one of the witnesses in the film, turning him into a figure she links with the Nazi's term *Figuren*. Though her rhetorical move to make the living witness a figure instead of a person (and moreover a figure she labels with the Nazi's label) is meant out of respect for the testimony, it instead profoundly discounts the actual person appearing in the film. Much as Caruth does in *Colonel Chabert*, Felman finds dehumanization where there was a human to engage.

One of the survivors interviewed in Lanzmann's *Shoah* is Simon Srebnik, a boy at Chelmno who kept himself alive by singing songs for his guards; though he was ultimately shot, he survived (Felman 254). The scene LaCapra notes as overinterpreted in Felman's chapter is set up at a location from Srebnik's past: "Lanzmann places Srebnik in the center of a group of villagers before the church in Chelmo, which, at the time, served as a prison-house for the deported Jews and as the ultimate waystation on their journey – via gas vans – to the forest, where the (dead or living) bodies were being burned away in so-called ovens" (Felman 259). In this scene, Felman recounts, a Polish man inserts himself in front of the camera and in front of Srebnik to say the Holocaust "was God's will" and a consequence of Jesus' crucifixion (Felman 264). Felman reads this moment as the fact of the witness's death:

what the church scene puts into effect and plays out, not in memory but in actual fact (and act), is how the real witness, in returning back to history and life, is again *reduced to silence*, struck *dead* by the crowd ... But the Polish villagers ... are unaware of the precise ways in which they themselves are actually *enacting* both the Crucifixion and the Holocaust in *annihilating* Srebnik, in *killing once again the witness* whom they totally dispose of, and *forget*. (267)

Without making light of the silencing Felman points out, one can see the problem in conflating that silencing with the "actual fact (and act)" of being "struck *dead*," of "actually *enacting*" the Holocaust. Silencing is, of course, not the same thing as "actually" "*annihilating*" and "*killing once again the witness*." Felman's focus on the actual betrays the metaphorical import of what she is saying. The way that the witness is metaphorically "dispose[d] of" is deeply important, but Felman's insistence on literality obfuscates that import.

This claim for Srebnik's death is perhaps meant to be all the more compelling because, Felman argues, Srebnik has only just come alive, thanks to Lanzmann's film:

it is only now, today that Srebnik can become a witness ... only today that he can situate his witnessing in a frame of reference that is not submerged by death and informed solely by *Figuren*, by dead bodies. It is therefore only now, in returning with Lanzmann to Chelmno, that Srebnik in effect is returning from the dead (from his own deadness) and can become, for the first time, a witness to himself. (258)

Felman does not offer evidence that Srebnik has never in the course of his life re-situated what he witnessed in new frames of reference. Her assumption that he has lived, until now, a dead life and only returns from his deadness because of Lanzmann's film seems to presumptuously account for his life. Such presumptuousness is perhaps unavoidable in reading Srebnik as an archetypal figure of a traumatic history.

Further, Felman's claim that Srebnik comes alive when he returns to Chelmno with Lanzmann competes oddly with her other claim that he is a ghost who improbably returns. Srebnik, for Felman, "is himself rather a ghost of his own youthful performance, a returning, reappearing ghost of the one-time winner of chained races and of the boy singer" (257). Of course, Srebnik is not a ghost of his original performance but the adult living through his life with that performance in his past. Even if we allow for a traumatization that may have made that performance an unclaimed experience, an experience that is not fully registered and incorporated within that life, Srebnik's return to the place where he did not die does not in any meaningful way make him a ghost. A more appropriate reading would understand as the ghostly return the song Srebnik sings again now as an adult. Felman, though, needs to make Srebnik a ghost so that she can argue that "his improbable survival and his even more improbable return (his ghostly reappearance) concretizes allegorically, in history, a return of the (missing, dead) witness on the scene of the event-without-a-witness" (257). Rather than turning a person into an allegory, she could read this scene as what it is: a return of a literal witness (not missing or dead). Instead, Felman makes Srebnik's song a literal fragment of the past and Srebnik, the living person, an allegory. Strangely, then, the song is real while the agent singing it is only a symbol.

Referring to the church scene, Felman claims that Srebnik's testimony is lost but for his song: "In spite of his own silencing and of his silence, the return of the witness undertaken by the film nonetheless persists, takes over, and survives in the return of the song" (268). The "element through which the very silencing of Srebnik's voice can be somehow reversed" is not Srebnik's singing, but the film's inclusion of "the song" (268). It is not so much the "return of the witness" but the "return of the witness undertaken by the film" that "persists." In this argument, Srebnik does not survive the death Felman says he experiences in front of the church, but the film "takes over" from his silence. The song's agency is part of the film's agency; Srebnik himself seems reduced to a silence that is a necessary condition for the film's powerful witness.

By making Srebnik – not the song – the ghost that returns, Felman privileges the song (the art) at the expense of the person (the witness). Certainly, art helps give witness to atrocity, but there is no reason to privilege art and its abilities at the expense of individuals

and their agency (or at the expense of the circulation of their stories in ways that adequately present them as individuals). Srebnik
is oddly removed from his own singing because it is the "*place* to
which, at the beginning of the film, the song in fact *gives voice*" (269),
but not to Srebnik nor he to his song. Indeed, "this contemporaneity
between present and past, between the singing voice and the silent
place remains entirely incomprehensible to, and thus noncontempo-
raneous with, the witness" (269). Yet, Felman asks, "can we in our
turn become *contemporaneous* with the meaning and with the significance of that enactment? ... Can we, in other words, assume in earnest, not the finite task of making sense out of the Holocaust, but the
infinite task of encountering *Shoah*?" (268). Who took the first turn
if not Srebnik? Why should we get to assume this task in earnest, but
cannot consider Srebnik to be working on this infinite task as well?

Felman's analysis is not about Srebnik, but only about what Srebnik's material presence can do for the film and its viewers. Though
"what constitutes the power of the singing ... is ... the uniqueness
of the singing voice" (277), the contradiction between this emphasis
on uniqueness and Srebnik's absence from this discussion as a person
who owns that unique voice is perplexing. I find it astonishing that in
a chapter nearly eighty pages long there is no consideration of what
singing this song might mean for Srebnik. Felman makes his relation
to the song a non-relation, a ghostly noncontemporaneousness that
elides him – his reality as a person – from the film. Indeed, Srebnik's voice becomes art he cannot sign because it signs itself: "Like
Lanzmann, Srebnik ... is in turn a sort of artist: an artist who has lost
his words but has not lost the uniqueness of the singing voice and its
capacity for signature" (278). He is only "a sort of artist" because the
voice is self-signing.

In Felman's account, Srebnik is much more like the materials out
of which art is built than he is an artist: his bodily presence is "the
material, singular concretization of the testimony" (255). As material
of art, Srebnik can be transformed into a figure:

It is indeed the living body and the living face of the returning
witness that, in *Shoah*, becomes a speaking figure for the stillness

and the muteness of the bodies, a *figure* for, precisely, the *Figuren*. What the film does with the *Figuren* is to restore their muteness to the singing of the artist-child, to revitalize them by exploring death through life, and by endowing the invisibility of their abstraction with the uniqueness of a face, a voice, a melody, a song. (281–2)

This use of the Nazi term strikes me as odd. Felman gives the origin and meaning of the term on page 210 and then on 226, so when she uses it again more than thirty pages (258) and then nearly sixty pages (282) later, the word has been decontextualized in her chapter from this explanation of its source. If when Felman identifies the dead here with the term *Figuren* she means to reclaim a word that denied the humanity of Jewish people, it is not clear that this *figure/Figuren* wordplay respectfully approaches Srebnik's humanity. At best, this strategy seems counterintuitive – this term that denied humanity through abstraction seems hardly countered by abstracting the witness into a figure for that humanity-denying term. Though Felman emphasizes the witness's uniqueness, aligning Srebnik with the *Figuren* must make him, by Felman's own definition, "a mere *figure*: a disembodied verbal substitute which signifies abstractly the linguistic law of infinite exchangeability and substitutability" (210). Indeed, in Felman's chapter, once Srebnik becomes a figure of the absent witness whose existence is the material for powerful art, once his voice becomes not *his* voice but a voice that signs itself, once his song becomes the film's song, his contribution to Lanzmann's film becomes the "disembodied verbal substitute" of a song that invites the "infinite exchangeability and substitutability" of "we in our turn" becoming contemporaneous with the witness. Felman restricts Srebnik from this meaningful experience, except insofar as he is the material out of which our encounter with significance is premised upon.

These negative consequences for how suffering others are understood occur when preconceived ideas supplant close attention. Felman's argument shows this adherence to theory over text in her first chapter's engagement with poetry's relationship to trauma. She follows Caruth in understanding trauma in terms of the accident one realizes only belatedly. Though she ostensibly evidences this idea through comments by Stéphane Mallarmé, Felman uses Caruth's argument as a formula that obscures and runs over Mallarmé's text.

In "La Musique et les lettres," Mallarmé writes, "It is appropriate to relieve myself of that news right away – to talk about it now already – much like an invited traveler who, without delay, in breathless gasps, discharges himself of the testimony of an accident known, and pursuing him" (qtd. in Felman 18). Felman reads Mallarmé's news of a new kind of poetry as the news of an accident. However, it is clear in Mallarmé's words that the news is not like an accident; rather, he, the teller, will speak about the news like one who knows of an accident. The comparison is between the two tellers and takes as its subject the mode of telling. The comparison does not indicate that the poetry is an accident, but that he, telling about the poetry, has the breathlessness of one who tells of an accident.

Even taking all that aside, the comparison is not one of identity but of likeness. Despite Mallarmé's use of simile, Felman comes to speak of the change to poetry as literally an accident:

> The revolution in poetic form testifies, in other words, to political and cultural changes whose historical manifestation, and its revolutionary aspect, is now noticed accidentally – accidentally breaks into awareness – through an *accident of verse*. The poetic revolution is thus both a replica and a sequence, an effect of, the French Revolution. What free verse picks up on, therefore, is not merely former poetry which it now modifies, but the formerly unseen, ill-understood relationship which the accident reveals between culture and language, *between poetry and politics*. (20)

Her claim that the relationship between poetry and politics was "formerly unseen" seems to need some sort of historical evidence and discussion. Further, her claim that poetry changed through accident – that the historical changes emerged accidentally in poetry – rather than through poets' explorations of their historical time and personal experiences is consistent with readings of witness poetry and other art as holding and transmitting unconsciously written trauma.

Indeed, Felman pursues this line of thought. She argues that "since the accident 'pursues him,' he has got to speak '*already*,' almost compulsively, even though he has not had as yet time to catch his breath. He thus speaks in advance of the control of consciousness" (21). We can see here that Felman brings her interpretation far afield from the original statement. There is nothing in breathlessness that signifies a lack of control of consciousness; speaking more quickly than one's breath can come is not equivalent to speaking more quickly than one's thoughts can come.

Felman next attributes Mallarmé's breathlessness to the poetry he speaks of:

> Such precocious testimony in effect becomes, with Mallarmé, the very principle of poetic insight and the very core of the event of poetry, which makes precisely language – through its breathless gasps – speak ahead of knowledge and awareness and break through the limits of its own conscious understanding. By its very innovative definition, poetry will henceforth speak *beyond its means*, to testify – precociously – to the ill-understood effects and to the impact of an accident. (21)

Felman makes a claim about poetry's "very principle" through a series of misreadings based on a preconceived idea of trauma, as an accident of which one is only belatedly aware. Now it is poetry that speaks, as its "very core event," "ahead of knowledge and awareness." This idea of poetry's essence is precisely the problem in studies of poetry of witness where it is assumed that writers do not consciously and deliberately use poetic means and devices but are instead used by poetry, that its fragments and omissions are not, as in other forms of poetry, artistic ways of expressing meaning, but erupting signs of trauma.

To demonstrate more specifically how this conception of trauma's relationship with art can play out in the analysis of witness poetry, I use Armenian-American poet Peter Balakian's "The Oriental Rug" as an example, examining its recent treatment by one scholar in the field. Alongside Walter Kalaidjian's reading of Balakian's poetry, this chapter concludes with my own reading of Balakian's "The Oriental Rug." This poem, from the collection *Dyer's Thistle* (1996), features a speaker who can be understood as a secondary witness – a witness responding to suffering felt by others. In the poem, Balakian's American speaker engages with his grandparents' suffering through the intermediary of a rug from their Armenian home. The poem is organized through the metonymical relation of that rug to the Armenian landscape (it is associated with the landscape through its design and with Armenian culture as a household object and memory-piece carried to a new country). This metonymical relationship guides the structural metonymy of the poem which forms a reader's positioning. My critique of the assumption, in the critical work surrounding witness poetry, of readerly substitution and identification comes out of the poetry's organization around such contiguous relations.

Around secondary witnessing is a great deal of scholarly conversation about distances, something that I find to be missing from discussions of witness poetry more generally. Descendants of survivors, or those otherwise accessing the testimony of experience from others, are considered secondary witnesses who are able to represent what others endured only through their own relation to first-hand accounts. In *At Memory's Edge: After-Images of the Holocaust in Contemporary Art and Architecture*, James E. Young discusses secondary witnessing in relation to a "post-Holocaust generation of artists" which "does not attempt to represent events it never knew immediately but instead portrays its own, necessarily hypermediated experiences of memory" (1). The secondary witness is not "willing, or able, to recall the Holocaust separately from the ways it has been passed down" (1). Similarly, Susan Gubar, in *Poetry after Auschwitz: Remembering What One Never Knew*, explains her term "proxy-witness poetry":

> In stark contrast to poets of witness, poets of proxy-witnessing often acknowledge their belated dependence on after-the-fact accounts of extremities never within their purview. They do so in order to avoid any confusion between victims in their vulnerability

of "then" and poets or readers in the safety of "now," to concentrate on the disturbingly specific details of experiences decidedly not their own. (146)

Also considering poetry, Kalaidjian explains that "coming after the event, the secondary witness assumes not just an historical but, more importantly, an empathic stance toward traumatic memory" (9–10). Though Young, Gubar,[5] and Kalaidjian express similar sentiments about recognizing the distance involved in secondary witnessing, trauma studies' influence does not always lead to this recognition in practice. Because Kalaidjian prefers poetry that plays out the relationships to trauma that trauma theory expects, his assumption that the poem's speaker simply is the poet – without space for the construction that is involved even in the cases with the deepest connection between poet and speaker – leads to the substitution not only of trauma theory's concepts but also of Balakian's other work, words, and life for what happens in a given poem.

In *The Edge of Modernism*, Kalaidjian considers secondary witnessing from a trauma studies approach. Thus, his readings are founded in the idea that "trauma breaches discursive representation and eclipses thought itself" (3) while poetry is a special medium through which testimony to trauma can move "across the generations otherwise separating primary and secondary witnesses" (9). Kalaidjian understands the secondary witness as one who witnesses what "escapes cognitive mastery"; in the secondary witness, "the sublime, inchoate excess of trauma touches upon the mind precisely as that which eludes consciousness" (10).

Following these definitions, Kalaidjian's work shows a bias against poems making clear their distance from traumatic events through content or formal technique. In his chapter on poetry responding to the Holocaust, Kalaidjian argues against "any realistic representation" (65) in which "the impossible heart of the Holocaustal event is translated into discursive conventions that render it all too readable" (64–5). He argues that "much of Holocaust poetry lapses into the stock images and stereotypical scenes" (65). At the same time, the criticism around witness poetry relies precisely on stock images and stereotypical scenes belonging to the event's *un*representability. A trauma studies approach to literary analysis characterizes witness literature in terms of stereotypical assertions of absent traces, fragmentation, and unknowability. These stereotypical discursive conventions render the poetry under analysis "all too readable" and, indeed, misreadable.

For example, Kalaidjian judges Balakian's poetry to be lacking where it is too realistic. In his chapter about the Armenian Genocide, Kalaidjian affirms Balakian's "responsibility of remembrance" in the form of the poetic recording of the "particular incidents of atrocity" (43). In this affirmation, though, he includes the caveat, "Yet, that politics of testimony also assumes that we possess, rather than are possessed by, the agency of genocidal witness" (43). In this analysis of Balakian's "After the Survivors Are Gone," Kalaidjian denies the poem's strategies because they contradict what he believes about witness and trauma. If this otherwise acceptable witness poem does not use the strategies the critical discourse assumes it should use, then it seems plausible that the critical discourse could use the poetry's correction rather than the other way around. At the least, the critical discourse ought to make space for approaches and perspectives aside from its own. Certainly the idea that there is only one appropriate representational strategy for suffering does not serve anyone.[6]

Yet trauma studies' tenets suggest that since trauma has its own agency to move contagiously across generations and through texts, it will be written by all witnesses at all removes in the same fashion: as the "sublime, inchoate excess" that "breaches discursive representation and eclipses thought itself." Thus, in his discussion of "After the Survivors Are Gone," Kalaidjian asserts that Balakian's "poem forgets that the surviving remnant of those earlier generations can never clearly differentiate themselves from the phantom transmission of their revenants" (43). For Kalaidjian, Balakian's poem does not adequately demonstrate the idea that trauma's "inherent latency always already eludes conscious memory" (42). Yet, if Balakian wrote the poem without the eruption of phantom revenants, might he not be accurately engaging with his own experience as a secondary witness? Does a critic better know what individual descendants of genocide survivors are haunted by and how? Does a critic better know how that haunting ought to be represented? Are conventional representations of the breaching of conventional representation adequate to the job of signalling the eclipse of thought? Along with the "conscious commemoration" that he allows is important but also criticizes, Kalaidjian suggests that "the other, and less consoling, lesson of Balakian's poetics of memory" is that "the trace of the traumatic moment comes in its own time and presences its reference in excess of what we would choose to recall or repress" (43). Yet, from the perspective of trauma theory, this is the only lesson possible for witness poetry. In contrast, Balakian himself understands a poem that is a "mode of historical exploration" to be "an act of commemoration" (*Black Dog of Fate* 143). For Balakian, commemoration "is a process of making meaning out of unthinkable horror and loss" that is necessary for "redemption, hope, and community" (279). From this perspective, Kalaidjian's denial of poetic meaning-making is a denial of an important form of commemoration.

My point is not that literary critics should not criticize poetry. Kalaidjian's demand that we not celebrate a poem simply because it addresses a topic (like genocide) that holds a kind of untouchable position is a demand for real engagement. I agree that "criticism may be ethically bound to ask the tough questions of value" (68). Yet to critique a poem, one must first think with it, and Balakian's poems offer an alternative to trauma theory for thinking about how they address their topics.

Balakian's "The Oriental Rug" compassionately engages suffering across distance, and it offers forms of representation that are occluded by trauma studies' dominance. Balakian explores his relationship to his grandparents' experience in the Armenian genocide through a speaker who accepts the responsibility of witnessing. The speaker engages with this atrocity through the mediation of the rug originally from Armenia and now lying on the floor of the speaker's American home. The poem begins with the speaker's memory of himself as a boy lying on the rug associated, through its floral patterns, with the Armenian landscape. These patterns have been dyed onto the wool by the "roots and berries" of the Armenian environment

(I.6) and, through this association, the speaker imaginatively enters a landscape of flowers, vines, and insects.

The rug represents the Armenian nation through this relationship to the land's dyeing products. The rug stands in metonymically for Armenia's people both through this association to the physical landscape and through its place (as artifact and household object) in Armenian culture. The string of depictions here is complex; the rug does not simply take the place of a people by standing in for a geography. Rather, the literal rug is continually reintroduced in the poem, calling for an ongoing reconfiguration of the complicated relationships between rug and people, rug and land, land and people, while also disrupting the speaker's connection to all of these entities. This frequent interposition of the rug reminds readers that it is the rug that provides the speaker with his always distanced access to the geographical location and the genocide that occurred there. His association to the witnessed suffering is metonymical in that he never reaches the pain itself. The speaker can only approach that which is associated with that pain. Metonymy, then, is a trope of distance and difference but it is also a trope of association, of finding a closeness that allows critical specificity in its refusal to negate difference, to blur into oneness two things that are not one.

In "The Oriental Rug," this metonymical relationship is also erotic. While eroticism is not the only or primary way to express compassion, it is one persistent conceptualization of the witness-sufferer relationship in witness poetry. To demonstrate how erotic relationship evokes compassionate witness, I now turn to eroticism's role in poetry by Joy Harjo and Seamus Heaney before returning to Balakian's poem. Writing from a Muscogee Creek perspective, Harjo offers witness to suffering brought by colonization: "My work in this life has to do with reclaiming the memory stolen from our people when we were dispossessed from our lands east of the Mississippi; it has to do with restoring us" (*Reinventing the Enemy's Language* 59). In the first poem of *A Map to the Next World* (2000), a collection of poetry and tales, Harjo's speaker tells us, "We are ascending through the dawn / the sky blushed with the fever / of attraction" (1–3), "[t]he sun lean[ing] on one elbow after making love, / savoring the wetlands just off the freeway" (28–9). While this pink sky describes a sunrise, these lines also imagine the sun and sky as personified bodies whose pleasure includes us all. This description of erotic encounter becomes apparent as a form of witness through the accompanying tale's explanation of "this moment of reconciliation, where night and morning met" when, for the tale's speaker, it "didn't matter that I didn't know ... how I was going to make sense of a past that threatened to destroy me during those times when I doubted that I deserved a place in the world" (15). This celestial reconciliation suggests balance and partnership between one day and the next and gives the speaker hope in "that city where we were defining what it meant to be Indian in a system of massive colonization" (14). Robert Warrior writes in "Your Skin is the Map: The Theoretical Challenge of Joy Harjo's Erotic Poetics" that "Harjo's erotic poems provide the fullest expression of her commitment to embodiment" (340). He continues, "For those of us committed to theoretical approaches that seek to address and make changes to the material realities that people in Native communities face, then Harjo's erotic poetry is a challenge to understand that our bodies, including our intellects, are connected to those material realities" (340). In the material reality defined by colonization, the speaker finds sense and solace in the overarching pleasure of environmental bodies.

In "earthly desire," Harjo returns to an eroticized environment to define community: "The ocean and sky meet out on the horizon for the love of touch. To speak like this isn't simplification, or personification for the sake of making intimacy where there isn't – this is the truth of the matter. We are all here in this place because we desired it. Desired each other" (115). Like the reconciliation between night and day, the horizon offers a place where different bodies touch. Harjo suggests that the erotic is not a metaphor for the intimacy of connection, but one place in which the truth of connection writ large is expressed. Writing about this essential desire for each other is, for Harjo, inseparable from writing about compassion. When Pam Kingsbury asks Harjo "What do you believe/feel/know lies at the heart of your body of work?" in an interview, Harjo responds: "Compassion. Joy" (*Soul Talk, Song Language* 45). The "love of touch" is a form of compassion and joy that is the premise for our contiguity. Harjo's conception of our nearness to one another is a desire for that nearness that is not only a human truth but a truth at the heart of material reality.

Much as in Harjo's poetry, and as we will see in "The Oriental Rug," in Seamus Heaney's "Bone Dreams" the speaker's erotic inter-action with another's body is filtered through a landscape connected to the experience of a marginalized group. "Bone Dreams" is from *North* (1975), a collection very much a project of witness. As Joseph McGowan explains more broadly, "the immediate context in which [Heaney's] poetry is so often seen" is the "continuing 'Troubles' of the post-Partition North of Ireland" (25). In this context, Heaney works within a complex of language, literature, and nation: "At school I studied the Gaelic literature of Ireland as well as the litera-ture of England, and since then I have maintained a notion of myself as Irish in a province that insists it is British. Lately I realized that these complex pieties and dilemmas were implicit in the very terrain where I was born" ("Belfast" 35).

In "Bone Dreams," Heaney digs into this terrain to engage these dilemmas through his speaker's eroticized investigation of skeletal remains. The poem begins with the moment of initial contact:

> White bone found
> on the grazing:
> the rough, porous
> language of touch
>
> and its yellowing, ribbed
> impression in the grass (I.1–6)

The bone is found "on the grazing": the phrase refers to the grazing grounds but has the doubled meaning of slight contact. The bone is found on the speaker's grazing it, on this light touch. At the same time, "grazing" can be a touch that breaks the skin – the rough graze can be brief and indefinite but also painful and lasting. This tactile witnessing, the communication through the "language of touch," does not evoke the bone with finality since a "rough" language suggests inexactness. Likewise, if the language is "porous," it is permeable to the context of its use, the particular time and place of this touching.

The bone's impression in the grass, like its porousness, evokes the context through which the bone must be articulated; "impression" can refer to the physical dent in the grass as well as to the speaker's response to finding the bone. Our understanding of this relic is limited to the speaker's "impression" of it. This personal and contextual engagement is important in thinking about Northern Ireland where, Mark R. Amstutz argues, memory has played a "problematic role" as "the Nationalist-Unionist dispute has been sustained by perceptions of injustice and in particular by memories of victimhood" (183). Since "history" in this context "has been used as a tool of conflict by helping to ossify memory and to sustain opposing worldviews," Amstutz proposes the need to "foster a memory that is inclusive and adaptable to conflicting perceptions" (183). In "Bone Dreams," the speaker's perception of the bone as an ossified fragment of the past is subjective, individual, and intimate. This perception brings movement to the ossified: "I touch it again, I wind it in // the sling of mind / to pitch it at England" (I.11–14). A reader accesses the bone through the speaker's personal imaginative engagement – the winding of the bone in the sling of his mind – with the past's continuing context within the present. That is, the fact that we are accessing the bone through the speaker's imaginative engagement is dramatized and taken as an explicit topic. We are not getting the speaker's repetition of an ossified narrative, but his exploration of the bone and the "strange fields" it falls into (I.16).

Yet the speaker tells us, after searching through a history of language, "I found *bān-hūs*" (III.4). He finds this name for skeleton, bone-house, "in the tongue's / old dungeons" (II.3–4). Once he releases this bone-house, or body, from its place in historical sense, it grows into a body-as-house with an interior "where the soul / fluttered" (III.7–8). With the help of an exploration of language's historical uses and changes, the engagement with the bone expands from

the initial brief touch into a house which contains the opportunities for emotional, physical, and intellectual states implied in "love-
den, blood-holt, / dream-bower" (III.15–16). Yet the speaker moves
beyond the metaphorical image of the word "bone-house," taking the
bone itself as the image of a human life, and inviting the reader to

> [c]ome back past
> philology and kennings,
> re-enter memory
> where the bone's lair
>
> is a love-nest
> in the grass. (IV.1–6)

In the sling of the mind, the speaker goes beyond language to re-enter
a tactile memory. Outside of the history of language, this memory is
the personal imaginative engagement of the sling of mind. It is in this
memory outside of ossified structures (like language but also presumably like the history of violence this land holds) that the speaker
engages in an erotic relationship with the bone as his "lady." The
speaker replaces the abstract body that houses literary and linguistic
traditions with the trope of a woman who is also a part of the present
landscape. In the move from within to beside, from "old dungeons"
(II.4) to "cradling each other" (V.2), the speaker creates a space – a
"love-nest" – in which he enters into relationship with the bone as a
synecdochal piece of the skeletal body:

> I hold my lady's head
> like a crystal
>
> and ossify myself
> by gazing: I am screes
> on her escarpments (IV.7–11)

The body, likewise, is metonymically connected to the physical land,
which itself provides a conceptual and literal ground for a sense of

national belonging; for, as Heaney says, "when we look for the history of our sensibilities I am convinced, as Professor J.C. Beckett was convinced about the history of Ireland generally, that it is to what he called the stable element, the land itself, that we must look for continuity" ("The Sense of Place" 149).[7] Through the bone, the speaker moves into a kind of timeless history but then back into a narrative of historical belonging. The speaker is hardened, ossified, into scree, but, in this erotic dialogue, the land (as the escarpments that suggest this stable element of Irish sensibility, though pictured through the shifting transformations of bone-as-lady-as-land ridge) is unmoving. Nevertheless, the speaker does not harden into immobility. Rather, the speaker writes himself as the running continuity of dialogic response to that land. Again, the communication with the bone-lady-land can only be understood, as the first stanza suggests, roughly, or – as the speaker "estimate[s] / for pleasure / her knuckles' paving" (V.5–7) – in what we can read as a rough estimate, but one that involves an intimate engagement of the self.

Thus, the erotic engagement between the speaker and the artifact does not function to define the other that stands in for a troubled national history, but, rather, allows the speaker to work through his own position as a witness to that history. Though "Bone Dreams" is not one of *North*'s more popular poems, Anthony J. Cuda considers it in "The Use of Memory: Seamus Heaney, T.S. Eliot, and the Unpublished Epigraph to 'North.'" For Cuda, this erotic engagement is identificatory. He reads this moment as the speaker's act of "assuming" the skull's "death-like qualities," which allows the past and present "to collapse in a single act of remembering which transcends them both" and "transcend[s] the ego's limiting qualifications" (165). That is, Cuda understands this transcendence to involve the transformation of sexual desire into "the 'self-forgetfulness' of love" (166). I argue quite the opposite here, with the self-consciousness of desire preventing the merging that would foreclose compassion in identification. Though Cuda concludes that "Heaney's speakers often refuse to renounce the erotic particularity of their visions for the reverent transcendence of pattern and archetype," his suggestion that Heaney's poems are tempted toward T.S. Eliot's "abstraction and universality"

forgets the grounded nature of Heaney's poetry (169). As Magdalena
Kay argues, Heaney does not want "to write too abstractly of moral
choices, which would imply 'culpable detachment' (*Government* 58).
His knowledge must be embodied. Its embodiment is physical and
cultural. This is why Heaney is so frequently tempted to re-open local
wounds" (110). The speaker's erotic engagement with the skull in
"Bone Dreams" is engagement with this embodied physical and cultural knowledge of local wounds.

   To return to Balakian, "The Oriental Rug" features engagement
with cultural wounds through its speaker's explicitly erotic encounter with a rose. The eroticism of this encounter is compassionate;
the section ends with a touch to soothe the rose's damaged parts – a
tender action in response to suffering – as the speaker

   back-rub[s]

   the remains of sepals
   which kept the rose alive
   in blighted April when Adana
   and Van were lopped off the map. (IV.21–5)

The back-rub may be difficult to recognize as tender in relation to the
violent lopping off of Armenian geographies, though it is the touch
to the remaining protecting walls of the sepal that helps reinforce the
rose. The erotic is a surprising enough marker for compassion, and
the poem's strategies are even further complicated by the combination of the erotic and the violent.

   In *The Edge of Modernism*, Kalaidjian notes that this poem erot-
icizes a traumatic history (45). Kalaidjian does not, though, offer his
explication of the poem's eroticism. Rather, he explains how the erot-
ic-traumatic works for Arshile Gorky. Kalaidjian is right to note that
"Balakian borrows this pictorial inmixing of trauma and sexuality,
arguably, from the painterly art of Armenian émigré Arshile Gorky"
(46). Balakian refers to Gorky in this poem (as Adoian). However,
Kalaidjian uses this connection to come to a conclusion about the
poem that the poem does not warrant: "Indeed, both for Gorky as

painter and for Balakian as poet, the maternal archetype inflected by genocide is at once a source of bereavement, a symbol of cultural exile, and a lost love object" (47). For Kalaidjian, this archetype demonstrates psychoanalytic theorist Maria Torok's argument that "the dead mother is powerfully cathected by desire" (47). Yet Balakian's poem does not contain a maternal archetype or any reference to a mother. Since the poem does specifically mention a father (Balakian I.26) and grandfather (I.40), Kalaidjian's analysis might consider how this poem approaches a generational cultural exile not through bereavement from a mother but through a patrilineal lineage (which Balakian continues with a difference when he dedicates the poem as another father to his daughter). Claiming the presence of "a lost love object" in this poem requires further discussion. The Armenian landscape, represented through the rug, functions perhaps as a lost love object, but its erotic relationship with the speaker is complex and shifting, and saying anything significant about that relationship requires sustained attention.[8] Insofar as Kalaidjian replaces close reading with theory and criticism (even if in part with Balakian's own engagement with another's representation of trauma), he demonstrates again the occlusion of a poem's actual strategies in the application of a strong commitment to certain ideas about trauma and its transmission.

To move more systematically through "The Oriental Rug" and its specific articulation of compassion, I suggest that the poem begins by establishing its speaker as a witness of suffering. The rug is introduced as "the brushed and bruised / Kashan" (I.2–3), making explicit its relation to pain. Further, the speaker's position as secondary witness is clear when he imagines his grandfather "staring at the few goats / that walked around the carnage" while "[o]utside my [the speaker's] house the grass / never had such colour" (I.44–5).[9] Moreover, the speaker naps on this rug which he imagines as the Armenian landscape, while his grandfather sits, staring, on the "mossy pillow" of the real land (I.39). This contrast, recognized by the speaker remembering his childhood rug-naps, is the beginning of a dialogue between the speaker as distanced witness and his grandparents in their experience of atrocity.

Entering into this engagement with his grandparents' world through sleeping on the rug, the boy is not yet consciously a witness but recognizes the pain's ongoing presence represented through the "splintering green wool / bled from juniper berries" that "seemed to seep, even then" (I.17–19). He remembers its dyed vines "leaving a shadow like filigree / on [his] eye as [he] closed it" (I.15–16). He calls his sleep a "night gazing" (I.36), indicating that this closed eye is already a kind of witnessing. Moreover, though the eye closes against this contact, the shadow of the rug's pattern remains across his face. This remnant is the first instance we get of the rug figuratively dyeing the speaker's skin. The exposure goes beneath the surface; after he closes his eye, the dyed wool seems to bleed into a "breathing […] inside [his] ear" (I.21–2). This breath within the ear suggests communication, but communication that is at this point wordless and nearly silent.

This breathing functions in the poem as an expelled silence, or near silence which, in its inarticulateness, signals the need for language. First appearing when the speaker feels "the wasp-nest cells / breathing in their tubular ways / inside [his] ear and further back" (I.20–2), the targeting of a deep consciousness – of the further back of his mind – is the call for his translation of that breathing. The image of cells, as units that work as part of a larger whole, within the careful and functional pattern of a wasp-nest, suggests the possibility of organized and discernible signification. In connection to this potential for analysis, the transmission of this sensation as breath through a tube indicates a directed offering of oral and aural communication, beginning inside the ear and travelling to the interpretive and imaginative further back of the mind. This dialogue seems more likely in the next reference to breathing as it moves to an orifice associated with speech:

the sea of ivory

between the flowers
undulated as if the backs

of heavy sheep were breathing
in my mouth. (I.29–33)

While the image of heavy sheep in the mouth suggests gagging, an
inability to speak, the association with the mouth nevertheless indicates the potential for communication and also sets up the more intimate connection that will come later in the poem. Thus, when the
speaker "feel[s] the wool give way" (II.5), it is the weave of the rug
giving way to the Armenian landscape, but it is also the giving way
of the wool in his mouth.

As the poem progresses, the speaker becomes increasingly open
to the communication of a suffering that is not his own. In this process comes a transposition of sensory information signalling the distinction between the suffering he witnesses and his own suffering in
response; this shift in perception suggests the gap between the rug's
pain and the speaker's responding pain. In this particular passage,
the rug, often appearing figuratively as the Armenian landscape, is a
literal rug:

The heavy mallet a Parsee boy
once used to beat the knots
beneath the pile so
the weft would disappear

vibrates in me
as a knelling bell (III.1–6)

The rug feels pain through the sense of touch (being beaten) while the
speaker feels the same action of the mallet as the vibration of a sound
(the knelling bell). Yet, while both sufferer and witness feel a tactile
force (beating and vibration), the speaker feels vibrations rather than
the actual mallet. There is an acoustic mediation in that the (tactile)
pain is transmitted to the speaker via a different (auditory) sensory
modality – importantly, one that suggests verbal communication.
This shift to the auditory is emphasized in the near-rhyme of "knelling bell." The assonance is put off only by the gerund, the indication

that this sound occurs in the present and not at the time of the original suffering.

As the speaker feels the vibrations as though they are a sound, the other's touch becomes a kind of speech that the witness hears as his own pain. This communication is difficult to enact; the speaker has to "pry" his way into the rose to "undo[] its blighted cliché" (IV.1–3). Cliché, by definition familiar and expected, functions to relay information without being noticed itself. Balakian makes the cliché available to our attention in reading intimacy against this conventional expression of it. In this entrance into the rose and disruption of its clichéd symbolism for intimate romance, the speaker makes literal the intimacy which the rose represents; rather than functioning as a symbol, the rose acts out the romance. When the speaker "strain[s] for the symmetry / of its inflorescence" (IV.4–5), he does not strive for the flower's balanced blossoming but for that of the cliché. When the cliché does what it means, when its poetic action is symmetrical to its symbolic meaning, communication is no longer blighted. With the strain for symmetry Balakian suggests the speaker's desire, in this intimacy of witnessing, to feel *with* rather than *for*. In this desire, there is a response to suffering rather than a replication of that same suffering in another. That is, symmetry does not occur when two sides are exactly the same, but when one side is a mirror image of the other. In compassionate witnessing, there is a reflection of one's pain in the other rather than one shared pain produced through a melding of the witness into the sufferer. Choosing intimacy over identification, the speaker breaks through the resistance to communication and "slide[s] along the smooth / cup of a petal" (IV.6–7).

It is here, when the resistance falls away, that the poem becomes explicitly erotic. I understand the erotic here as an expression of conversation or engaged relation, shown through the equal give and take in the speaker's alternating active and passive stance as he both "feel[s] the tubey walls / muscle [him] to the ovary" and "suck[s his] way into the nectaries" (IV.10–11, 15). In this give and take, the reader is privy to the flower's actions, but the speaker describes only his own feeling, repeating the word "feel" twice in this section to emphasize that his sensation is the focus of his depiction (IV.10, 16). The witness does not appropriate the other's suffering by presuming to know how it feels. In this eroticized relationship, the importance is not to know the other's pain or pleasure, but to feel one's own suffering or enjoyment in response to the other's signs of feeling.

Despite the erotic imagery, to be "[w]rapped this tight" in the flower is not entirely pleasurable. At the end of this stanza, the speaker loses himself in a moment that reminds the reader that the eroticism points to an engagement with suffering:

> I come apart in the thorn
> (the spiky side that kept the jackal out)
> and disperse whatever's left
> of me to the earth. (IV. 26–9)

The plant's spiky defence against malicious intrusion breaks the speaker into dispersible pieces. Though the stanza ends here, the speaker asserts his return, beginning the next stanza with "I walk" (V.1). Throughout the poem, the speaker posits his own pain, loses himself in his pain, and then reasserts his active presence, suggesting that witnessing requires both a self to receive communication and a giving up of the self to one's own sensation, to allow oneself to suffer together with another.

This give and take is also expressed through repeated images of carrying. From the poem's start, the speaker carries the rug's pattern as the filigree shadow over his eye. Later, he carries the pattern of the rug's pain more permanently as he feels "six centuries of Turkish heels / on [his] spine-dyed back" (II.9–10). While he carries the rug's dyes, however, he is also painfully carried by the landscape they illustrate:

> safflower, my Dyer's Thistle,
> carry me on your burr
> so I may always feel
> dry gusts on my neck. (V.13–16)

These gusts on the speaker's neck are like the earlier breath, but the speaker is no longer an involuntary recipient as he asks for the perpetual painful carrying on the burr. The rug's capacity to carry is related to its symbolic status; a metonymical depiction is one in which something nearby the thing approached is carried closer through the trope's action. In addition to understanding the rug in this rhetorical way, we can also investigate its presence in the poem as materiality. The rug operates as an icon: it stands for the landscape by resembling it in its patterns. Yet through the rug's physical connection to the land – its production through the dyes of the land – its relationship to that land becomes indexical. As the rug bleeds these dyes, it is set up, in this animate indexical connection, as a living object available for an engagement imagined as physical and erotic. The "bleeding," the term for the leaking of dyes into water before they are set, along with the earlier breathing of the sheep (and, here, the echo of bleating in bleeding), gives life to the wool so that it becomes active and embodied. As a metonymical and indexical object, then, the rug carries the speaker closer to another's suffering in two ways. First, the rug allows the speaker a proximity to things from which he is actually distant, and, second, the rug, as it becomes a breathing and bleeding part of the land, appears as an object available for intimate engagement.[10] Significantly, the idea of symmetry re-emerges in this engagement as the speaker also carries the rug in return: "I walk with a rug on my back. / Become to myself a barren land" (V.1–2). Throughout the poem, the speaker has gone deeper into the images on the rug in order to enter the Armenian landscape. In this last stanza, however, the rug and speaker change positions, rendering the speaker and rug equals in this dialogue; the speaker has been carried by the rug as figurative land and now carries the rug as his own land.

Compassionate witnessing is a kind of carrying. Witnessing carries the cause of someone else's suffering into the effect of one's own suffering in response; one carries over another's feeling into relationship with one's own. Compassionate witnessing is also a kind of being carried. Insofar as my feelings are an effect of your suffering, my feelings are carried by yours as secondary, belated, and contingent. As I discuss in relation to the speaker's request to "carry me on your burr," "The Oriental Rug" moves between witness as carrying and being carried, suggesting its combination of active and reactive elements.

To carry the rug here is to hold the responsibility for the translation of Armenia's tragedy into something affecting in present day America. Thus, when

> [d]ust from the knots
> fills [his] arms
> and in the peaceful New World sun
> becomes fine spume (V.3–6),

the speaker carries the dust – the original suffering of the genocide. Through this contemporary witnessing, the carried dust becomes wet spume of fresh pain. In this act of carrying, the pain from another time and place becomes active in the translation from dust to spume, an action related to the shift from dried to dyeing pigments. Thus, when the speaker has earlier "suck[ed] [his] way into the nectaries" (IV.15), it is significant that it is "[t]hat wet, [he] wash[es] / to the cool leaflets" (IV.18–19).

The poem ends with this connection between dye and communication, as the speaker makes a request: "Tyrian purple, from a mollusk shell / lodged in Phoenician sand – / gurgle all your passion in my ear" (V.24–6). The purple dye he asks to gurgle to him derives from a shell lodged in sand that is associated with a people (the Phoenicians) known for spreading their alphabet in sailing from land to land. There is a kind of language in the dry sand that is linked, through the dyeing shell, to the gurgle of the sea's passion. The shell next to the speaker's ear lets him translate from the language of the dry, historical pain to the gurgle (wet in its association with the sea) that makes that dye seem fresh even if it is really dried (it is not the real sea, after all, but its noises). This gurgling shell is reminiscent of earlier images of the rug's pattern breathing inside the speaker's ear and mouth. Both here and earlier, the speaker imagines a translation, a carrying over or across or, in this case, a carrying into his ear suffering which he translates into poetic response. The speaker connects imaginatively to the pain of an atrocity he did not witness himself and so opens himself to a kind of dialogue, troped here as erotic and dyeing.

Part Two

Compassion and Representation

Community and Poetry's Maps

Joy Harjo's "A Map to the Next World" (2000) and Adrienne Rich's "An Atlas of the Difficult World" (1990–91), both the title poems of their respective collections, explore the relationship between poem and community. As title poems, these two explorations of mapping serve as important commentaries on each collection's relationship to poetic guidance. Both poems use images of maps, landscapes, and bodies to navigate the heuristic and hermeneutic qualities of a poetic guide to nation. The communities in these two poems – the United States and the Creek Nation – are depicted through images of shared space characterized by the entwining of place and body. Yet, at the same time, these poems use mapping images to suggest the distance involved in positions of witnessing.

In the same way that the framework of intimacy will not suggest easy communality, the distance points not to disconnection but to the potential of travel. A map points to a place so that its readers might position themselves in that place. That is, a map is a point of connection between "here," one's current location, and "there," the location one might occupy. Every depiction of place on the map is offered with the potential of becoming the location for one's presence. The map, then, is a tool in the way that the poem is a tool; both offer guidance, the map in leading the reader to a place and the poem in leading a reader to an experience, thought, or feeling. The poetry is itself map-like and presents the image of the map in an act of self-theorization; the map and the poem have a conceptual relationship in that the map offers a theory by which this poetry can be read. Using literature as a map for navigating experiences beyond one's own involves taking a position of engagement along a continuum of nearness and farness. Such engagement recognizes literature's capacity to represent experiences or realities and to direct its readers through representation, not to achieving for oneself another's experience, but to navigating the distance between one's place and that of another in order to offer one's engaged presence.

In this chapter's argument about engaged presence, community, and witnessing, I understand the maps in these poems to have two registers of meaning, one metonymical/heuristic and the other metaphorical/hermeneutic. The images of maps depict the metonymical relationship of the land to the nation. These maps are heuristic tools to understanding the literal relationship between place and community. The map also depicts the metonymic connection between physical presence and the presence of mind necessary to take something into consideration or to offer one's attention. The map becomes hermeneutic in the relationship between place/community and emplacement/consideration. The map is a metaphor for "being there" for another or "being here" in an attentive relationship. In bringing together the concepts of emplacedness and place with community and consideration, the map acts as a conceptual framework for understanding the relationship between a position of attentive and considerate presence in a place (literal or figurative) and the communality of that place.

The roads, rivers, and trails in Rich's and Harjo's poems depict travelling across distance. This distance is in space (actual nearness or farness in the landscape) but also in knowledge. Knowledge can be distanced or intimate. Intimate knowledge knows particularity and details. Distanced knowledge is acknowledgement of the relative and changing distance from which one might witness that which is not one's own or where one is not. Distanced knowledge might be conceived as a sort of meta-knowledge governing the relationship between knowledge in the empirical sense (knowledge in practice) and knowledge as epistemology (knowledge in theory). Yet distanced knowledge, in its acknowledgment of itself, is also the conceptual travelling toward more intimate knowledge. Remembering that these two knowledges are not separate but move along a shared spectrum and thus differ in degree rather than in kind, we can use two terms from Rich's poem to consider intimate knowledge to be "moored" and distanced knowledge to be "behooved." Distanced knowledge is, then, not in contrast to intimate knowledge. Rather, distanced knowledge is a recognition of the necessarily diverse starting positions (and consequent perspectives) that exist in relation to various contexts; intimate knowledge must also recognize its own relative distance from its object. Distanced knowledge can be usefully recognized as the place from which empirical intimate knowledges might initially be approached. Intimacy refers not only to this (literally or figuratively) spatial element, this closeness to a person, place, or event, but also to an affective position out of which comes attention and consideration. Distanced knowledge can be affectively intimate though it approaches intimate knowledge of particularity from elsewhere.

I use the term *mindful presence* to indicate the presence of mind involved in this intimate attention. Mindful presence suggests the metaphorical presence of the mind (consideration, attention) as well as the literal presence sometimes involved in attention (being in attendance, emplacedness).[1] The deictics of the poems' "heres" point to both the physical presence typically suggested by community but also the mental presence that does not depend on bodily attendance to build communality, a witnessing that is not dependent on proximity. While this non-proximity is inherent in any written communication, witness poetry has a generic relation to proximity and distance. The implied reader present in any poem is the presence of a general category, not of an individual. This position is structured by a particular poem's strategies for communication; each poem accepts readers in its own way. This impersonal category of the reader is counterbalanced when a poem's communicative strategies invite a reader to feel in his or her own particularity. Witness poetry commonly positions readers into remembrance of themselves. As Rich writes in "Someone Is Writing a Poem," "I can expect a reader to feel my limits as I cannot, in terms of her or his own landscape, to ask: *But what has this to do with me? Do I exist in this poem?* And this is not a simple or naive question. We go to poetry because we believe it has something to do with us" (85). This idea combined with the claim that immediately follows – "We also go to poetry to receive the experience of the not me, enter a field of vision we could not otherwise apprehend" – speaks to the relationship of distance and intimacy in Rich's poetic theory but also in witness poetry more generally.

In Rich's and Harjo's poems and their maps, issues of distance and intimacy come through a consistent tension between metaphor (a constructed, conceptual relationship that requires interpretation) and metonymy (a literal relationship that requires only knowledge of the referent). The poems construct chains of metonyms that come to form metaphor. The images of maps as heuristic tools to navigate the actual details they represent – details of place, of community, of witnessing, and of witnessed lives – combine to create a conceptual relationship requiring interpretation. Knowing the details (through the poetry's heuristic or metonymic actions) comes in connection with interpreting the larger emplacement of the details (through the poetry's hermeneutic and metaphoric suggestions). Knowing that involves interpretation always involves distance because interpretation is translative – and knowing is also always interpretive to different degrees. Much as distanced knowledge is still intimate, intimate knowledge is still distanced. Interpretation, in this moving and combining of details, involves the process of distance that the map represents; it involves the walking of roads not one's own. Thus, distanced, metaphoric, hermeneutic knowing is anageographic, or out of its own place. Anageographic knowing is interpretive, but the interpretation comes out of the combinations of the particulars in their contexts. A witness might, then, attend well to a context outside of his or her experience, place, or time. This definition of distanced knowledge follows from my discussion so far. However, the idea of distanced knowing as a hermeneutic and metaphoric endeavour suggests that distanced knowledge can be understood additionally as an interpretive knowledge of a possible interaction of details. The details of community are removed from the places of community and held in thought in the theoretic place of the poem. The details might be gained through heuristic tools of understanding (engagement with particularities in their contexts) but their combination into potential difference is achieved through hermeneutic interpretive activity (interpretation of the possible interactions of particularities from various contexts).

It is not coincidental that attention is the return for an offer to enter into a lyrical "here." "Attention" is related to "attendance," a word which includes the idea of being "here" and also of offering consideration: "The action, fact, or state of attending or giving heed; earnest direction of the mind, consideration, or regard; *esp.* in phr. to pay or give attention. The mental power or faculty of attending" (OED). "Consideration," connected with attention, makes even clearer my understanding of "giving attention." Consideration is linked to generosity in its definition as "regard for the circumstances, feelings, comfort, etc. of another; thoughtfulness for another; thoughtful kindness" (OED). It also clarifies my use of attention: "The keeping of a subject before the mind; attentive thought, reflection, meditation" (OED). Consideration further gets at a sense of conscious witnessing, as "the action of taking into account" (OED) or the action of understanding something to be of "importance, consequence" (OED). These words collectively evoke the multiple registers of meaning in the word "presence," and the distinction "mindful presence" that I use to distinguish the extra mental action that can be added to (or come without) being "here."

In this framework of witnessing, attention, and affective, interpretive knowledge, the map is an icon (it resembles the landscape for which it stands). However, once one mentally inserts oneself into the map, it becomes an index (as a means of navigation – one imagines oneself moving down the representation of a road and this imagining allows the successful movement in reality). This action of reading changes the map from being figuratively representative of a space to being directly connected to navigation of that space. The heuristic action and the representation combine to produce this indexical quality. If one is not "here" but looking at the map in the absence of its referent and the need to navigate that referent, then the map is not transformed into this metonymical, indexical relationship with the space. When one interprets the map through the perspective of distance (when one is not in and will not be in the space the map depicts), the map is metaphor. One is not in direct knowable connection to the details the map represents but rather is in a position of interpretation. In this case, one reads the map hermeneutically as revealing possibilities of particular emplacements within various considerations of the represented details of the space. A map exists whether one uses it or not, but once one does use it as a means of navigation – heuristically or hermeneutically – one is responsible for reading it well. Witnessing is a deictic moment of inserting oneself – or being inserted – "here," even when this insertion is into a possible or potential "here," an insertion preceded by the hermeneutic process of travelling distance.

Like a map, a poem might also be read both heuristically – as guidance in one's own life – or hermeneutically – in the navigation of experiences one has not had. While both kinds of reading are needed, reading for what is familiar comes more easily than reading to learn to better connect to, understand, or feel with unfamiliar experience. The approach to distanced knowledge, to something lacking the familiarity that marks it as something having to do with you, might require practice. Yet, again, intimate and distanced knowledge are part of a continuum. The heuristic approach seems often to come first, but can lead to the hermeneutic. Attention to what affects one personally might prepare one for being affected personally by something outside of one's personal experience.

This interaction of heuristic and hermeneutic processes is relevant to considering Rich's and Harjo's speakers as witnesses. The speakers often emphasize their emplacedness and include deictic reference, positioning themselves "here." Yet the speakers also travel, suggesting both the heuristic and hermeneutic approaches to knowledge of the contexts they explore (remembering still that the hermeneutic derives from the heuristic, that the two do not represent a dichotomy). In either case, this poetry features a deictic accountability. A poem offers a metaphorical, hermeneutic representation of the community with which it engages. Yet the representation of the community may also be an index for the real, lived community this poetic community represents and might impact. While the communities are not co-identified (they remain known separately and are distinguishable within the poem), the represented community is occupied as a map (used as a map, a tool) to navigate the lived community, thus creating a literal, metonymic, heuristic connection between the poetic community and the lived community, one that depends upon an ethical obligation of the witness to navigate well.

Witnessing is primarily associated with sight. To witness is "to experience by personal (esp. ocular) observation; to be present as an observer at; to see with one's own eyes ... (In loose writing often used merely as a synonym of 'see')" (OED). But witnessing also involves giving testimony of what has been seen, "to testify to, attest; to furnish oral or written evidence of" (OED). In the poetry I study here, the ekphrastic action of verbally representing the images of maps is a witnessing action. The speakers call attention to their acts of telling when they disrupt moments of mimetic showing by diegetically telling what is shown. The poetry represents, and the speakers sometimes narrate, their acts of representing. In the ekphrastic moments especially, mimesis (what is told) is subsumed in diegesis (the telling).[2] Ekphrasis offers an icon as it represents through a relationship of resemblance. The ekphrastic responsibility (much like the responsibility of testimony) would seem to be one of accuracy to the original. However, in the poetry included here, the witnessing ekphrastic ethic is indexical. I do not mean index in the sense of conjuring the original, but in the sense of "that which serves to direct or point to a particular fact or conclusion" (OED). Rather than the telling leading back to the seen, the witness's verbalization of the visual leads away from the details represented (but precisely through the representation of those details) to response.

The context for my investigation is the poetic concern with national community in Rich's and Harjo's collections. The relationship between intimacy and distance functions as an overarching structure to my reading of the poems. The central image is the map. My key terms – mooring, behooved, presence, gift, knowledge – come out of the poetry itself, though I add mindful presence (to differentiate between physical attendance and attentive presence of mind), attention and consideration (to describe the witnessing action of these speakers), and communality (to emphasize at times a sense

of a "communal state or condition; solidarity" [OED]). I use the latter
term in contrast to community, which suggests belonging as limited
by place or identity: "A body of people who live in the same place,
usually sharing a common cultural or ethnic identity. Hence: a place
where a particular body of people lives" (OED). In this context of
nation, community indeed limits belonging. I use both "communality" and "community," depending on what is most appropriate for
the particular context. I move between Rich's and Harjo's poems as I
consider mapping, community, and continuums of intimacy/distance,
heuristic/hermeneutic, and metonymy/metaphor. I turn to poems by
Elizabeth Bishop, Walt Whitman, and Hart Crane as they are relevant to a reading of "An Atlas of the Difficult World."

Maps

For Rich, the national setting is the United States and, for Harjo, the
Creek Nation existing within the borders of the United States. Both
poets explore national belonging through linked landscape and
body imagery. Rich's "An Atlas of the Difficult World" more specifically explores American patriotism. Terre Ryan's *This Ecstatic
Nation: The American Landscape and the Aesthetics of Patriotism*
elucidates a long tradition of conceiving of American patriotism
through the linked images of land and body. Tracing landscape
imagery through American history, Ryan argues against Jonathan
Foreman's claim that, as "a people dedicated to a proposition,"
"American patriotism has almost nothing to do with notions of
blood and soil" (128). Ryan notes the multiple references to both
blood and soil in important American documents like the Gettysburg
Address as well as in "our enormous body of landscape imagery
and our frontier and war mythologies, all intertwined and active in
contemporary culture" (128–9) as indicative of the historical and
continuing prominence of these terms for articulations of patriotism in the United States.

Land and blood, as figured in Rich's "An Atlas of the Difficult
World," do not participate in these associations of the tamed landscape and the nation united by its citizens' shed blood. Rather, images

of land and blood in this poem function to explore the relationship between an embodied individual and a place. In *Blood, Bread, and Poetry*, Rich writes of "the facts of blood and bread, the social and political forces of my time and place" ("Blood, Bread, and Poetry: The Location of the Poet" 171). In this account, blood and bread together mean a particular embodiment in a particular context: "I need to understand how a place on the map is also a place in history within which as a woman, a Jew, a lesbian, a feminist I am created and trying to create" ("Notes toward a Politics of Location" 212). In "An Atlas of the Difficult World," Rich presents the nation metaphorically as a body, but she does so in relation to literal bodies. Mary Eagleton argues that Rich "rejects not only high theory but also – and this is somewhat strange for a poet – metaphor in favour of a soberly literal view of her body and its relation to institutions and historical events" (303). While I do not agree that Rich goes so far as to reject metaphor, Eagleton's claim highlights Rich's attention to literal relationship, which is also the attention of metonymy.

Harjo mentions Rich in her response to poet Marilyn Kallet's question about her "true teachers of poetry, those who have influenced [her] work" (Coltelli 115), and indeed both poets approach nation through embodied experience. For Harjo, though, this attention to embodiment has to do with a history of colonization. Robert Warrior writes that, for Harjo, "our bodies – or our skins, which are the parts of us that most immediately touch and relate to the rest of the world around us – are not only the most immediate site of the battle for our selves, but also the primary guide to where we ought to be headed. Our skin, as Harjo puts it, is the map" (345). Thus, Harjo's connection of land and blood in her responses to colonial violence shapes the images of landscape and body involved in broader questions of knowing self and community. Harjo's landscape in her poetry, as she tells interviewer Joseph Bruchac, is that which is "between a woman and all the places I've ever been" (Coltelli 30). In the same interview, Harjo indicates that this personal positioning is tied to her concern with community at a global level: "I really can't help but think that at some point ... the community will be a world community" (32). In an interview with Sharon Stever, Harjo describes "a moment of global awareness and therefore global responsibility ... The differences are not points of division; rather they link the whole. What you see is one fragile, luminescent, tender, little place, or home" (Coltelli 82). Harjo's version of witness, in which "what you see" is "one ... little place, or home," involves a movement from the heuristic to the hermeneutic. Home is what "you" can see from your perspective, but that witnessing opens up into a global scale in the recognition of home as "fragile, luminescent, tender, little." The intimacy of home – its tenderness, its brightness as a focal point in the realm of the witnessable – is balanced by its fragility and littleness on a larger scale of increasingly distanced knowledge. Harjo recognizes the tender feeling of one's own home along with the fragility that special closeness involves in relation to all places.

While these comments move toward the abstract, Harjo's engagement with concepts of home and travel are tied to the particular context of the Trail of Tears. Earlier with Stever, Harjo discusses the trope of travelling in her poetry in this context: "I've also considered it in light of the removal of the Muskogee people from Alabama to Oklahoma. It was a forced walk away from our original homeland. Perhaps that is also why I am always traveling" (Coltelli 75).[3] Craig S. Womack – in a chapter of his book *Red on Red: Native American Literary Separatism* that demonstrates the importance of the specific Muscogee Creek content of Harjo's poetry – makes clear the significance of the image of the map in terms of its connection to Creek culture. Womack references "the story of Creeks carrying the embers from the square grounds all the way from Alabama to Oklahoma during Indian Removal and rekindling the sacred fire on their arrival in their new home" (235), arguing that Harjo, in her poetry collection *In Mad Love and War*, "suggests that one can take up migratory paths if these sacred relationships are held in active memory, if one remembers these story connections, the act of memory itself a cleansing and rekindling of old fires" (235).[4] As Harjo tells Stever, "I've had to learn that my home is within me. I can take it everywhere. It's always there" (Coltelli 76). The idea of home recurs in her interviews, and she tells Kallet that home is a place that is "more than land – but of the land – a tradition of mythologies, of ongoing history ... it forms us" (Coltelli 112).

Adrienne Rich's "An Atlas of the Difficult World" also pursues the relationship of land, self, and nation through the image of travelling. The long, many-sectioned poem comprising the first half of the collection by the same title begins with the "declarations" of others who are struggling (I.13). The speaker is uncomfortable with the suffering of a woman murdered by a man who appears to be her lover: "I don't want to hear" (I.39); "I don't want to think" (I.45); "I don't want to know" (I.48). Yet this section ends with the speaker's positioning as a witness, as she delineates a witness's space as paths that have not been one's own: "These are not the roads / you knew me by.   But the woman driving, walking, watching / for life and death, is the same" (I.75–7). If she was known before ("you knew me") and still "is the same," then the speaker has always been this witness, but the roads have changed. The violence against the woman is a violence the speaker doesn't want to hear and think and, in this witnessing, know, but she clearly has heard and thought and witnessed, and does know: she tells us the details she does not want to know at the same moment that she tells us she does not want to know them. Her move to new roads suggests an openness to know suffering; this move indicates the choice to know what she does not want to know. This change in roads is a widening of her witnessing to, we find, a national scene. As Maeera Shreiber argues in her article "'Where Are We Moored?': Adrienne Rich, Women's Mourning, and the Limits of Lament," Rich "is a poet for whom 'change' is an operative condition of being, a poet for whom the 'road' serves as a dominant image, a way of representing a commitment to an ongoing interrogation of the terms of belonging" (301). The speaker's repositioning into this interrogation is emphasized in the repetition of her earlier claim that "[t]his is no place you ever knew me" (I.62). It is in this place to which she comes to know (arrives in order to know and approaches knowing) and has not been known that she grounds herself: "– this is where I live now. [...] I fix on the land.   I am stuck to earth" (I.60–6).

Having established herself as a witness grounded by the task of "walking," "watching," and knowing, the speaker articulates this witnessing as an availability to alternative and unexpected ways of seeing: "I promised to show you a map you say but this is a mural / then yes let it be   these are small distinctions / where do we see it from is the question" (II.22–4). Her map is a mural that points to this "where" from which we might see. The difference between a map and a mural is significant; our guide is a picture rather than a plan for direction. While Rich's speaker describes her roads for us, readers are deterred from merely replicating the speaker's path. A mural is, however, like a map, in the sense that both are particularly connected with place. While a map aids one in navigating a space through its symbolic replication of that space, a mural changes the quality of a space. A map points to ways to be in a space from outside of it, while a mural shapes the experience of a place as a part of it. For Joshua S. Jacobs in "Mapping after the Holocaust: The 'Atlases' of Adrienne Rich and Gerhard Richter," Rich's mural suggests "grassroots creation" in contrast to "the map's authoritative view of American history" (np). Similarly, Shreiber considers the mural "as a prospective prototype for public, collective expression" (310). As murals frequently perform a commemorative function, this shaping incorporates intangible aspects of a place – the memories of a community – into large-scale availability.

The distinction between map and mural calls into play a cartographical aesthetics, or an aesthetics that seems cartographical but turns out not to be after all: Rich offers us one kind of representation only to clarify that we have ended up with another. At least, the "you" here understands the speaker to have promised a map and delivered a mural ("I promised to show you a map you say but this is a mural"). This interlocutor seems imagined by the speaker in order to voice the objection she expects when her words promise to be metaphorically a visual representation of space but might in fact provide a more aesthetic than prescriptive or directive representation of that space. Yet her response to this objection is likewise not definitive. It seems that she includes the objection only so that it can remain active, so that readers cannot simply re-classify the map as a mural and move on. The indication that "this is a mural" is deictically ambiguous: the speaker might indicate that she has a mural rather than a map or that, forgetting about the map altogether, she tells us a poem that is a mural. If her poem is a mural, we might expect not the description of images found elsewhere, but the presentation of images making up a poem. If the map is the mural (rather than a map), then we might consider the poem to be explicitly ekphrastic and expect diegetic access to the map-mural. In the first case, the poem refers to itself and gives us its images. In the second case, the poem refers to something else and describes those already-existing images. In "The 'Words Are Maps': Traveling the Poetry of Adrienne Rich," Jeanette E. Riley considers Rich's poems to be maps in that both are social tools involving ideological and cultural practices (121–2). The hermeneutic (poem and mural) becomes difficult to differentiate from the heuristic (map). Functional guiding is made inseparable from artistic creation, from imaginative production. And indeed, the speaker tells us that "these are small distinctions / where do we see it from is the question" (II.23–4). Important to consider as we continue is how the poem (or map/mural) structures our seeing, our position as readers.

Joy Harjo's speaker in "A Map to the Next World" is likewise making a map for a space to be achieved through the figurative travel of both speaker and reader: "I wished to make a map for / those who would climb through the hole in the sky" (1–2). In "Poem and Tale as Double Helix in Joy Harjo's *A Map to the Next World*," Angelique V. Nixon argues that the collection "incites a world-making journey that encourages readers to be active participants in knowing and learning" (16) because "in order to engage in the interdependence between poem and tale, a circular reading is required to see the double helix created by this unique relationship" (3). Significantly, much like Rich's disinclination to produce a firm and transferable guide, Harjo's poem ends with the direction, "You must make your own map" (53). Indicating a concern with the relationship between experience and representation, the speaker asserts that "[w]hat I am telling you is real and is printed in a warning on the / map" (21–2). It is more common to hear a declaration that something told is "true" rather than "real." While truth is conceptual, reality indicates actual existence. This realness of what is told suggests a heuristic investigation of community through a testimony of experience. We might say here that these *are* the roads she's been known by.

What the speaker tells is both told in the poem and represented on the map the poem describes. Yet we can access what is on the map only through the telling. In a poem that is already a description of the map, what is the distinction between the moment the speaker tells us something about the map and the moment she tells us again that she is telling us something about the map she is describing? When she tells us that she is telling us something real, and that this reality can be found on the map, the speaker emphasizes that this telling is a representation. Diegesis takes over from mimesis and we are directed to focus on the telling rather than the told, the act of testimony rather than the story as completed object. Though the poem describes a map, our access to the map is mediated. This mediation occurs not only because we are reading a representation, and not only because we get a verbal description rather than an actual image, but also because we are reminded that the concept of a map that we receive is not our concept of a map, but the speaker's. Since "[y]ou must make your own map," the speaker's sharing of her map is more demonstrative than definitive. Mapping her direct experience that the reader cannot access, the speaker also offers the image of a map with which the reader can engage. Yet even this image is largely withheld as readers are reminded so insistently that they are only told of this image, not given it directly.

Harjo's poem is not the map itself: the speaker says that she "wished to make a map" but does not claim that this is that map or that its creation has indeed occurred. Within the poem, the map is a mediated object and, even further, it is often not an object at all, but an experience. Thus, the map is at times tangible and material and, at others, it is a figurative way of reading land, bodies, and inherited knowledge. We can see this progression over the first half of the poem. The speaker first explains that "[t]he map must be made of sand and can't be read by ordinary light. It / must carry fire to the next tribal town, for renewal of spirit" (6–7). Here the map is figurative, a metaphor for that which will keep alive cultural tradition.

The idea of the map as a metaphor for memory and story shifts in the very next line of "A Map to the Next World": "In the legend are instructions on the language of the land" (8). The presence of a legend invokes the image of a literal map rather than the abstract and conceptual image of sand that can be read and carry fire. Yet, again, the legend could indicate both the key on a physical map and the narrative of a people. Womack argues that Harjo's poetry "demonstrates the ways physical and spiritual realities are constantly rubbing up against each other" (224). A nation, likewise, depends upon recognition of both physical and spiritual realities. Womack suggests these dual components of a nation, explaining the legal and political aspects of the Oklahoma Creek Nation that make it a "sovereign country existing within the borders of the United States" (25) and also arguing that "a key component of nationhood is a people's idea of themselves, their imaginings of who they are. The ongoing expression of a tribal voice, through imagination, language, and literature, contributes to keeping sovereignty alive in the citizens of a nation" (14).

Creek national community seems in crisis in the poem's next reference to the map where we find ashes rather than symbolic fire: "Trees of ashes wave good-bye to good-bye and the map appears to / disappear" (16–17). Saying "good-bye to good-bye" seems final; it is the last good-bye if good-bye as an option is dismissed. The destruction appears permanent and the map "appears to disappear." Yet the map returns, literalized as an object "printed" with what is "real" (21). Just as quickly, the map becomes the life one enters through the physical union of one's parents (25–6). The map, "interpreted through the wall of the intestine" (28), is now the understanding of one's life through one's own embodied existence.

Interpretive cues for this reading through the self are not plentiful as, at the next world to which this poem titularly guides us, "there will be no X, no guidebook with words you can carry" (35). There will be no guidebook to carry because "you" are now in the map. The guidebook can carry one who lives its guidance but cannot be carried by one as an abstract authority for navigation. The absence of an "X" indicates that the identification of the correct place, a meaningful symbol, cannot be carried from one kind of knowledge to the next, but must be selected and created through the process of living.

Reading back with this lack of guide in mind, that "the map appears to disappear" seems more hopeful; now it may be read to mean that the map appears in order that it might disappear. The map will disappear once it achieves the speaker's goal as stated at the start of the poem: "In the last days of the fourth world I wished to make a map for / those who would climb through the hole in the sky" (1–2).[5] The map as a material, tangible object will disappear, becoming an integrated part of a living existence rather than an external aid. This reading indicates another difference between the real and the true: what the speaker is telling us is real and printed on the map, but the map will disappear when its readers can live what is true in their own experiences. For now, though, the image of the map becomes, again, material as "[f]resh courage [...] // lights the map printed with the blood of history, a map you will have to / know by your intention, by the language of suns" (38–40).[6] The map is given tangibility, though its materiality is metaphoric as it is printed by history and known by intention and by cultural belief.

When it is presented as materiality, the map is an icon in its met-aphorically mimetic representation of the nation. However, the diegetic interruption of this mimesis reveals the speaker creating her poem-map as she uses it to place herself within the community it represents. The map then becomes an index as it is a real part of the community: the poem-map's description of the community helps to uphold the community. Since "[y]ou must make your own map" (53), any use of this map must be indexical.

In Rich's "An Atlas of the Difficult World," the map similarly shifts between the tangible and the immaterial. The speaker "fix[es] on the land" (I.66) that becomes the "map of our country" (II.1). In relation to the country, this land functions both metaphorically (as a terrain to unite across) and metonymically (as the location of the United States).[7] "An Atlas of the Difficult World" is not composed of images of a mate-rial or tangible map. Rather, we are given a poem that calls itself an atlas or operates as one. The poem does not visually evoke an atlas, leaving open images aside from a book of maps. Like the Atlas of Greek myth, "An Atlas of the Difficult World" holds up – holds up for its readers to see and upholds a community spirit in the action – images of the places of the United States. In sequence, the poem describes fields (I); roads real and metaphorical (I.54–77); the interior of a room (III); a flower that "binds / the map of this country together" (IV.1) – so that here the country is its own map through its landscape; its "road-sides from Vermont to / California" (IV.4–5); a history of the places and monuments of battles, whether of war (V.2–4), of prison (V.12, 22), of migration (V.10, 21–38), or of prejudice (V.49–63); American promises of work for Irish emigrants (VI); New York (VII); the Pacific ocean and the mental terrain of an emotional struggle (VIII); places of loneliness, stories of lonely travels and a grave of a lonely death (IX); a prison cell (X); a Pacific bay at the freeze of winter and the country investigated through lists of its citizens' efforts and livelihoods, and of its options for patriotism, for where these citizens might be moored and bound (XI); one woman's beauty and "blueprints of resistance and mercy" (XII.2); and the imagined places where various "you"s "have landed" and read this poem (XIII. 41).

Rich does offer one image of "a map of our country" (II.1), but this image is the one that, as I mentioned earlier, shifts the map into the new form of the mural (II.22). The written image of a map is nearly ekphrastic, especially when we find that this map is actually a mural. Yet neither the map nor the mural is described in the poem; they are invoked diegetically without being evoked mimetically.

The ekphrastic element is even more apparent in Peter Balakian's "The Oriental Rug," which I discuss in chapter 1.[8] Balakian offers a written representation of a visual representation: the speaker describes the patterns of the rug, which is itself a metonymic representation of the Armenian landscape. As I note in my first chapter, the speaker also takes this pattern onto his body (I.15–16), making the poem a verbal interpretation of the representing function of his own physicality. Further, Balakian's poetic interpretation in part reads the rug's visual and tactile interpretation of the landscape through the lens of another visual representation of the same land. The speaker describes "the dark balm / of the marshy hillsides // of my faraway land – the poppied acres / of Adoian's hands" (III.14–18). As Balakian's notes explain, "Adoian" is the "family name of painter Arshile Gorky" (176). The speaker's "faraway land" is not only faraway; the land is also the creation of the Armenian painter's hands.

Ekphrasis is a procedure of mediation: words stand in for an absent visual entity. Ekphrasis is, then, especially appropriate in the witnessing genre. Witnessing, as its definition makes clear, is primarily understood to be engaged in moving from the visible to the verbal. The secondary witness – like Balakian and his speaker – has to work with the translation of what was seen into what is told. It is this process of mediation and translation that particularly suggests the appropriateness of a genre emphasizing the absence of the visual object. As scholar of English and Art History W.J.T. Mitchell explains, "A verbal representation cannot represent – that is, make present – its object in the same way a visual representation can. It may refer to an object, describe it, invoke it, but it can never bring its visual presence before us in the way pictures do. Words can 'cite,' but never 'sight' their objects" (152). What Mitchell does not make clear is that the difference between citing and sighting an object is not the same issue in verbal representation in general as it is in deliberately ekphrastic strategies specifically. These strategies (not found only in poetry with a fully determined ekphrastic goal but also in many poems with moments of ekphrasis) have a particular goal of *re*-presentation. Verbal representation can never make present its object, but one might argue that ekphrasis does not wish to achieve this presence. The ekphrastic object, already presented in one form, is translated into a new form rather than presented again as a new original.

So, when Rich leaves her atlases and maps at the level of ambiguous description, and when Harjo invokes a material map only to suggest that it will disappear in the face of lived experience, we find an emphasis on words as things that do not bring us their objects and do not seem meant to do so. Both descriptions avoid the icon: neither poet presents us with a graspable image of a map. In their privileging of diegesis over mimesis, the poets assert the map as an indexical object. In the hermeneutic structure of these descriptions in which the map itself is not much present, the reader is required to be more present, to follow the descriptions into his or her own creation of the map. In this indexical use of the map, Rich creates a hermeneutic community by writing of particular lives in the United States and recombining these details into a hopeful, potential community, one that is metonymically related to the lived community of the nation. This metonymical connection comes out of the aspect of nationhood that relies on the conceptual understanding of the nation by its members. Community is similarly hermeneutic for Harjo. As the last line of her poem indicates, the map must be created by each individual. The hermeneutic community here is formed by each individual interpretation of the details of this nation in relation to the self.

Rich speaks in similar terms about Elizabeth Bishop: "More and more, her poems embodied a need to place herself in the actual, to come to terms with a personal past, with family and class, and race, with her presence as a poet in cities and landscapes where human suffering is not a metaphor" ("The Eye of the Outsider," *Blood, Bread, and Poetry* 126). Though Rich says, "some of the poems in her first book ... I found impenetrable: intellectualized to the point of obliquity (e.g., 'The Map')" (125), Rich's central image (the map) and one of her central terms (mooring) resonate with this precursor map-poem's interest in the border of water at land and the border of depiction at the original. According to Sara Meyer in her article "'Another Attempt at Mastering Infinity': Elizabeth Bishop's Art of Map-making," "The Map" "maps a reading, drawing boundary lines between sea and land, 'printer' and reader, fact and fiction, landscape and fantasy. The result is a multitude of questions about relationships, representation and referentiality ... The map as picture devours the map as sign. Here signs receive meanings which exceed the world of reference they are supposed to serve" (237). Like Bishop's "The Map," Rich's poem engages with the boundaries of meaning-making through overlapping, provisional forms as they are filtered through the actual form of the poem. As she verbally creates a map, Rich's speaker offers interpretations of it, thus producing a map that is concerned with its own function. Her poem offers a map that becomes a mural – the map is described in words that proclaim it to be a picture, thus complicating the map as sign. The idea that this poem is a reflection of a referent but also a tool to act on that referent is engaged through its description as a sign (a map, whose referent is the landscape or the political boundaries it depicts) and an interpretation (a mural, whose pictures may represent or refer, or do neither).

Bishop's "The Map" likewise investigates the boundaries of artistic depiction.[9] Her speaker comments on her own interpretation of the map: "We can stroke these lovely bays, / under a glass as if they were expected to blossom, / or as if to provide a clean cage for invisible fish" (11–13). The ocular, mental, and tactile disruption of stroking represents our interpretive shaping of these bays under our glass. Our own looking – setting apart space with the glass, this decision about the boundaries of focus – has expectations that structure meaning. Yet, since we look "as if" something "were expected," the recognition that we expect something turns that expectation into a simile of itself: our expectations stand in for themselves as if those expectations existed. Thus, we set these boundaries without really believing we can control what we can expect. The affection with which this analysis works – in the stroking of lovely things – suggests a tenderness toward and enjoyment of such boundaries that might be in line with Harjo's "fragile, luminescent, tender, little place, or home." Bishop's poem and Harjo's comment each approach interpretation through an affectionate move that also dismantles the perspective into its composite pieces, or reduces its magnificence. Bishop's speaker can stroke lovely bays into an almost blossom within the borders of a glass she holds, much as Harjo can recognize a place as luminescent only in the midst of its fragile, tender littleness.

That it is "as if" we expected the provision of a cage suggests that there was some need beforehand, that these invisible fish required us to "provide" a cage whose cleanliness indicates its own invisibility. This invisibility is "as if" our restrictions to meaning go unnoticed as the unremarkably clear response to a need. If invisible fish are as yet unknown meaning, then stroking the bays with lyrical attention and ekphrastic energy might restrict meaning so cleanly that we do not see it happening. In the relegation of this expectation to the realm of the "as if," it seems that the actual role of interpretation here is not to reproduce meaning but to be aware of our interpretive ability to restrict it or to make it more open[10] (more open being the other option the poem gives: the bay's blossoming, that conceptually unclear transformation of bay to flower, or, perhaps, the excitement of the bay to overwhelm its mapped boundaries by flood). Bishop makes visible the expectations of interpretation, thus changing them. Readers of Rich's poem likewise become aware of their own expectations of interpretation when Rich changes her poem to an atlas to a map to a mural. The poem positions its readers to consider boundaries of meaning in interpretation, and the way that an interpretive community – as far as it is structured by the object of interpretation – constructs those boundaries.

Bishop's under-glass bay waters also suggest Hart Crane's "chained bay waters" (4), a line from "To Brooklyn Bridge" that Rich quotes in "An Atlas of the Difficult World" (V.12). For Paul Giles, in *Hart Crane: The Contexts of "The Bridge,"* this line might indicate the "bay of NY harbor – chain bridge is another name for suspension bridge" (226), but also "water chained or imprisoned by poet" (226). Rich's borrowing of this line indicates her own glass or chain: she writes as if we expected "Liberty" but her reader can only "catch [it] if you can" (V.6). In the context of "To Brooklyn Bridge" and (more obliquely) "The Map," this section of Rich's poem examines interpretation as something that inserts the reader into the poem as one who contains its meaning, as the arranger of a glass cage or chain. In this imperative to "catch if you can," the reader is sent out into the poem to catch liberty, to stroke its loveliness, to imprison in the poem's representation of the United States a meaning of liberty. This positioning makes the blossoming of a prison out of what should have been the Statue of Liberty all the more affecting: Rich marks Crane's line "over the chained bay waters" as borrowed through italicization and an endnote. Yet Rich omits the line's final word, "Liberty," which she repositions in her own poem: "catch if you can [...] / these pilgrim ants pouring out from the bronze eyes, ears, / nostrils, / the mouth of Liberty / over the chained bay waters / San Quentin" (V.6–12). She does not note "Liberty" in its relationship to "To Brooklyn Bridge." Rich recontexualizes the word "Liberty" so that it seems only to refer, with its bronze orifices, to the Statue of Liberty, depriving the word of the doubled meaning it holds in Crane's poem as potentially both a symbol of freedom (referencing the Statue of Liberty) and freedom itself (referencing "liberty's" ordinary definition). Rich replaces "Liberty" with "San Quentin" so that the juxtaposition of Liberty with chained bays and a prison interrupts Crane's contiguous ocular chain – a view of a bridge with a view of a sign (statue) of Liberty – that builds up from the chained bay waters. If in Crane's poem Liberty might "forsake our eyes" (5), in Rich's poem it stands clearly in ironic juxtaposition to detainment.

In contrast to this reading, Joshua S. Jacobs in "'An Atlas of the Difficult World': Adrienne Rich's Countermonument" argues that Rich makes us "see Liberty as an occupiable icon" (731) because "the statue is tied to the experiences of Native Americans, women, Vietnam veterans, and other groups who have marched on symbolic places in order to claim a place in American historical narratives" (732). Although Jacobs earlier quotes Alice Templeton's argument that this poem is not made to be received as an icon (729), he considers Rich's poem as a countermonument like this occupiable iconic Liberty, particularly as the Dedications section "enacts individual readers' experiences" (744). Yet, once a poem invites a reader's use, it becomes indexical rather than iconic. Rich's poem strives not to be an icon of individual experiences it monumentalizes, but instead to imagine experiences that allow readers to use the poem as an indexical guide to engaging those experiences, whether their own or others.

Rich's poem begins with the evocation of place, of walking, of the "terrain" (I.53) that becomes linked to the American state in the poem's second part with the introductory phrase, "Here is a map of our country" (II.1). The deictic presentation of the land as a map of the country evokes a sense of presence. This presence is both spatial – in terms of being "here" or moored somewhere – and mindful – in terms of mooring as an emotional presence or presence of thought or, perhaps better, as I have been tweaking a figure of speech into the notion of attentiveness, a presence of mind. Mindful presence is also the knowledge experienced in the act of witnessing. The speaker is mindfully attentive to the "here" of the map of the country as she uses the map to interpret the country's flaws: "Here is a map of our country: / here is the Sea of Indifference, glazed with salt / This is the haunted river flowing from brow to groin / we dare not taste its water" (II.1–4). This map of the country continues over the land's physical and immaterial spaces: "This is the desert [...] breadbasket [...] birthplace [...] cemetery [...] sea-town of myth and story [...] These are other battlefields [...] here are the forests primeval

[...] These are the suburbs of acquiescence [...] This is the capital of money and dolor" (II.5–18). The evils are "missiles [...] "foreclosed farms" [...] "bankruptcy" [...] "battlefields" [...] "silence" (II.5–16). The spatial country is evoked from the position of the witness, the mindful presence of attention to these places and their losses and lackings. The list ends with the switch from map to mural that I have already discussed: "I promised to show you a map you say but this is a mural / then yes let it be   these are small distinctions / where do we see it from is the question" (II.22–4). The "where" created by the presentation of the map or mural is important in terms of the space that presentation creates. In this offer of the map's presence, readers are brought into the position of witness, so that we too see this map from watching roads.

Bodies

Rich's "fissured, cracked terrain" (I.53) is, as literal land, metonymically connected to the country as its location but also metaphorically to the disintegrating community. In this dual signification, the landscape operates in parallel to the concept of the map or atlas in the poem, metonymically representing community much as the rug in "The Oriental Rug" does the Armenian nation. Yet, while the land is both a literal and figurative grounding of the national community, in "An Atlas of the Difficult World" it also becomes a body that is mapped as the nation: "Here is a map of our country: / here is the Sea of Indifference, glazed with salt / This is the haunted river flowing from brow to groin / we dare not taste its water" (II.1–4). This representation is curiously shifting: the image of a map depicts a landscape which we understand symbolically as a body, or the image of the landscape functions as a map when we read it as a body.

Rich maps her nation's flaws through these waterways – this sea and river become important in relation to her repeated question, "Where are we moored?" (XI.63–5; V.17–19). If "we" can be moored on this map, we are boats at sea (of indifference). It is significant that Rich does not focus on the seas bordering the nation, but rather, since the river flows from brow to groin into this sea, on a body of water largely surrounded by the body of the nation, fed by this river traversing its core. Mooring seems not to be important for situating the nation within its fixed borders, but rather for providing a stabilizing influence for a community within water that flows and connects, much as the speaker must be fixed to the land that holds roads to be walked. This river and its sea are positioned at the centre of this road map.

Yet, if the river is haunted and flows only into indifference, then the river needs to be exorcised through the drinking that is not dared. This communal drinking, this acknowledgment and remembrance of national ghosts, this taking into individual bodies the failures of the nation, is an intimate mooring. The acceptance of the landscape-as-community into one's body is precisely the kind of mooring that allows for movement, for walking and witnessing the roads not one's own.

Harjo also makes this connection between body, land, map, and community. In "Joy Harjo and Her Poetics as Praxis: A 'Postcolonial' Political Economy of the Body, Land, Labor, and Language," Azfar Hussain considers two decades of Harjo's poetry. He argues that her poetry across collections "differentially but continuously focuses on those four crucial material-discursive sites – the body, land, labor, and language – in ways in which they keep intersecting as the crucial sites of struggle" (36). In this focus on labour, Hussain refers to the many references to giving birth in Harjo's work that correlate with other aspects of material reality and struggle. In "A Map to the Next World," the map is life – you enter it because you are conceived: "The place of entry is the sea of your mother's blood, your father's / small death as he longs to know himself in another" (25–6). This form of entrance into the map suggests its unavoidability, but the fact that you must make your own map suggests that its interpretation is a choice, the undertaking of a responsibility. One enters onto the map in entering life, but the map is also a part of the person and can be read through his or her body: "The map can be interpreted through the wall of the intestine – a / spiral on the road of knowledge" (28–9). Moreover, the landscape and the body are entwined on the map: "You will see red cliffs. They are the heart, contain the ladder" (43). Harjo's image of an intestinal spiral on the road to knowledge demonstrates the kind of making a map might take. Knowledge might be a road, with a start and an end point, but the kind of coming-to that is a deep internalization – organ-deep, metaphorically speaking – is a spiral, a re-turning to the same ideas. A spiral follows back in on itself into a density around an inner point or a deepening toward some central concept. The image of the heart as red cliffs containing the ladder seems another rendition of this idea (the poem itself spiralling around the concept of the spiral of the road to knowledge) from the opposite perspective. The heart-cliffs have a ladder for climbing back out of the depth, for thinking back up and out. The multiplicity of cliffs comprising the heart suggests a span of truths through which one might climb for perspective.

But this map is not only personal internalization and traversal of knowledges; as I have already discussed, the map addresses the Creek nation, carrying in it Creek-specific symbols. The map shows the connection of the community as well as the individual to the land: "In the legend are instructions on the language of the land, how it / was we forgot to acknowledge the gift, as if we were not in it or of it" (8–9). Harjo's individual map is likewise made communal in its connection to both physical body and physical geography: the individual's interior map is made up of the individual body – intestines, heart (28, 43) – as well as features of a terrain – red cliffs (43). Moreover, the map must be interpreted "by your intention, by the language of suns" (40). The phrase "your intention" suggests personal interpretation while "the language of suns" evokes cultural understanding as an important aspect of Creek belief;[11] here the two are linked appositionally by a comma, suggesting the connection of the personal and the communal as a shared motion rather than as separate endeavours. Harjo's landscape is something that can be carried within the person, indicating a focus on the place of individual within community, while Rich's landscape as a shared social body indicates an exploration of community itself.[12]

Rich's speaker demonstrates a desire to achieve a certain kind of public life through a national body. Harjo's kinship ties are important in relation to cultural continuance (song, fire). Both poets use similar images in similarly metaphoric and metonymic ways, though in importantly divergent contexts in terms of Rich's pull of the country toward community and Harjo's investment in a nation within that country's borders. Another difference (though I will qualify it later on) occurs in the spatio-temporal operation of these images. Rich's poem foregrounds an understanding of public life and social ties, of people living and acting together in a shared place, while Harjo's poem is linked to a shared history of discrimination. Consequently, the common body in "An Atlas of the Difficult World" operates more spatially, notably in the introduction of the image of the map: "Here is a map of our country [...] *where* do we see it from is the question" (II.1, 24 emphasis added). Moreover, this section is an anaphoric list of various places in the present day country, establishing a repeated, deictic "This is the ..." formulation that further suggests presence in this current country (II.3–21). Harjo's map image is more temporal, as, for example, it is "printed with the blood of history" (39). Moreover, the call to remember the historical moment of forced removal looks both forward and backward in time while also indicating a concern with place as unavailable as a secure cultural grounding: "Remember the hole of our shame marking the act of abandoning our / tribal grounds" (46–7). For Rich, then, these images of shared embodiment correspond to the context of shared space and national discourse, while for Harjo images of passed-on embodiment through reproduction correspond to a shared history of experience and a future of passed-on stories. The current lived story, premised on the shared context and shared proximity in Rich's poem is, in Harjo's, a shared ongoing story in a shared temporal context of memory and continuation.

Rather than a succession of figurative substitutions, these poems deliver a concatenation of simultaneous metonyms: the metonym of the land for the country also becomes, for Rich, the metonym of the land as a national community via the human body and, for Harjo, in opposite container-content relationship, the metonym of the individual body as that which holds the nation as land and community. These shifts are not subsequent because the land remains land while it is also the body-public, and the body is still a body while it houses the land that underpins national identity. In each moment that the nation is understood through the trope of the map, it is also understood through both figurative and literal conceptions of a geographical location and the physical bodies of its occupants.

Gifts and Dedications

These figural and literal registers of land and body are recognizable in Rich's speaker's repeated question: "Where are we moored? / What are the bindings? / What behooves us?" (XI.63–5). An answer to these questions seems linked – in its similarity to wandering other roads – to the kindness of straining to see another from outside of one's own perspective, as well as to questions of intimacy and distance. The earlier openness in trajectory becomes a kind of kindness when a "desperate man [...] / experiences his first kindness, / someone to strain with him, / to strain to see him as he strains to see himself" (X.50–3). The image of one straining to see another as he strains to see himself suggests the distance involved in knowing. The image makes apparent, though, the continuum of intimate and distanced knowledge as even the man straining to see himself finds his most intimate knowledge – his own seeing of himself – distanced from himself.

The speaker's questions are repeated in separate sections of the poem. In their first instance, the lines are typographically offset from one another: "Where are we moored?   What / are the bindings? What be- / hooves us?" (V.17–19). The large spaces suggest a lack of bindings, a lack of mooring, but "An Atlas of the Difficult World" works within the tension between wandering and fixedness, walking and mooring. The striding over of the enjambed lines contrasts the long stillness of the caesura – caused by the question mark and extended space – in the middle of the lines: the formal aspects of these questions juxtapose moving with stopping, wandering with mooring, roads with "here."

In contrast to the first iteration of these questions in a right-aligned stanza with enjambed lines and extra spacing between sentences, in their repetition the questions are asked with a firmer form, presented in end-stopped lines and centred on the page (XI.63–5).[13] These prominent lines end this section. The first time the questions are asked, the enjambment and spacing make them seem tentative; the right alignment and separation from the rest of the section make the lines appear jotted in the margin, a commentary on the rest of the section rather than the main point, the conclusion, the call to action. In their restatement, the questions seem rather like an envoi, both in its conventional place as a concluding offering in certain poetic forms, as well as in its more literal meaning as a "sending forth," a call to be answered, a call heightened beyond the call a question mark already makes for a response.

In asking where "we" might find mooring and what behooves "us," Rich's speaker interrogates the possibility of a nation as a community. "An Atlas of the Difficult World" maps the positions those in the United States might be behooved to take in order to answer to the conception of a nation moored in community. Rich's speaker suggests that this nation is lacking as a community: "Catch if you can your country's moment, begin / where any calendar's ripped off [...] / – catch if you can this unbound land these states without a cause" (V.1–6). These "states without a cause" can be the country's regions, but "state" can also be read as a condition or situation. These states are, then, the literal politically bound communities of the nation, lacking a cause in the sense of the interests or goals that might be taken up in relation to the states' status as communities. At the same time, the states are also the condition in which the speaker finds her country. These conditions might be understood as a disengaged emotional and political state if "cause" here refers to something producing an effect or consequence. To catch the country's moment is to begin in the past, to recover the page ripped from the calendar. The imperative form paired with the address to a "you" – rather than being spoken by the "I" of the poem or addressing the "we" of the imagined community – makes a demand of the reader, though this demand is pessimistically framed as potentially unfulfillable. It might not be possible for the reader to catch the present moment through this remembering. Indeed, the alliteration and assonance of "catch" and "can" leaves "catch" connected so closely to its conditionality that the action cannot be considered aside from the uncertainty. The "if" intrudes before we can even find out what it is we ought to be catching. The repetition of the phrase increases its urgency while simultaneously increasing its unlikeliness.

In "The Nation-State: A Modest Defense," political theorist David Miller, in answering "What does it mean to think of oneself as belonging to a national community?" (138), suggests that one aspect of this belonging has to do with catching your country's moment in the binding of historical obligation:

> The historic national community is a community of obligation. Because our forebears have toiled and spilt their blood to build and defend the nation, we who are born into it inherit an obligation to continue their work, which we discharge partly toward our contemporaries and partly toward our descendants. The historical community stretches forward into the future too. This then means that when we speak of the nation as an ethical community we have in mind not merely the kind of community that exists between a group of contemporaries who practise mutual aid among themselves and which would dissolve at the point at which that practice ceased; but a community which, because it stretches back and forward across the generations, is not one that the present generation can renounce. (139)

I earlier discussed Harjo's poem as the better example of this historic obligation. "A Map to the Next World" focuses often on remembering and forgetting (9, 12, 18–19, 22, 46) and is a future-oriented passing on of obligation, as the speaker instructs that "You will have to navigate by your mother's voice, renew the song / she is singing" (36–7). Yet Rich also engages with a historical conception of community (thus my formulation of Rich's poem as spatial and Harjo's as temporal is not firm but offered as a heuristic frame). The speaker reflects on a house of personal memories, where the "old medicine bottles" (III.80) dug up years ago by the speaker's children resonate with the "time-hurtling wind" that "has a voice in the house":

> I'm not talking of ghosts. The ghosts are here of course but
>   they speak plainly
> – haven't I offered food and wine, listened well for them all
>   these years,
> not only those known in life but those before our time
> of self-deception [...]? (III.97–104)

The "time-hurtling wind" brings voices from the past back into the house to join the ghosts to which the speaker has long tended and attended. The present time of "self-deception" and the obligation to plain-speaking ghosts from "before our time" suggests a present behooving to truths ignored. Listening well is an offering just like the gifts of food and wine.

Moreover, in this house where gifts sit on "shelves of things / both useful and unused, things arrived here by chance or choice" (III.54–5), the speaker describes a "broken-spouted" teapot from her grandmother (III.56, 58) and one from "a refugee who killed herself" (III.61) which "cannot be used because / coated inside – why? – with flaking paint: / 'You will always use it for flowers,' she instructed when she / gave it" (III.62–5). The interjected "why?" is an emphasized aside that goes unanswered, but in being asked and set apart, it indicates an important concern with the object's history as well as its future. While the gift from a family member of an older generation resonates with Harjo's poem as dedication, the gift from a refugee suggests a need for witness to past suffering. That neither teapot can be used for its proper purpose indicates that this attention to suffering might involve the thoughtful creativity required by "things arrived here by chance or choice." Thus, though some of these things were unchosen, they are "useful"; though some are "unused," they are not use*less*. The instruction to use the teapot otherwise than for its usual purpose suggests the operation of the gift as an object of possibility – here, the possibility of remembrance. The refugee's instructions are not phrased as instruction but as prophecy: "You will always use it for flowers." To play out this future-tensed statement as reality, the receiver of the teapot must use it in remembrance of the refugee's comment on this future.

The gift, then, creates an obligation. Sociologist Marcel Mauss in *The Gift* suggests that to offer a gift is also to deliver a commitment. In her foreword to Mauss's work, Mary Douglas writes, "What is wrong with the so-called free gift is the donor's intention to be exempt from return gifts coming from the recipient. Refusing requital puts the act of giving outside any mutual ties ... According to Marcel Mauss that is what is wrong with the free gift. A gift that does nothing to enhance solidarity is a contradiction" (vii). For Mauss, "it is not individuals but collectivities that impose obligations of exchange and contract upon each other" (5). The gift of the teapot necessitates that the speaker look back toward its causes and forward to its use, to remember the refugee and to respect her instructions, inside of an understanding of interpersonal ties. There is an implication in the idea of a gift that one must use the useful and attend to what arrives in the context of relationship. Especially in relation to a gift that comes with instructions, there is an element of trust that the receiver will accept that obligation.

Yet, as Margaret Canovan explains in *Nationhood and Political Theory*, professor of religion Adam Seligman questions whether there is, at the national level, a "sufficient sense of mutual trust and obligation to generate and support effective sharing" (30). Canovan notes that, although "Seligman argues that the 'generalization and universalization of trust'" is necessarily involved in civil society, the "process of abstraction and universalization that created the Western liberal nation and made possible the autonomous individual and civil society may in fact be continuing to destroy social bonds to the point of undermining itself. Perhaps it is the case that 'the very universalization of trust ... vitiates the mutuality and communality upon which trust must be based'" (40–1). Thus, Canovan explains that while "civil society was made possible ... because individuals had been released from communal identities, and had instead become members of new, more abstract national communities that transcended ethnicity," the thinning out of this trust to span a nation may undermine the communality it requires (40).

Rich suggests fragmentation in the American nation as she describes its citizens as "each [...] now a driven grain, a nucleus, a city in crisis" (XI.24). While these citizens are, however, *both* "touched and untouched in / passing" (XI.22–3), the "crisis," not contained by any punctuation, carries into the next line that begins a long invocation of the nation's citizens, of whom "some [are] busy constructing enclosures, bunkers, to escape the com / mon fate" (XI.25–6). This long anaphoric list gives various categories of "some" that make up the country. The first stanza of this section of "somes," separated from the section proper by a blank line, describes "the death-freeze of the century: / a precise, detached calliper-grip holds the stars and the quarter- / moon / in arrest" (XI.1–4). This frozen, detached state works as an epigraphical metaphor for the following section. The "hardiest plants" have had their "juices sucked awry" and are "slumped on their stems like old faces evicted from cheap hotels / – *into the streets of the universe, now!*" (XI.4–9). The italicized imperative offers a different understanding of the speaker's earlier wandering of roads. This image of eviction into the streets operates as a counter-call to the demand, or shifts the demand onto the reader, implying the need for the purposeful wandering of the roads; from these roads, kindness might mean seeing the "old faces" that are "sucked awry" by unjust demands. Noticeably, the juices aren't sucked away, but awry, or "away from the straight" (OED). "Awry" means as well, though, "to fall into error" (OED). The sense of injustice in this passage comes from the idea that people are frozen "out of the right course" (OED).

The list shows people working with conflicting tactics – "some who try to teach the moment, some who preach the / moment" (XI.28–9) – and from conflicting experiences and options that preclude shared goals – "some for whom peace is a white man's word and a white man's / privilege" (XI.38–9). The list ends, though, in the description of

> some who have learned to handle and contemplate the shapes of powerlessness and power
> as the nurse learns hip and thigh and weight of the body he has to lift and sponge, day upon day
> as she blows with her every skill on the spirit's embers (XI.40–4)

The seamless shift in pronoun, from "he" to "she," indicates a move out of the individual into a group of nurses, a "some." The nurse's particular kind of help offers the possibility of community, linked here with dying fire much as it is in Harjo's image of trees of ashes. Again Rich, also like Harjo, imagines community through physicality as the nurse's help is focused through the "hip and thigh and weight of the body"; this physical and intimate proximity suggests presence in its literal meaning of attendance as well as in the kindness of attention.

This encounter between a diversely imagined nurse and the weight of a body is not used to achieve a general rule or abstract understanding that is removed from particularity. Rather, Rich creates a scene of juxtaposed details. Witnessing can provide this juxtaposition first through the act of attending and second through the interpretive connections coming out of the combinations of the known particulars. Attention to the particular lives making up a community is an attention that culminates (culminates continually, that is, always knowing but never reaching to an ultimate and final knowledge) in an interpretive knowledge of the possible interaction of these details. The materiality of "powerlessness and power" suggests that power and its absence take "shapes" that can be rearranged by those who "handle and contemplate" them. Rich imagines a lyric community of such witnesses, and, though her speaker "knows you are reading this poem" and knows the conditions under which various imagined readers do this reading, she can only posit this knowledge because of her attention to the details of particular experiences of the United States. This poem gives us the hermeneutic community it envisions: we have the speaker's or poet's interpretation of the details of the country that could be recombined to foster community.

In contrast, Shreiber argues that though Rich "writes with enormous insight of Whitman's failure to represent difference and its attendant discontinuities," she is, in this poem's Whitmanesque lists of individual lives, "culpable in some of the same ways. While she works hard to avoid Whitman's invasiveness, she nonetheless ends up duplicating his tendency to make universal sameness the grounds for sympathetic identification" (314). Yet Rich makes clear her desire for community outside of identification. In *Blood, Bread, and Poetry* she writes of "we who are not the same. We who are many and do not want to be the same" (225). Indeed, in "An Atlas of the Difficult World," her community is based not on common identity or identification, but on the offer of mutual obligation. Much as the gift of the teapot comes with the obligation to fulfill a particular future use, the speaker's offering of the map serves as a gift asking for something in return: "I promised to show you a map you say but this is a mural / then yes let it be   these are small distinctions / where do we see it from is the question" (II.22–4). The "promise" holds a community in its temporal operation from the moment it is spoken, forward into an expected future. Though the speaker breaks this promise – she does not present the reader with the object the reader expected to have to use – she suggests that there is a small distinction between what comes by chance and what by choice; it seems the reader might benefit from understanding this creative flexibility. Further though, despite the speaker's promise of mimetically showing the map, her actual act of diegetically telling it leaves an absence of tangible images through which readers play a role in constructing the map. In giving the poem as a gift, the speaker requires readers to put themselves into the walking of roads. As in Harjo's poem, this is not a map that one can carry.

The idea of gifting provides a context for understanding this poetry's dedications. The last section of "An Atlas of the Difficult World" is titled "(Dedications)." In contrast to Harjo's dedication to her daughter, this dedication is contemporary (and beyond) rather than generational, and open rather than specific, as it is available to any reader of this poem as he or she reads it. A dedication is a way of giving over and Rich gives over this poem to an imagined community. She posits a community of readers by joining them with a goal: "I know you are reading this poem listening for something, torn / between bitterness and hope / turning back once again to the task you cannot refuse" (XIII.36–8). The speaker presumes that this goal already exists in the lived community as the lyric community of "this poem" is created by those "listening for something" in the poem. Philosopher Ernest Renan suggests that "a nation's existence is, if you will pardon the metaphor, a daily plebiscite, just as an individual's existence is a perpetual affirmation of life" (53). Readers can choose to listen for this dedication and to receive the obligation for becoming part of this community in connection to life in the United States. The readers have to "turn[] back" from the poem: the poem is something aside, something to which one can turn (ask of, rely on), and, in contrast to the individual's "task," a turning that can be refused.

A dedication is like a gift insofar as both ask for something in return. Rich proposes that readers give listening in return for the gift of her dedication. Listening is necessary for the community the poem describes, and the dedication is a gift because it provides a "here" for all those who come to it by chance or choice. This open dedication is not a gift given directly to each person; it is available to any reader, thus offering a form of belonging that is non-exclusive. As the community is formed by the generosity of the dedication and by the mutual obligation to listen, the poem's written dedication is a gift like the gift of the teapot that can be repurposed: you will always use it for listening. Listening, as opposed to reading, suggests the physical presence associated with the togetherness of community. Moreover, the assumed emotional response – not just between bitterness and hope, but emphatically "torn" between the two (as emphasized by the line break after that word) – imagines readers to be emotionally in motion, unable to rest at either end of the spectrum. The "you" here might function, not as an individual, but as the general category of the reader inside of which any individual reader might be affected at any point of the spectrum of emotion. Since this "you" stands in for the whole picture of response, the poem only assumes that the reader feels something. Even apathy, or indifference, falls on this scale between bitterness and hope.[14]

Though the speaker, it is true, is imagining the connection, Rich, as the writer of the poem, does have some control over what its readers might find in it, and so some control over that for which readers might reasonably look. A dedication might be considered a kind of trust in this moment where the poem offers something through the assumption that its readers will want to find it. There is an implication of community in knowing a need to the extent that the speaker is willing to offer fulfillment of that need and to the extent that the poem, designed to fulfill this need, will gather readers who need that fulfillment. Thus, the declaration "I know you are reading this poem in a waiting-room / of eyes met and unmeeting, of identity with strangers" (XIII.21–2) is not a presumption but a reaching out.

Rich's pronoun use has been a topic of concern for scholars far beyond this section alone. In "Someone Is Writing a Poem," Rich articulates a preoccupation in her work: "Self-reference is always possible: that my 'I' is a universal 'we,' that the reader is my clone ... But most often someone writing a poem believes in, depends on, a delicate, vibrating range of difference, that an 'I' can become a 'we' without extinguishing others" (85). Eagleton writes in "Adrienne Rich, Location and the Body," "The impulse towards relation and connectedness is *the* underlying structure of Rich's work and, hence, the constant oscillation across binary divisions – 'I' and 'we,' the rational and the emotional, one's own pain and the other's pain, horror and hopefulness" (311). Scholars trace an upward trajectory in Rich's career-long struggle with this difficulty, as Eagleton puts it, "to establish the legitimate connections while making the necessary distinctions so that one does not slide into taking equivalencies for granted – identifying with an experience is not the same as having an experience" (306–7).[15]

Even as Rich's critics define her career by her attempt to avoid problematic identification, many of these same critics nevertheless read identificatory strategies into the poems that they claim avoid them. Shreiber, for instance, glosses the speaker's time in the house full of ghosts in "An Atlas of the Difficult World" as the outcome of "Rich's only resource": "to carefully display those personal credentials that perhaps entitle her to speak on behalf of others. Such is the ideological premise of the poem's third section, where she returns to Vermont to a house filled with broken, mismatched, profoundly unusable objects and memories of her failed marriage" (311). Of course, Rich's speaker, not Rich herself, makes this return within the poem. More importantly, I have shown that the objects in this section are in fact profoundly usable in the task of witnessing. The speaker travels to this house not to hold up her suffering as a personal credential that lets her speak the suffering of others, but to elucidate this speaker as a witness through some materials that have shaped her as one.

For another example, Jacobs reads Rich's poetry through the identificatory approach of trauma studies. He argues that in "Contradictions," by rendering those killed in the Holocaust as "still physical," Rich creates a basis "for a present-day artist to experience that world [of the Holocaust] in his/her own physical being in the manner suggested by Felman" ("Mapping after the Holocaust" np). In other words, she creates the basis for "the imaginative capacity of perceiving history – what is happening to others – in one's own body" (Felman qtd. in Jacobs). Despite this reading, Jacobs explains in the same article that Rich is not guilty of the "presumption of identity" with which many have charged her. As proof, he notes that the poem "Eastern War Time" "culminates with an I demanding to inhabit Rich and the reader with a force of discomfiting alterity" (8). Yet, if this were the poem's demand, the suffering speaker would still create a reader who can presume to have experienced what it is to be another, even if the power relations are ostensibly reversed. Moreover, Jacobs's account of this demand is inaccurate. The "I," though figured as a traumatic historical memory fitting nicely with trauma theory's idea of an agential trauma that moves through literature to infect readers, does not seek to enter the speaker. Rather, this memory says it holds a mirror within the poem: "I am standing here in your poem unsatisfied / lifting my smoky mirror" (qtd. in Jacobs). The voice shows a reader his or her relation to the poem; it does not obscure that relation by collapsing it into identity with another's memory.

For Jacobs, a speaker can justly speak for others if she presumes to be inhabited by them (in contrast to speaking for others whose experiences she presumes to inhabit), and Miriam Marty Clark makes a similar argument in "Human Rights and the Work of Lyric in Adrienne Rich." Clark writes that Rich's poem "North American Time" shows what she is "most interested in here: how the poet, *sans frontières* – stripped of the immunity time and place and identity provide – stands before the endless, boundless, and increasingly visible troubles of the world" (52). This is not a possible position: the poet is never immune to time and place and identity. An individual must encounter the world's troubles through the borders of her life. By reading the poet as "*sans frontières*," Clark loses the importance of the position the speaker engages from, a position to which Rich certainly attends. The stanza Clark uses to make this claim begins, "Words – / whether we like it or not – / stand in a time of their own" (51). Words may be said to stand in their own time since words exist beyond the point of writing. However, the relative boundlessness of her words does not allow the poet to stand without the context of boundaries.

Returning to the "(Dedications)" section, I understand the condition of this poetry's readers differently than does Piotr Gwiazda in "'Nothing Else Left to Read': Poetry and Audience in Adrienne Rich's 'An Atlas of the Difficult World.'" In a similar vein as Jacobs and Clark, Gwiazda claims: "Like Whitman, Rich envisions her audience as a matter of perpetual potentiality ... Like Whitman, too, she insists on the transcendental connection between poet and reader, an act of extra-verbal communication between two strangers. Poetry is somehow more than words; it is not only a form of art, but also a mode of intimate attachment" (182). However, there is nothing transcendental nor extra-verbal in this connection. Rich offers something to her potential readers. This something is, probably through Rich's choice more than chance, a poem, and the reader's position is structured by that form. Poetry can only make a connection through its words – it does not overcome words, it *is* words. Of course words are always more than words (this is their point – they are signs to indicate something else; they are always attached to something beyond themselves). Yet, if poetry achieves this intimacy, it does so precisely through its words and whatever attendant "more" those words hold.[16]

I understand the direct address in Rich's "(Dedications)" section to be not overcoming its own mode, but exploring the limits of poetry's communicative ability. This section's relationship with the poem's readers has echoes of Walt Whitman's "Whoever You Are Holding Me Now in Hand," which features a speaker likewise aware that he speaks out of a poem and to a reader unknown yet nevertheless addressable. Whitman and Rich both write out of a desire to create a sense of national community, a desire which requires a public audience but one that is made up of individuals who feel themselves to be parts of this wider group. Michael Warner, editor of *The Portable Walt Whitman*, reads "To a Stranger" as an address to a generic public and an individual reader:

> this "you" is, after all, not you but a pronominal shifter, addressing the in principle anonymous and indefinite audience of the print public sphere. At the same time, you know that you are not being addressed by a complacently generic you, of a kind that I am using to address you in this sentence. In "To a Stranger," while we remain on notice about our place in nonintimate public discourse, we are nevertheless solicited into an intimate recognition exchange. (41)

This "you" manages the different levels of address through its indication that, in speaking to a community, it speaks to a community of individuals, each of whom is necessary in his or her individuality for the community to exist at all. And, similarly, it is through the presence of the whole – a community of readers who, together, are "the reader" of the poem – that any individual reader might be addressed as "you." "The reader" becomes the heuristic guide to any particular reader's hermeneutic navigation of the poem. The direct address serves as a map through which readers can chart their particular responses through the possibilities provided by the poetic terrain.

   The effectiveness of this address is dependent on the foregrounding of its context. What Warner says about "To a Stranger" I think is even more applicable to "Whoever you are, holding me now in hand": "we cannot possibly *be* the self addressed in second-person attributions. But we also cannot simply fictionalize either the speaker or the scene of address, in the manner of 'My Last Duchess,' because the speaker himself indicates the genericizing conventions of publication" (41). Though such an address always comes through the space of the general reader role that might be occupied by any real reader, the poem's awareness of the nature of its own address makes clear its boundaries. Within these boundaries, we cannot discount the address as impossible – merely general, artificial, undirected – or imagine it as transcendent – overcoming itself as poetic address to become direct contact.

Thus, when the speaker "know[s] you are reading this poem in a waiting-room," it is the concept of the waiting room which indicates the potential for intimate connection. Like a *waiting* room, in which nothing is meant to happen but the potential of something happening later, a poem is a space in which an address does not really happen (at the moment of its creation there is no one to be actually addressed) but in which waits the potential for the realization of that address in a future reader.

Through the eyes in the waiting room that are both "met and unmeeting," this section of Rich's poem moves toward a community among strangers that is not yet established. Though there is already "identity with strangers" here, the kind of community I read in this poem is not dependent on identification. The unmet eyes of these strangers suggest that shared identity – whether through the common activity of reading this poem, the common place of a waiting room, the common status of stranger, or the common place of the United States – is not enough to posit community. The poem does not address a reader synecdochally – as part of the whole, as though any reader might be substituted for another – because no one reader can stand in for the whole national community. While both Whitman and Rich look to establish national identity in these poems, there is a suggestion in these lines that a multiply shared address cannot establish a shared identity without the mutual meeting of eyes – that is, without a form of witness that also establishes difference within the general address of shared identity.

Bishop's "In the Waiting Room" is, like "The Map," a useful pre-text for Rich's "(Dedications)" section and this "identity with strangers." In the poem, the speaker (named Elizabeth), reading an issue of *National Geographic* in a waiting room, experiences a cry of pain which seems to her to be shared by herself and her aunt. When Elizabeth feels a destabilization of her self in a profound moment of identification, she becomes unable to meet the eyes of the others in the waiting room:

> I scarcely dared to look
> to see what it was I was.
> I gave a sidelong glance
> – I couldn't look any higher –
> at shadowy gray knees,
> trousers and skirts and boots
> and different pairs of hands. (64–70)

The "scarcely dared to look to see" is a nearly tautological emphasis on sight that signals a breakdown in the kind of witness through which a community between selves might be established. In "The Weirdest Scale on Earth: Elizabeth Bishop and Containment," Lee Zimmerman comments on this troubled sense of what it is to be a person among other persons: "Coming in out of the cold, blue-black, isolating space means renouncing any degree of the crucial difference necessary for relatedness. Self and others, inside and outside, aren't *related* but are 'just one,' a realization Bishop is loathe to confront, as she 'scarcely dared to look' at the other people in the waiting room 'to see what it was I was' (160). If she *is* the others (if they are 'all just one'), she isn't *like* them, a distinction she quietly insists on by calling this experience of ostensible kinship 'unlikely'" (513).

The sudden sense that a cry of pain might be shared as one common experience breaks down Elizabeth's ability to learn about the others around her as it fragments them into body parts and articles of clothing. The identification arising from the felt shared experience is here dissolving rather than unifying. Elizabeth tries to read the frames of the people around her – their bodies, their coverings – but the cry of pain that can't be singularly attributed produces for her an inability to contextualize people in the experiences of their own bodies. The texts of people are unframeable, and the lack of framework makes them unreadable.

In "The Geography of Gender: Elizabeth Bishop's 'In the Waiting Room,'" Lee Edelman, working from his reading of Elizabeth's reading of the *National Geographic* magazine in which she "studies the cover, the margins, and the date in order to construct a frame for her reading experience that will circumscribe or contain it" (193), writes that "to gloss this passage as the young girl hearing 'her aunt cry out in pain' is surely to ignore the real problem that both the girl and the text experience here: the problem of determining the place from which this voice originates. Since the poem asserts that it comes from 'inside,' the meanings of 'inside' and 'outside' must be determined, their geo-graphical relation, as it were, must be mapped" (185–6). Edelman, though, points out the difficulty in determining this distinction, and of the model of "reading as mastery" (188): "Though only in the course of reading the magazine does 'Elizabeth' perceive the inadequacy of her positioning as a reader, Bishop's text implies from the outset the insufficiency of any mode of interpretation that claims to release the meaning it locates 'inside' a text by asserting its own ability to speak from a position of mastery 'outside' of it" (188).

The "you" indicating simultaneously *the* and *a* reader points precisely to this difficulty of being inside and outside the text. *The* reader is the position created by the poem. While *a* reader approaches the poem from outside, he or she is invited by the poem into this internally shaped position. The nature of this "you," as Warner makes clear, is one that comes both from the inside – as a general and public call shaped in the poem – and from the outside – as an address actively seeking the real response of individuals. The difference between the shared identity of the generic "you" in Rich's and Whitman's poems and the shared identity which Elizabeth experiences is this: a reader reading as "you" is afforded a framework from which to read that eliminates the problem of inside/outside while still maintaining the boundaries of that framework. These poems call attention to their own status as poems, highlighting the possibilities and limits of poetry through which the address explicitly operates.

In contrast, Elizabeth is herself in the space of a reader within Bishop's poem and her call to identity comes from outside of the frame of what she is able to read. The call is incommensurably outside and inside herself, incommensurably outside and inside the waiting room. In Rich's and Whitman's poems, the explicit ground-ing in the language of a poem provides a frame to make clear the con-text of the address to shared (national) identity. A particular reader is not lost within Rich's collection of depicted "yous" or Whitman's intimate "you" because these "yous" exist within the framework of words waiting for the actual readers whose acceptance of such a role extends the address outside of the poem and into the possibility of the community it seeks to create. It is only in the indication that no one reader is the only one that the poem looks for readers in plural-ity, that such an address can maintain its insideness (its continued waiting for "you," the general category of reader) at the same time that it is completed outside of itself (in its particular call to "you," an individual reader).

The speaker in Whitman's "To a Stranger" is – like Elizabeth in Bishop's poem and a "you" in Rich's – in a condition of waiting: "I am to wait, I do not doubt I am to meet you again, / I am to see to it that I do not lose you" (Whitman 15–16). For Rich and Whit-man, the "identity with strangers," with readers, is always a kind of waiting, a waiting in words. If a poem is a space like a map, it is also a space like a waiting room. "I am to see to it that I do not lose you" suggests Rich's meeting of eyes and Elizabeth's inability to look up to eye level. Seeing is necessary to not losing "you," losing an individual reader in the assertion of *the* reader. "I do not doubt" – rather than "I am sure" – affirms through negation much as the address affirms its facility through its incompletion in waiting. Like the promise to show a map and its fulfillment in the telling of a mural, the waiting room is a promise fulfilled by this dedication of another, poetic, space. A waiting room promises the coming or happening of something else; it is a space designed for the time before the next thing. A dedication is "the giving up or devoting (of oneself, one's time, labour, etc.) to the service of a person or to the pursuit of a purpose" (OED). The poem itself – Rich's labour – is dedicated to the readers who wait still for the map of the country as a community. As the section is titled parenthetically – "(Dedi-cations)" – it makes room for readers to take the dedication as an aside, to approach the section without it. If the poem is offered as a gifted communal space to its readers, its surround of parentheses makes it a gift that an individual reader can choose to unwrap or not; each reader can choose to bring it outside into a completion in oneself as reader or to open it as a map in an acceptance of the dedication's terms of poetic navigation.

Compassion across Contexts: Substitution, Incorporation, and Juxtaposition

Compassion seems most available as a reaction to the suffering of a particular person or group. Feeling in response to another's suffering is necessarily particularized in the sense that this suffering must occur in some specific context. Thus, we might expect compassion outside of a circumscribed set of details to take the form of an abstract value. What happens in poetry engaging multiple contexts? In this chapter, I examine a bridging compassionate response in three collections of poetry whose authors depict compassion as a feeling that might transcend a given circumstance. Adrienne Rich's *An Atlas of the Difficult World* (1990–91), Joy Harjo's *A Map to the Next World* (2000), and Rachel Tzvia Back's *On Ruins & Return: The Buffalo Poems* (1999–2005) each differently approaches compassion's extension beyond a single context. In addition to the three poets I focus on in this chapter, I more briefly consider poetry by Lee Maracle – who, like Harjo, presents an indigenous perspective from North America and, like Back, engages with Palestine – and by Walt Whitman, whose poetry influences Rich's engagement with American patriotism.

Rich's *An Atlas of the Difficult World* examines her country from the position of a citizen who cannot abide the oppression she witnesses in the United States. To show the uneven experiences of belonging within this whole, she maps constellations of relationships. In *A Map to the Next World*, Harjo offers "Poems and Tales" engaging with Muscogee history and culture. As she explores ongoing effects

of colonization, she considers abuse of power more broadly. Back's
On Ruins & Return gives in fragments a personal account of life as
an Israeli citizen. In examining the ongoing violence in Israel-Palestine, Back brings the colonial history of her birthplace, the United
States, into comparison with her current home, seeking resonance
between two contexts of suffering.

Rather than an isolated instance of a feeling, compassion operates
here as a disposition that is tied to one's way of being in the world.
As a mode of life, compassion can exist as a general state with the
capacity to become particularized at any instant. Poetry engaging
at once varying levels of particularity and abstraction may, in both
its successes and failures, aid in a conceptualization of compassion
that is broad enough to navigate between contexts without being
dissociated from lived details. Rich, Back, and Harjo differently work
through the interaction between abstract concept and particular
example. In investigating the underlying mechanisms through which
these particular poems bring together their elements, I find Rich and
Back each to employ juxtaposition in contrast to Harjo's substitutive
approach. Harjo's method of substitution depends upon replacement
through similarity, and this similarity operates through the omission
of particularized detail. In contrast, Back's presentation of an image
shared across contexts allows for the inclusion of separately contex-
tualized detail while Rich's images gather a diversity and plenitude
of details into their purviews. Back's image is one of juxtaposition
without equation, while Rich's images create juxtaposition through
incorporation.

Through linguists Roman Jakobson and Morris Halle's understanding of metonymy and metaphor,[1] we can consider juxtaposition
as a metonymic strategy and substitution as a metaphoric one. In
juxtaposition, elements are contiguous, working through combination. In substitution, elements work through selection; one element
can take the place of another.[2] Through juxtaposition, Rich creates a
single context through which multiple elements signify. Back juxtaposes separate contexts, creating a new meaning in their interaction.
Harjo, I argue, presents an idea of compassion without depicting the
feeling itself. Though her speaker identifies compassion as her mode

of being, this compassion comes across as an abstraction in its assertion, without specific demonstration, of the role of feeling in a way of living.

While these particular collections present these differences, however, I choose them also for the similar frameworks in which this concern with compassion operates: each of these poets depicts an idea of waste which might be reconceptualised or recycled into generosity. Thus, this chapter's investigation includes compassion's specificity, its relation to borders, and its wasted reach. This vocabulary of waste and generosity comes from the poems themselves, but points, for me, to an interest in theorizing compassion in terms of excess. Compassion is not solitary; it is a feeling in reaction to another. Compassion is in some sense excess (surplus) feeling because it is premised on feeling with another. Feeling compassion is about how my feelings join another's feelings. It is also in some sense excess (wasted) in that the concept of compassion depends on a separation between the one suffering and the one feeling compassion: though compassion is "participation in suffering," it can only be participation in one's own distinct suffering in relation to what another feels. In contrast to empathy, with its sense of imaginatively joining another in his or her pain, compassion is a feeling in response to and separate from the suffering of another.

My suggestion of compassion's excess is clarified in relation to the concept of a "we-intention," which Oren Izenberg explains in his essay "We Are Reading: Collective Intentions across Poems." As "work on social-action concepts like collective intention has aimed to recover the individual basis of collective life" (100), Izenberg says that the question to ask is, "How is it possible that individuals, with their single minds (minds that must be understood in some relation to individual brains and bodies) are nonetheless capable of formulating collective intentions and undertaking cooperative actions?" (101). He turns to an "account of collective action" termed

"summative," because it argues that collective intentions consist exclusively of individual intentions plus something else. Thus, according to the influential summative account put forward by

Raimo Tuomela and Kaarlo Miller, what it means to say that
"we intend" to act together is that I intend to do something, that
I believe that it can be done (that it is logically and empirically
possible), that I believe that you intend to do it, and that I believe
that you have a set of beliefs equivalent to mine (that is to say,
that you also believe both that I will do it and that it can be
done). (101)

If I suffer together with another, I intend to participate in his or her
suffering.[3] But the other's suffering does not have the same intention:
the other suffers first. This suffering cannot include my intention to
suffer together. Though I intend to suffer with you, my suffering is
more individual than that: I suffer that you suffer, but I do not par-
take of your suffering with you. My efforts are wasted in the sense
that this we-intention (we are suffering) is predicated on its partial
failure. This we-intention is also generous because it is the urge for
and belief in the value of compassion as surplus suffering – unnecessary, additional suffering whose effect is to make another's suffering a collective one, even as my additional suffering does not come
through a sharing and subtraction of your suffering.

First Nations author and poet Lee Maracle dramatizes a form of
wasted compassion in her poem to Nelson Mandela. While any compassion is defined by wasted surplus in the way I have just described,
Maracle presents a particular "wasted" compassion in the sense of
weak or frail as well as in the sense of expended uselessly. Despite
this wasting, the compassion is nevertheless significant. "Mister
Mandela" comes in the collection *Bent Box* (2000),[4] where Maracle considers compassion across many borders. For example, "Song
to a Palestinian Child" uses an identificatory strategy to pair suffering in Canada and in Palestine. The speaker hears "a voice calling
from a place far away / The voice of a girl child very much like my
own" (1–2). Maracle's speaker "answer[s] in kind" (11). The collection's next poem, "Women," complicates the aligning of the experiences of a First Nations child in Canada and a Palestinian child
from "far away." Without negating the alliance across this distance
("Women" ends with "womanly resistance" that sends "the warm

winds of change [...] to the shores of my decadent home" [25–8]), "Women" contrasts the difficulties faced by Palestinian women with the comparatively minor worries the poem attributes to the women of "Can-America." In the juxtaposition of the two poems, Maracle complicates a substitutive strategy with a contrastive one. That is, she puts the substitutive strategy in reverse to observe the details it must occlude.

In contrast, Maracle presents a compassion in "Mister Mandela" that is weakened by the identification it cannot overcome. In this poem, the speaker fixates on the similarities between her own suffering in a racist and colonizing system and Mandela's suffering under apartheid in South Africa. The similarities between prison and "the windowless room / of [the speaker's] childhood" (6–7) produce an unwanted substitution that prevents the speaker from imagining Mandela's experience. Because "the memories of an empty belly / force themselves to fill the space / where thoughts of you ought to live" (14–16), the speaker concludes, "You shall have to be happy, Mr. Mandela / with my humble tribute" (27–8). The speaker's potential understanding is wasted because her own experiences block her attempts to consider another's suffering. Her compassion is wasted in the sense that she achieves a response more "humble" than the one she hopes for. "Humble" is repeated in the last line of "Song to a Palestinian Child"; what I am calling "wasted," Maracle names "humble."

Her compassion is also wasted in the sense of being unheard. The poem is set up as an apostrophe to "Mister Mandela" who may never read this poem directed to him. If he did read it, he may not "be happy" with the tribute, as the speaker demands. By directing the poem to a public figure and by requiring a specific response (feeling satisfied with what the poem offers rather than, say, feeling sad at the suffering the speaker experienced, feeling disappointed at the way that her experience occludes his own for her, or feeling compassion of his own that might engage more deeply with the particulars of the speaker's context), Maracle sets up the compassionate engagement for various forms of failure. Indeed, the opening "Forgive me Mister Mandela" becomes "You shall have to be happy, Mr. Mandela." The

shift from "Mister" to "Mr." suggests the transition from the familiarity of a sort of nickname to the impersonal distance of a letter's
salutation. This transition corresponds with the speaker's inability
to leverage the similarities in the two sufferings into a compassion
that successfully connects her feeling to Mandela's feeling. Moreover,
unlike the Palestine poems, this poem has no partner to add the missing particularities. This compassion fails to create itself fully and fails
to deliver. The poem sets up and witnesses that failure.

Further, Maracle's poems consider as waste the suffering that disrupts compassion. In "Song to a Palestinian Child," the ampleness of
"green grass and rich soil" (3) contrasts the bombs that "crash about
her levelling her home" (4). In "Women," "mothers use ivory /and
the rising price of 'HUGGIES' / is our most serious problem" (5–7).
These products' wasteful cleanliness suggests a false purity hiding the
suffering within Can-American consumption. In "Mister Mandela,"
the speaker's suffering makes a waste of the joy nature offers: "When
I look at you in prison, Mr. Mandela / I can't feel the power of mother
sea" (21–2). This sight likewise "draws the drapes on the ray of light /
left me by a thousand rain-soaked days" (19–20). As her compassion
causes her additional wasted suffering, Maracle's speaker connects
compassion to the suffering she figures as waste while nevertheless
suggesting that the relationships created in the humble response are
significant.[5]

I consider compassion in relation to its surplus of suffering and suffering's waste in Harjo, Rich, and Back. I begin with Harjo and Rich
in my demonstration of compassion as a surplus suffering involved
with community. The speakers in Harjo's "The End" and Rich's "An
Atlas of the Difficult World" extend compassion within and between
communities. Rich's speaker articulates an idea of patriotism which
works through the relationship between a felt connection to the
abstract American nation and a felt connection to the diverse individuals and groups making up the country. Harjo's speaker engages with
atrocity in Cambodia by comparing it to atrocity in the United States.
I will consider this comparative poem in relation to other poems in
her collection that are written specifically about the context of Creek
history and community.

Both Rich and Harjo indicate tools or materials that might build generosity from waste. Rich's speaker desires ignorance, but waste is the material that might allow her to remedy that which she wishes not to know: "I don't want to know / wreckage, dreck and waste, but these are the materials" (I.48–9). This assertion that "these are the materials" is repeated (V.56), suggesting that the lists of national mistakes, harmful choices, and individual suffering are those things available to be worked into community. What remains in destruction, the wreckage, is what might be reworked into value. Harjo's speaker, when constructing her map in the poem "A Map to the Next World," finds tools in the desires that remain through suffering: "My only tools were the desires of humans as they emerged / from the killing fields, from the bedrooms and the kitchens" (Harjo 3–4). The idea of turning waste into persisting community is prominent in Harjo's collection and is even more explicit in "Returning from the Enemy" where the speaker posits "the ability to make songs out of the debris of destruction" (14.3).

Rich's speaker witnesses destruction or wreckage in the divided- ness of her country, its isolations and marginalizations. In line with what Piotr Gwiazda calls Rich's "growing preoccupation with the idea of civic responsibility" (166), compassion in this poem takes the form of patriotism, love of one's own.[6] Rich, in an interview with Bill Moyers, says that *An Atlas of the Difficult World* "reflects on the condition of my country, which I wrote very consciously as a citizen poet, looking at the geography, the history, the people of my country" (qtd. in Gwiazda 165). Rich's speaker is "bent on fathom- ing what it means to love my country" (XI.12). She sees "some busy constructing enclosures, bunkers, to escape the com / mon fate" (XI. 25–6). This observation begins a list of "somes" referring to groups and their actions or experiences in living within this common fate. The anaphoric "some" indicates a proliferation of tactics for living in this country, tactics shaped by their relationships to power. The division of "common" suggests the divergences within the common, particularly in the near mirror image of the syllables that nevertheless alter into a new shape at the last moment. It is the "some who have learned to handle and contemplate the shapes of / powerlessness and power" (XI.40–1) that lead into the study of what it is to be a patriot: "A patriot is one who wrestles for the / soul of her country / as she wrestles for her own being" (XI.46–8). Access to the soul unifying the country comes through the "handling" of these shapes. Indeed, fathom means, etymologically, "the outstretched arms" (OED). The sense of fathoming as "thoroughly understand[ing]" is thus related to "encircl[ing] with extended arms." This wrestling embrace suggests inclusivity of the "somes" without asserting a false "common" that refuses to work to understand the "shapes of powerlessness and power."

Rich's image of tangible access to the intangible soul of her country is reminiscent of Whitman's concluding section to "Crossing Brooklyn Ferry." The poem's final line is "Great or small, you furnish your parts toward the soul" (12.14). Much as Rich's speaker "wrestle[s]" for the communal soul, in Whitman's poem "we" "realize the soul" through tangible means, through "solids and fluids" (12.2). However, wrestling for the soul is not wrestling the soul itself; tangible parts are not equivalent to a tangible whole. Further, Whitman's lists move from material to immaterial parts: "Through you color, form, location, sublimity, ideality; / Through you every proof, comparison, and all the suggestions / and determinations of ourselves" (12.3–5). "Color, form, location" seem aspects of the "parts" leading "toward eternity (12.13)," the soul of "sublimity, ideality." As the use of asyndeton omits any conjoining words which might indicate a shift in relationship between the first words and the last, the juxtaposed elements seem to combine as the soul.

Yet, in "Crossing Brooklyn Ferry," each element does not come together to create the soul. Instead, each individual provides its parts "toward the soul." Each individual "furnishing" his or her parts is "accomplish[ing], complet[ing], or fulfill[ing]" ("furnish" OED), not the soul itself, but "toward" such "sublimity, ideality." Moreover, the individuals in this trans-temporal community "have waited" but also "always wait" (12.6). The accomplishment of the soul is ongoing "toward eternity" and so it is always in completion rather than complete. Similarly, for Rich, a patriot is one who wrestles "for" the soul of her country, not one who wrestles the soul itself. The soul remains immaterial as the surplus that is the conception of community; it is not the "solids and fluids," but the "proof, comparison, and all the suggestions and determinations of ourselves."[7]

The unity of the communal soul is akin to the surplus figuring compassion in Rich's poem. Rich's speaker is a witness to her country and her compassion (as a form of patriotism) extends to all its contexts. These juxtaposed contexts together create something more than the sum of the parts, a surplus depicted as a soul. Individuals are metonymically related to the soul of the community since this surplus – the concept of the unity of the nation – is created *through* but not *of* the individuals belonging to community. The soul of community is not composed of the community's individuals but of their desire for community, their conceptual movement toward its existence as an operative idea.[8]

This communal soul, for Whitman and for Rich in these poems, is constructed rather than inherent. Useful here is Benedict Anderson's insight that a nation is "an imagined political community" and is so "because the members of even the smallest nation will never know most of their fellow-members, meet them, or even hear of them, yet in the minds of each lives the image of their communion" (6). In "Crossing Brooklyn Ferry," first "We arrest you" but then "We receive you with free sense at last" (12.1, 12.7). It is in arresting the parts for this purpose of unity that the parts become free in determination. Once a whole is proposed, the parts can be already a part of that whole. Then the sense is free: meaning is unarrested insofar as the meaning is already invested in the part as it signifies in relation to a whole. That is, the meaning is "you" as "you" belong to "we" and in "we" as the idea of "we" (a group of individuals) is implicated in an overlapping concept of "we" as community (a meaningful group). While Rich's speaker is "bent on fathoming what it means to love my country," for Whitman, "We fathom you not – we love you" (12.11). Rich's desire to understand what it is to have patriotic love contrasts with Whitman's assertion of love in the place of fathoming. Rich's speaker wants to know what loving this country means, how to fathom belonging, precisely because she loves a country made up of individuals who are not all able to participate in the national community. Anderson argues that a nation "is imagined as a *community*, because, regardless of the actual inequality and exploitation that might prevail in each, the nation is always perceived as a deep, horizontal comradeship" (6). Rich's focus in this poem is on how this sense of comradeship can be moved from the projected notion of community into an actual functioning of the country through addressing the inequality and exploitation in her nation.

"An Atlas of the Difficult World" links its idea of national community with a readerly community in a section entitled "(The Dream-Site)." As the centre of the poem (the seventh section, with six sections on either side), this section can be read to underpin the poem as a whole. Only this section and the last ("(Dedications)") are titled. The link of the central section with the concluding section indicates that the dedications to those reading the poem are a way of asserting this communal dream-site, directing it out of the poem to those who the speaker "know[s] ... are reading" (a knowledge she repeats throughout the section). Moreover, the bracketed titles indicate their own superfluous status. They are not necessary for the structural logic of this poem, but additional. The surplus of these two sections (the centre and the conclusion) indicates the essence (the soul) of the poem, an essence dependent on community with readers. In this move, the poem particularizes the realm in which it might be effective, a realm proper to its mode (this written art suggests its hope for effect on readers). As with the soul of a national community, the soul of this poem only exists if readers take the speaker's suggestion of its presence and join in believing in the poem as an effective force.

It is in this way that the poem is a dream-site, a symbolic realm. As a dream-site, the poem's centre is not the depiction of particular lives, but an evocation of their connection. In "every known constellation" are the particularities of the lived community, the lives that construct it (VII.5). These constellations are "coherently hammocked," separated by "avenues" (VII.8). The poem's "you" "could distinguish all" (VII.6) and "you knew your way among them, knew you were part of them" (VII.9) until the change in perspective, "until, neck aching, you sat straight up and saw: // It was New York, the dream-site" (VII.10–11). This change sets things "striding" and "streaming" into a "webbed and knotted" "living city" (VII.17, 24, 25, 24). This new knowing involves insertion; we "went striding the avenues in our fiery hair" leads to "we felt our own blood / streaming   a living city overhead" (VII.17, 23–4).

We can return here to the account of hermeneutic and heuristic navigation I introduce in the previous chapter. This section of Rich's poem begins with a hermeneutic tactic of interpretation. The speaker has knowledge derived from moving between examples. Walking the avenues alone, she makes connections from a distance. As the section continues, the speaker creates a new kind of understanding through heuristic encounter. Her map is created through direct encounter with the environment through which she moves. This section repeats various forms of "to know" until the "until" and an indication of a new perspective. The initial knowledge is physically separated from this new perspective by a line break. The speaker was confident of her own belonging in her travelling among groups "coherently ham-mocked" – knowable, understandable – until the "blueblack ave-nues" became instead a "lost city" of "dreadful light" (VII.8, 12). This dreadful enlightenment is the insertion into a different heuristic; it comes through another kind of seeing, an "aching," a sitting up. This moment of affective and active realization is both grounding (the speaker sees New York instead of the sky) and also figuratively ungrounding (it is a dream-site).

The separate "you" turns into the group experience of the "we" after the line break. Now, "striding the avenues," there are no longer hammocked groups, distinguishable and known; however, the stars remain "coherently webbed" (VII.25). While coherently connected, groups are not hammocked aside, but live "knotted" and "bristling" (VII.25). Attention to the places of this community occurs bodily as "we" are "pressed against other bodies / feeling in them the maps of Brooklyn Queens Manhattan" (VII.19–20). Though maps are felt in other bodies, the semiotic field actually exists in the relationship between bodies. It is the haptic "press" that holds the maps of the cit-ies. The "we" here do not read maps but feel them. This felt relation-ship emphasizes a heuristic rather than a hermeneutic understanding. In the space of contact between the bodies, the maps are the sign of the something extra of community, the significance that exists as something felt and lived between people.

This section is reminiscent of sections five and six of Whitman's "Crossing Brooklyn Ferry." The speaker asks, "What is it, then, between us?" (5.1). The distance "between us" is a signifying space. It is precisely in this "between" individuals that the unity of community exists. Yet, this space between, "Whatever it is, it avails not – distance avails not, and place avails not" (5.3). The speaker depicts the abstract notion of community through the identity of his material body: "That I was, I knew was of my body – and what I should be, / I knew I should be of my body" (6.9–10). As Rich's poem similarly highlights the bodies which press together in a haptic experience, the focus of both poems is less the concept of community than it is the work of creating the concept. Both poems explore the lived experience that leads to the concept. The nation's unity is felt through a heuristic experience of living in proximity to the lives of others. The meaning created through this juxtaposition is the surplus of community.

Likewise, in Rich's lines, feeling something of the whole through the individual body is emphasized in the physical inclusion of the striders in the "living city." The city lives as those individuals living in it "darkly [...] felt our own blood / streaming" (VII.23–4). The blood that is shared as ours is also reflexive as "our own"; this collective possessive dislodges the sense of blood streaming from the individual body into an abstract communal entity, emphasizing a shared space among people, a space mapped as though the avenues become arteries. It is in feeling this blood as a heuristic to community that the community comes to life. Izenberg finds a we-intention of community in "Crossing Brooklyn Ferry" that I find to be similarly evident in Rich's dream of "we and all the others / known and unknown / living its life" (VII.26–8). Izenberg argues that "Whitman's will to act jointly – and his confidence that the world will permit it – license his belief in other people and their motives, even when those other people are at the greatest imaginable distance away (the distance between actual present and notional future)" (103). Rich's speaker displays this same confidence in these unknown people who – no less for being unknown – live together a life. Rich's living city operates as a microcosm for the country as a whole, depicting togetherness in a dreamily defined locality in order to point toward a larger belonging.

In her introduction to *Compassion: The Culture and Politics of an Emotion*, Lauren Berlant is critical of imagining an abstract togetherness for a country founded on local interaction:

> The problem of social interdependence is no longer deemed structural but located in the faith that binds to itself a visible, lived-in community. In this view all occupants of the United States are local: we cultivate compassion for those lacking the foundations for belonging *where we live,* and where we live is less the United States of promise and progress or rights and resources than it is a community whose fundamental asset is humane recognition. Operating powerfully is a presumption that the local is the same thing as the communal, both experientially and institutionally. This remediation of national life away from the federal state does not blank out the nation but sees patriotism as a feeling of abstract intimacy practiced from the ground up. (3)

Rich's "An Atlas of the Difficult World" indeed seems predicated on "humane recognition" but, significantly, the recognition is not limited to the local, though imagined through it here. In this poem, "where we live" is expanded along the roads that span the country to become a community premised on a patriotic questioning and critique of the "United States of promise and progress," "rights and resources." When the speaker says that "[t]hese are not the roads / you knew me by" (I.75–6), she follows Muriel Rukeyser in "uncovering her country: *there are roads to take*" (V.48). Rich foregrounds the travelling necessary to deny a myth of inclusivity based on locality; her image of community in the United States falls somewhere between the visible, lived-in community and an abstract intimacy.[9] Rich defines "abstractions" as "severed from the doings of living people, fed back to people as slogans" (*Blood, Bread, and Poetry* 213). In the depiction of the dream city, "living its life" is the idea that matters. Her theory of patriotism is grounding in its depiction as something that exists only because it is lived. At the same time, her focus on different ways of living and lives not included in common images of the nation ensure that "the doings of living people" does not become its own slogan.

Rich's speaker proposes a material reality of generosity that transcends local borders within the United States:

> Late summers, early autumns, you can see something that binds
> the map of this country together: the girasol [...]
> Is there anything in the soil, cross-country, that makes for
> a plant so generous? *Spendthrift* we say, as if
> accounting for nature's waste (IV.1–14).

The girasol binds the map – the symbolic guide to the country – but Rich presents a misinterpretation of the plant's generosity in the idea that the plant grows from "nature's waste." Our "accounting" makes the flower into currency: if nature is "spendthrift," one who spends money recklessly, then girasols are as money, a symbol of value. In this interpretation of the United States, the country is symbolically united, but this plant which might be read as generosity is instead symbolic of value wasted. Nature's waste, the plant's generosity, is the excessive proliferation of the flower. Yet Rich's speaker reads the flower as surplus: the flower is not the map representing the country but an additional element binding the map together. The girasol is not only a generously proliferating plant, but it here represents the "more" than the sum of the country's parts.[10] Negatively, the girasol is the land's excess expenditure; positively, it is the country's surplus value.

A symbol of the value of community and the surplus of the sum of the parts, this girasol is another manifestation of the soul of the nation. The speaker also names the girasol as "Jerusalem artichoke" (IV.10), Jerusalem being a corruption of girasol, the Spanish name for sunflower.[11] The plant is neither from Jerusalem nor an artichoke. This sliding of the name and its connotations emphasizes the space between the material flower and its concept. The girasol binds the country, literally covering its geographical expanse as the concept of the girasol binds the map. The map is a conceptualization of the geography of the country, but points in this poem to the more removed concept of community, or of a concept of the material land as the ground of community. Much like the emphasis on bodily presence in the dream-site, the girasols are invoked as a point of access to a conception of national community.

Thus, Rich juxtaposes several options for imagining the surplus of community. Temporality as the living cycle of the girasol (you can see it at one point – "late summers, early autumns" – in the year) matches the cyclic circulation of "our own blood streaming." The image of the living city is an image of the generous soil; the constellations are a star-map reflecting the map-binding flowers. Like the girasol's name, the symbol shifts. Several suggestions of the concept exist in juxtaposition. In juxtaposition, there is no tangible depiction of a national community but meaning created in the space between symbols. The interaction of these signs, the semiotic press of symbols, generates a concept of national community.

This interaction requires the removal of borders. Rich connects borders to waste: "Ours [our waste] darkens / the states to their strict borders, flushes / down borderless streams" (IV.14–16). The "strict borders" oppose not only the "borderless streams" of the space of the land (rather than the place of the country) but also the symbolically binding, symbolically generous proliferation of the girasol. If the girasol's cross-country presence is the surplus that binds the map, then these borders are the resistance to that symbolic unity. Rich's girasol section lists the elements of community that the speaker argues the country needs. This list's beginning of "Waste" (IV.18) indicates the importance of "those who could bind, join, reweave, cohere, replenish / now at risk in this segregate republic" (IV.20–1).

The contrast between waste and generosity is similarly apparent in Harjo's A Map to the Next World. In "Protocol," Harjo considers the obligation to remember generosity: "I will consider the gift / of those who kept walking though their feet were bloodied / with cold and distance, as their houses and beloved lands / burned behind them" (26–9). The speaker of "A Map to the Next World" depicts as waste a failure to recognize the gift of survival from the generation that walked the Trail of Tears: "Our forgetfulness stalks us, walks the earth behind us, leav / ing a trail of paper diapers, needles and wasted blood" (22–3). As with Rich's girasol, a shared conception of the land provides connection, here between a past generation and a present one: "In the legend are instructions on the language of the land, how it / was we forgot to acknowledge the gift, as if we were not in it or of it" (8–9). The significance of this language comes from the lived experience of a semiotic system (the land's language) and the inheritance of a previous interpretation of that system (the legend). The ambiguous pronoun reference here – each "it" might refer to the legend, the instruction, the language, or the land – makes it unclear what the community is of or in: the actual land, the semiotic register of language describing the land, the instructions for interpreting that language, or the framework of a legend for those interpretive aids. This ambiguity places community within an intersection of shared material conditions and the various ways in which these conditions might be interpreted. In its conceptual element, its hermeneutic level, the community is open to shifting lived relationships to the legend, its instructions, the land, and its language.

While Rich's generous national spirit seeks to unite through maps felt through contiguous bodies and cycling blood, Harjo's uniting through memory offers a similar, though temporal, juxtaposition of a past signifying system generating meaning with current experiences of communal belonging. Yet, in a poem offering shared feeling outside of a shared context, Harjo's approach can be contrasted to Rich's. Harjo's "The End," also in *A Map to the Next World*, explores compassion as her speaker imaginatively travels to witness the death of Cambodian dictator Pol Pot.[12]

This poem begins with an epigraph explaining the cremation of Pol Pot, "infamous leader of the Khmer Rouge, responsible for the killing of thousands" (24). In the accompanying tale "Compassionate Fire," Harjo indicates that "the end" for the speaker was of a "nine-year relationship" but posits the possibility that "that night *the end* slithered through the unconscious of the city ..., a monster from the waters of the deep conscious ..., dragging us through our fears at the deepest point of the night" (26). The speaker extends her mental state and circumstances to the strangers near her in the New York hotel. In this night she "tried to sleep in the hotel room, accompanied by the sounds of the thousands who surrounded me in that city, souls clammering in the present, from the past and present and possible future" (26). While the "sounds of the thousands who surrounded me" is euphonic, these sounds produce for a reader the tongue-twisting clammering of the difficult accumulation of similar sounds. In the speaker's "accompani[ment] by the sounds" of those nearby, "clammering" as a description suggests that those around her are intrusive with their difficult appeals to her attention. The shift from being "accompanied" to being "surrounded" seems a move from community (posited not only in nearness but in the identificatory dispersal of the speaker's pain to each of these nearby strangers) to claustrophobia. This reaction to the mingled voices comes in contrast to the earlier privileging of a shared understanding of the language of the land or of "the ability to make songs out of the debris of destruction." While the speaker at first imagines a community of the deep conscious, here she comes to find this extension of community to be claustrophobic in its inclusivity of voices. There is a sense here that the speaker wants to escape this surround of sound, this clammering for attention. Indeed, she comes to extricate herself from this mass as a compassionate traveller, as one with a special ability to move between contexts. Tensions between being a stranger and knowing others, between being an isolated stranger and "the myth of the lonely stranger" as a "lie / by those who think they own everything" (17–18), and between particular detail (the elucidated facts of the speaker's situation) and generalization (the extension of the speaker's feelings to the city of strangers) occur throughout this poem.

The speaker moves from the poem's setting in New York City where she "was a stranger" in "a room / of ten thousand strangers, in a city of millions more" (1–2), to "traveling // through the dark" (6–7), to the end of Pol Pot's life in Cambodia. Her own experience of a relationship ending brings the speaker to consider the aftermath of tyranny in another country: "What I had // feared in the dark was betrayal, so I found myself there / in the power of wreckage" (30–2). As she moves to this other context, the speaker differentiates herself from those around her by emphasizing her particular ability for "traveling" and seeing, when "[n]o one saw anything" (9). Yet the disruption to her personal life also brings her to align herself with the strangers of her current location, through the image of a monster that unsettles the sleep of all those in New York. In her hotel room setting, the speaker is like those around her as

> No one saw it. No one saw anything
> because it was dark and in the middle of the night and it was just
>
> a hotel room, one of millions of hotel rooms all over
> the world, filled with strangers looking for refuge,
>
> sleep, for sex or love. We were a blur of distinctions (9–13).

These strangers, like those creating barricades in "An Atlas of the Difficult World," miss the "blur of distinctions" in "looking for refuge." Yet the only distinction the speaker makes among these millions is that, while the grammar suggests all look for refuge and sleep in hotel rooms, some might be looking for sex while others are looking for love. This alternative recalls the speaker's recently ended relationship more than it does call up the particular experiences of others in hotel rooms. The "blur of distinctions" becomes a general indication of shared difference, and the poem offers a valorization of engagement with difference without engagement with actual difference. If the speaker moves outside of her own context, she does so to make a generalized comment about compassion.[13]

The speaker contrasts her attention to "every detail" with the city of strangers who did not see anything. For her, "Every detail mattered / utterly, especially in the dark, when I began traveling" (15–16). Yet, in defiance of its own assertion about the significance of details, the poem unsettles the specificity of Pol Pot's destructive reign in Cambodia by noting that she is in "Cambodia or some place like it" (20). The act of witness through which one might feel compassion is likewise vaguely indicated in the poem. The process of coming to witness occurs in the dark. The darkness of the transition between this place and the next creates a silence around the process of witnessing, around what might be involved in making connections between two contexts or in the process of moving out of one's own place to a place of visitation. The speaker is "traveling / through the dark" without a visible framework for making connections between details.

In the tale, Harjo links Pol Pot – through the idea that "evil often sit[s] in the chairs of rulers," after they are "chosen according to the ability to acquire power and money, not because of their outstanding gifts of service, compassion and love for the community" (27) – to a suffering closer to home: "Andrew Jackson was made president after being medaled with high war honors by the U.S. Government for killing Mvskoke women and children who were resisting being forced from their homelands" (26). The recognition of separate suffering as a shared issue of a larger and widespread lack of "compassion and love for the community" suggests community as an open category that might contain any community or all communities or existence itself as already community. If the comparison could be Cambodia or someplace like it, the point seems to be that suffering transcends borders. Yet how might this point be compelling if suffering is only abstractly invoked?

Though the poem and tale indicate that there is suffering in these two contexts, they do not depict that suffering. What is at stake in this connection between divergent contexts of suffering, then? Though the details "mattered utterly," they are not included. Why insist that details matter without providing any? What is emphasized in providing a blur of distinctions rather than the distinctions themselves? Details matter utterly here as those which are selected by the speaker to indicate something common in the suffering of one group of people and another. Details, then, are not so much what the speaker offers as what we are to understand to lie behind the speaker's assertions of similarity. The logic of details in this poem is the logic of similarity or substitution. The speaker does not evoke Cambodia in its detail but as Cambodia or someplace like it to figure a place in which evil reigned. Cambodia's history makes it an adequate example of non-compassionate leadership for which any other example could be substituted to make the same point.

In the tale, the speaker asserts that "there is an exact address of compassion and in this place even Pol Pot and Andrew Jackson will one day open their eyes. But it is sometimes difficult to translate this knowing into the here and now" (27). The "address" of compassion indicates compassion as occupying a place, such as the figurative place of a witnessing community, and also indicates that compassion speaks out, demanding its own attention. The speaker seems to have her eyes open, so to speak, to the compassion that speaks out, but the exact address of compassion is precisely this figurative or abstract place. Working from an exact address of compassion, she moves with a substitutive logic, filling and refilling this address with examples evoked through their detail-stripped similarity. This speaker makes an argument about what it is to be a compassionate person by positing herself as such a person. Readers, though, must accept this argument as self-evident.

If being compassionate is about "open eyes," the poem includes an unresolved contradiction in depicting witness as occurring "through the dark." If compassion has an "exact address," there is an inconsistency in leaving out the detail that matters "utterly." The poem translates the call of compassion, its address, into an openness that exists beyond any single context of compassion in this world, leaving eyes open to details that cannot be specified in the dark. The poem and tale offer a frank statement of compassion without any indication of how another person might see as the speaker sees, how another individual might cease to be one of the "strangers looking for refuge" (12) who cannot see "anything / because it was dark" (9–10). The poem provides the category of engagement (compassionate witnessing) without providing its elements (how one might aim to open one's eyes to suffering). The tensions in the speaker's positions – being a stranger and being one of many, being a special witness and being in the dark with everyone else, being grounded in context and detail and being able to move freely between contexts through a blur of distinctions – indicate a difficulty in seeing this speaker's special proclivity for compassion at the same time as understanding compassion as an address that everyone should both hear and find. This poem gives voice to compassion's address, but leaves its location for those who already know how to travel.

"The End" indicates a personal context of suffering alongside one not personally experienced by the speaker; however, her own heartache, the treatment of indigenous populations under Andrew Jackson, and Pol Pot's regime are not substantially connected through the speaker's representation of a condition of witnessing. In contrast, Rachel Tzvia Back's collection mingles two contexts in an investigation that includes the contexts themselves as well as what it means to witness them together. Back, a poet born in the United States and living in Israel, approaches compassion across contexts in a series of buffalo poems in her collection *On Ruins & Return: The Buffalo Poems*.[14] In these poems, the speaker witnesses the conflict between Israelis and Palestinians, a conflict she engages with through the image of a buffalo. In a review of the collection, Andrew Mossin writes, "Back describes the conflict in genuinely non-sectarian terms, mourning Palestinian and Israeli deaths alike" (np). The buffalo's wandering across space and time allows the juxtaposition of the violence in Israel-Palestine with the buffalo slaughter occurring during the colonization of the United States. In the collection's first part, "From Between Kastel & White Stone Quarry," the animal appears as an image drawing witness to its own slaughter while at the same time facilitating a poetic response to the violence committed and suffered by human groups in both the United States and Israel-Palestine: "On American plains there were once / sixty million, here / there were none / though now I see him   here / as though returning / remnant" (1.45–50). Like the materials of wreckage and waste in Rich's and Harjo's poems, the buffalo as returning remnant is left over from the wasting of the buffalo. This buffalo is valued here, as buffalo were not in the historical context of the American plains. It is also revalued in the context of Israel-Palestine. This buffalo is, then, the material of the surplus, the additional meaning created in juxtaposition. Back also attempts to write compassion across contexts by working the remains of violence into a generous extension of some version of poetic community. With the buffalo, Back takes an image of waste and makes it an image of generosity in its operation as witness across contexts.

In the collection's introduction, the speaker moves from prose to poetic lines to explain that she first sees the buffalo in the Jerusalem Hills: "Here, where there were / never buffalo – but here // it is" (10). She invokes the absent category – there never were buffalo – before moving to the singular "it." This buffalo is not one of a group, but a particular, cross-contextual image. It is a remnant of one historical situation that is in excess – in surplus – of that historical meaning through its presence in another geographic and political context. The line of empty space that occurs before this "it is" – an articulation of the buffalo's being – functions as a pause, a hesitation, that indicates the buffalo's complicated existence as it links two geographies and political contexts. The same hesitation (a blank space this time) and the same deictic "here" occur also in the section I quoted in the paragraph above. "Here it is" is a deictic indication of the buffalo's presence in the speaker's space and time. This presence is asserted against the pause, which signifies the complicated implications of the buffalo as an image that might be attached to a context in which it does not, in actuality, belong.

"Until we all see buffalo" (9) is the title of the prose-poetic introduction in which the pregnant speaker stops her car in the Jerusalem Hills and sees a buffalo. The buffalo becomes "mostly forgotten" (11) as life moves into the birth of the baby and the new millennium but is remembered "when the first riot erupts" in the Galilee and the buffalo returns "carrying the weight of violence on its broad back, in its vast and silent eyes – and it allows me to write what I could not have otherwise" (12). It carries the weight of violence, but it is not a trope or a translation – a carrying across – of one suffering to another. The broadness of its back suggests the generosity of carrying the weight of multiple sufferings while it does not take the place of – become a symbol for – the sufferings that are with it. Its vast eyes likewise mark the buffalo as an image of witnessing while their silence tells us that the buffalo will not speak for what it sees; it does not stand in for the violence it witnesses.

The buffalo's presence in the North American context is literal, but its non-literal presence in Israel-Palestine is not metaphoric. Rather, the buffalo operates as an image linking the two contexts. We might consider the buffalo to be a sort of conceit, but it is a conceit that involves no substitution. This buffalo is a conceit without metaphor, a conceit in which all terms stay separate, one context and another and an image that links them. Though neither context comes to stand for the other, they are held together in likeness through a common image. The image's presence makes them similar in a way that they are not (having to do with buffalo), not as a figure of speech but a figure of juxtaposition.

The introduction ends with another break into poetry as the speaker asserts that the image of the buffalo allows "me to write / what I could not have otherwise" (12). What she writes in this first part of the collection are seven sections detailing the image of the buffalo, the conflict and violence in Israel-Palestine, and the settlers' violence against buffalo and human in North America. In the first section, the speaker sees shot and killed a buffalo in her land that does not have buffalo. In the second, the buffalo is referenced only in the oblique way the speaker – threatened by "doubt // in a place of stonesteady / believers" (2.10–12) – describes "something of broad uncertain shape, / dragging a broken self" (2.25–6) that is "[a]lways misnamed" (2.12). This might be a buffalo, while it might also be a god, "[t]he past I didn't choose / that is mine" (2.1–2), or the speaker's own "mind clouded / down" (2.5–6). Section three describes "the quarry // [that] was a heap of dead bodies" (3.26–7) alongside the description of buffalo shot from trains. The fourth section offers two columns, side by side, one detailing the slaughter of the buffalo and the other giving the relationship between the buffalo and the indigenous peoples of the American prairies – "If it dies, / we die" (4.3–4, right column) – along with a list of names of those killed in a battle. The fifth section reflects the struggle with faith in the second section, as a lost soul is compared to a wandering buffalo. In the penultimate section, the focus is on a hurt child, with the buffalo appearing only at the end, "crouching low / before mourning houses" (6.52–3). Finally, the last section does not mention the buffalo but talks of the city of Jerusalem as "surrounded by the armies / of those who love her too much / love her weight her warmth her steadfast bulk immobile / behemoth" (7.30–3). In this too generous love, the city becomes like the wasted things in Rich and Harjo's poetry, and, in

Back's description of it as "bulk immobile / behemoth," also becomes like the shot buffalo, the "heap" of section one (72), the "broad uncertain shape" of section two (25), the "giant beasts" of section four (6, left column), the "breathing carcass" of section five (48).

In this oblique comparison, the poem approaches a symbolic register in the image of the buffalo. The poem records this approach as the ultimate erasure of the buffalo's presence – in the last section which has no buffalo – by the symbolic valence. Transformed into a symbol, the buffalo becomes like the too-loved Jerusalem in the overkill of destructive hunting. Yet this final section transforms the buffalo so tentatively – its disappearance here seems to flow from its lesser role in the previous section and the city, as a "bulk" or a "behemoth," is only subtly buffalo-like – that it seems more like a recognition of the temptations of this transformation of buffalo into symbol than the actual doing of it.

Likewise, earlier, "doubt / in a place of stonesteady / believers" (2.10–12) is only hintingly imagined through the image of a buffalo:

Always misnamed, he is

this: [...]

He is what I dream,
the black ropes

that will not hold, the blood
that flows unnoticed through the dirt

stained darker smells of fresh
kill, he is the someone,

something of broad uncertain shape,
dragging a broken self

into these jagged hills, my always
foreign horizon. (2.12–28)

It is merely the broadness of the uncertain shape that indicates the buffalo here. That the shape of this "someone" or "something" is "uncertain" and dragging into a "jagged" and "always foreign horizon" suggests the tenuousness of the buffalo as a symbol for the speaker's religious faith. It is suffering and its disregard that contribute to the speaker's doubt; the unwitnessed blood contrasts the observed smell of the fresh kill, suggesting an interest in the successful hunt rather than in its implications. The ambiguousness of the buffalo as an image of faith makes it an image of doubt as well: the image of faith wanes in the face of ongoing violence. If the buffalo is the faith, its blood that, unnoticed, stains the land with death (both literally and also metaphorically as a moral stain) is the doubt, and if it is the buffalo's blood spilling here, faith itself is the fresh kill (or dies with the new deaths). When the speaker dreams of doubt, she dreams of the "ropes" holding the buffalo as the image that "will not hold." Thus, as the speaker constructs the image, she simultaneously depicts its unravelling. Her doubt, "always misnamed," is in this tenuous naming as buffalo, a naming that dramatizes its own inability to hold, another misnaming.

The sequence later returns to the question of faith with a simile:

It is the soul
Suddenly

    wandering off

        like a butterfly

or a buffalo (5.1–5)

The comparison does not suggest likeness of being, but likeness of action: the soul wanders off like a butterfly or a buffalo, a comparison that breaks down in the contrasting alternative possibilities – a butterfly and a buffalo cannot be said to wander with much similarity. The simile seems to wander from its comparison into another line, a line disrupting an image of how the soul might move away from its body. The buffalo prevents any ease of comparison, complicating the idea of similarity even as it offers it. That it does offer it, though, suggests the conceit without substitution, the comparison that does not use one term to explain another, but combines items that remain mutually constitutive – both expressing the other, and neither disappearing into the expression. The soul wanders like a butterfly or a buffalo – not like both, but not like only one or the other either. In the available options, the soul becomes something which we cannot imagine to wander in one fixed way. The materiality of the description is both evoked and unsettled: the soul wanders like a tangible entity, but the surplus description makes imagining a concrete wandering difficult and uncertain. Like the maps felt in the press of bodies in Rich's poem or between the land, its language, and its interpretation in Harjo's, this soul is situated in a space generated between other elements. This soul is depicted through alternative rather than through combination. Yet the buffalo here is a descriptive option whose additive function defies the grammar of its suggestion: though it is an "or," its very givenness is already additive. Moreover, in the alliteration, assonance, and doubled double letters in "butterfly" and "buffalo" that suggest connection moving into difference, an idea of the soul is generated through complicated interaction.

Interrupting the speaker's lines are biblical quotations featuring buffalo,[15] as though matched contexts – words of faith to call back faith – might create similarity between the soul and the buffalo. Yet the words she might use "to call / the lost soul / back" (5.36–8), "furred words / lumbering forth [...] // are all wrong" (5.29–34). The quotations, in breaking through the speaker's words, are not integrated in her project, but, like the buffalo, simply assert their presence.

Section four puts the buffalo in its actual context of late nineteenth-century America. It is here that the shared context of suffering between human and animal is made explicit in a two-columned poem. On the left side is a story of the slaughter of the buffalo and on the right is a story of the slaughter of the people, "*All dead at Adobe Walls battle*" (4.19). Until we get this context halfway through the seven-sectioned poem, it seems as though the image of the buffalo is associated with the North American context more essentially than the Middle Eastern one – representing, through its own slaughter, the colonisation of the land on which the buffalo lived and the suffering of that land's first peoples. But the poetry fights against that synecdochal connection, not allowing the buffalo to stand as a part for the whole. This section takes the central image and breaks down the synecdochal relationship, preventing the production of a symbol. Here, both human and animal suffering are presented. The buffalo cannot stand in for what is not absent.

At some points, the buffalo and human suffering are juxtaposed in a manner suggesting association built of likeness rather than nearness; that is, in these cases, the buffalo seems close to taking over as a symbol of human suffering. In the collection's second part, "On the Ruins of Palestine," a father travelling a "besieged road to bring / his soldier son home // drives into a daylight ambush   death / rises from the roadside shadows" (15.8–11); the speaker explains, "there is no bringing him back // there is no bringing them back // the buffalo" (15.16–18). The "him" and "them" shifts to become as much applicable to the buffalo as to the humans to whom the pronouns first refer. Yet, again, the buffalo does not stand in for the father or son, but they all stand together, side by side, all terms in play. In an earlier juxtaposition, the killing of the buffalo and the human become entwined; a shooter "marks the lead cow" and "she drops to one foreleg then / to the other kneeling / in dust we are kneeling in dust / what do you / hear / what does the herd / hear // A rifle's rupture of space / across river ravine / ruminants and the land / at last stampeding / as again // we take aim" (12.5, 23–35). The buffalo begins beside the humans to indicate a similarity in violent conditions, but is moved aside as well to recognize difference. This "we" refers to both those kneeling in the dust and those taking aim, but not to the buffalo, which remains separate in the herd to hear the rifle. What "we" hear ostensibly differs from what the lead cow hears, though the speaker's question about what "you" hear goes unanswered. This pronoun recognizes readers who may need to contemplate what they do hear from their positions. "Ruminants" refers to a group of mammals to which the buffalo belongs but also to contemplative individuals. The rifle ruptures space across the herd and the land but also across "ruminants" in this other sense. While readers are included in the "we" behind the rifle, they may also – by contemplating the poem and its buffalos and what they hear – occupy the position of the ruminants, perhaps "at last stampeding" in mental reaction.

Examining these poems as a kind of bestiary, a collection of moralized fables about actual or mythical animals, the speaker, in "From Between Kastel & White Stone Quarry," again addresses the buffalo's role: "The air [is] thick with blood and dead / buffalo Bestiary with no moral" (4.21–2). A bestiary featuring actual animals is most fictional in the moralizing narrative into which the animals are inserted. The removal of this moral takes the animal out of the symbolic realm, placing it – in removing the purpose of the context in which it exists – into a literal realm in which there is no final end offering a clear moral.

This buffalo as "returning / remnant" (1.49–50), by the poem's concluding section, "had wandered across / continents // white corded waters / into roped-off histories // onto forgotten minefields" (5–9). The buffalo, in this role, becomes a kind of pervasive historical residue that might wander – despite these various borders and obstructions – into new possibilities for attentive compassion. Yet, to return to the collection's first part, this residue might be wasted: "The scene should be framed and hung on walls as // is, as / from anywhere / in these hills – / highpitch of air punctured – / single shot / in perfect flight through will / pierce fur / flesh and he too / will fall // another small / soon / indistinct / dark decomposing // heap / as ancient and pointless / as the rest" (1.58–74). The buffalo will decompose into an indistinct and pointless heap, adding to an ancient collection of killings suggesting an eternal nature to pointless violence. The unwitnessed death (in that the heap will not be recognizable as a buffalo) and the pointlessness of that death contrast the picture's visibility and purposefulness. To hang the scene as a picture "as is" would be to replicate the buffalo's function in this poem. The buffalo's function is to be; we are told that "it is." The simple presence of the scene contrasts the pointless destruction threatened by a "perfect" shot "from anywhere." The scene says "it is" to counter a history in which it is not, a history that nearly obliterated this presence. At the same time, to frame the scene "as is" suggests this poem's attempt to include the buffalo as an image but not as a trope. The speaker recognizes the impossible desire to frame something without changing its meaning. This attempt for the buffalo to move "as is" is observable throughout the buffalo poems, most particularly in the places where the image approaches a symbolic resonance that is immediately or simultaneously undermined.

The buffalo returns in the final section of the collection's third part "Pray for the Grace of Accuracy," and also completes the collection in "Bringing the Buffalo Back Home: (October 2005, Adirondacks, NY)." In the former, the speaker gives the image of the buffalo in a violent environment and a struggle for hope:

> her curved back its
> furred arch pushing against the unforgiving
> sky pregnant threats in the air it was rounded
> like a woman's lovely belly as though a baby could push
>
> out of her back into the day a different day (*"After five years of writing buffalo poems"* 8–12)

The pronoun changes that occur throughout the buffalo poems are evident here. The buffalo moves back and forth between a "her" and an "it," a living being and an image. In a similar way, the image of pregnancy moves between threats in the air and the hump that is like a woman's belly, in the first case a figure of speech in which threats become pregnant and in the other an assertion of physical likeness between buffalo and human. The simile moves from the conceptual level to the physical level, from a colloquialism of threats to a cliché of hope – or at least to something that is like a standard image of hope, since the buffalo is not an image of pregnancy, but an image of something that is like pregnancy. In this connection, then, the buffalo is an image of something like hope, but resists becoming a symbol of hope itself.

As the poem plays with the placing of the buffalo's figurative register, it also depicts an oscillation of the buffalo's presence. Though

"[o]ne day she was gone   disappeared / from the page" (2–3), the
buffalo's presence is undone only to be found again. In this poem,
when the buffalo disappears from the page, the speaker finds the
buffalo in her heart as "only / my heart   heard her stillness" (6–7).
But this "moment of *beckoned listening*" passes (4), and the image
returns to the page:

> I didn't even notice   until she was gone   and I
> kept calling   as though in her name   there was a moment   but
> not mine to keep   now   I write buffalo poems
>
> in her absence (21–4)

In holding a moment that cannot be kept, the buffalo's name holds
a memory. The speaker withholds the name (even from us, her readers) because these poems do not depict the image of the buffalo in
the speaker's heart (she was gone when the speaker writes the buffalo poems). Rather than present the buffalo's name that keeps the
memory of her presence in the speaker's heart, these poems produce
a poetic version of that personal image. The poetry's image of the
buffalo is a memory of the image the speaker held as her own.[16]

In the poem ending the collection, the speaker returns to the idea
that the buffalo is not a device that she uses, but rather an agent
within a moment which the speaker remembers and writes. Earlier,
in the third part, the speaker corrects herself when she said she found
the buffalo again: "I found her   no   she / found me though" (5–6).
The speaker is not engaging in a fantasy in which she has no hand
in the images of her own poetry. The buffalo presents herself to the
speaker, but does not insert herself into the poem; it is in the buffalo's
absence that the speaker writes her buffalo poems. The buffalo image
is, for the speaker – who finds herself a citizen of two contested lands,
the United States and Israel-Palestine – a part of the violent context
with which she contends. The buffalo is self-asserting because it is an
essential part of these contexts as the speaker experiences them; thus,
it is not incidental or additional, nor is it a different and separate
version or perspective.

In the final poem, the speaker depicts the moment in which the buffalo became this image: "I first saw her   there / she first stole // the image / broke open lies" (33–6). The buffalo stole the image and the image broke open the lies, and thus the speaker says, "[s]he // taught me to tell" (135–6). Or, these lines could be read differently: the buffalo stole the image, the image broke open, and lies shattered. In the first reading, this image, which is for the speaker a part of the scene of violence, stole into her poetry and allowed her to write something that felt true about the violence she witnesses. In the second reading, the buffalo stole into her poetry, destroying its central image but also opening it, revealing its inner mechanisms in its shattered availability. These two possible alternatives are consistent with the moments of tension throughout the buffalo poems between the presentation of an image approaching various modes of symbolic force and the breaking down of that image.

The speaker, writing in the Adirondacks, NY, "brought my heart's buffalo home" (83). Since, in this poem, the speaker "saw her leave" (142), this moment is different from the earlier one of sudden absence. She returns to the place "where her exile / my anger // took hold" (128–30). The speaker's anger caused the buffalo's exile, a displacement brought to pass by the speaker's need for its company in her heart. Eventually, the buffalo brings the speaker through her crisis by teaching her to write these buffalo poems: "Home // already then a place / haunted // by what / is untold She // taught me to tell / and in the end // she lumbered off / [...] // I saw her leave / My // solitary heart / did not weep // as I knew / this is exactly // as it should be" (131–48). Her heart is now solitary, the buffalo has been brought back, and the collection ends. The buffalo is no longer "my heart's buffalo." Although the image earlier in the poem was a memory of the image in the speaker's heart, it seems finally to be more like its shadow: a reflection causally attached to the heart's image. The poem's image is the heart's image again, but in a different form. For the speaker, the image in the poem does not stand in for the image in her heart. As with the multiple contexts the buffalo is associated with, the presence of both is required for the poetic image to function through its presence rather than through the substitution of its presence for something absent, and the marshalling of its presence towards that absence.

Back's use of an animal image to encounter two contexts of human suffering complicates the already difficult co-encountering of distinct situations of violence. The buffalo, as a part of one of these contexts, would seem, if operating as a symbol, to equate animal suffering with the suffering of people indigenous to North America. As a symbol, the buffalo would similarly equate the colonization of the United States with the conflict in Palestine-Israel. Such equation would occlude important difference – ontological between human and buffalo and political and historical between North America and Israel-Palestine. Instead, Back's buffalo functions as an image without equation. Her image is present alongside the separately depicted details of each context of suffering and brings divergent elements into connection without joining them.

In Back's poems, the buffalo's presence works as a process communicating the speaker's witness. Mossin, then, misses the significance of the buffalo image when he argues that Back's collection shows "the problematic context of" the term "poetry of witness" that "has been used to celebrate the first-person notion of testimony" because her poems remind us that "witness is not subjective" (np). Back's collection is profoundly subjective and personal. This witnessing is not separate from the rest of the speaker's life; it is no less an element of her life than the baby she carries as she begins the collection or the love for her husband that she records in the collection's fourth part, "What Is Still Possible (6 Love Poems)." While all the poets I have dealt with here consider compassionate communities, Back's poems are not about bolstering community within collectives (as in an inclusive United States) or between collectives (as in an abstract transnational or global community of compassion and just leadership). Back's poems are concerned with the process of communicating this speaker's witness to readers. A poem is already a medium of communication, but the buffalo is that communicatory function made an explicit topic.

Thus, the buffalo is an image that connects this speaker's compassion, as it arises from the framework of her life, with the poetic communication of that compassion. The speaker's heart's buffalo is not the buffalo that is in the poem. This poem's central image has meaning in relation to the speaker's personally significant memory, which it does not stand in for but instead stands with. The poem's buffalo image signifies and is significant insofar as it is not, but acts in relation to, the speaker's heart's image. A readerly relationship is not at all formed with the speaker's buffalo, but rather with a poetic image that works in relation to the image in the speaker's heart. Likewise, the poem's image cannot be one from any reader's life, but might have significance for any reader in relation to the images that he or she has held in heart. Not of the speaker and not of the reader, the poem's buffalo is a joining device, a creation of meaningful space between speaker and readers.

While the buffalo can be considered as an image of witness and an image of compassion, these can be understood to be part of the buffalo as communication. This poem engaging concerns of witness – involving a relationship to testimony – and compassion – involving feeling in community – is particularly conscious about its own modes of signification and address. The image of the buffalo is what can be shared between speaker and reader. The image is compassionate as it is com-signifying: the image means along with the speaker (with what she has held to be meaningful in living her life) and it offers to mean along with a reader. This buffalo, allowing fellow-meaning, can be considered as an image facilitating compassion (insofar as I will not separate this fellow-meaning from a concomitant fellow-feeling). As in compassion, in which one does not feel the suffering of another but feels one's own suffering in response, a reader encounters this speaker's personal meaning through its explicitly poeticized communication.

Earlier, I examined the buffalo image as a refusal to symbolize, an avoidance of becoming a rhetorical device that would displace a term in its construction. Though this image is in relationship to the image of a buffalo outside of the poem, the poetic image does not stand in for a referent. Consequently, there is wasted signification in the gap between the image in the world and the image in the poem, in the meaning that will not be carried over. At the same time, this poetic image offers surplus signification in its operation as (rather than standing in for) a process of communication. The image breaks open as an image and reveals itself to be a process. The poem is almost iconoclastic in its consistent breaking down of its central image at the same time as its meaning is dependent upon that very image. But it is dependent on the image showing its own mechanisms, on being an image that does not communicate by covering over or moving aside. This image does not deliver anything except itself as that which might hold open some signifying space. It only works because it is broken open.

The nearness between elements in "An Atlas of the Difficult World" is similar to the juxtapositional work of Back's buffalo. The strategies are, however, ultimately significantly distinct. Rich's tactic is metonymical; her act of witness has a logic of contiguity. The individuals in her poetry are brought into relation through a separately constituted whole. Her approach is a kind of binding as her images work like the girasol to bring together the elements of a nation. As in Back's buffalo poems, Rich's poetry works through the nearness of various elements, through placing things beside each other. Yet, while juxtaposition is the logic behind the image, the image itself works differently. Rich's images function as wholes encompassing all possible elements. These images bring elements into proximity, but the images themselves consolidate the elements into one overarching framework. The individuals encompassed by the image of national belonging are gathered into belonging by symbols, but first produce symbols through the desire to belong to a national community; there is a co-constituting relationship in this symbolic production. Back's poetry creates a relationship for her readers between contexts that are in personal relationship for her as her two homes: she makes a personal, coincidental relationship public and significant in the reality of a need for attentiveness and openness across contexts. Rich takes individuals in a nation, who share in reality the connection of living in the same country, by analyzing that relationship itself. What is it to be associated? How can we consider the association itself, that intangible surplus that is connectivity and shared significance? Rich emphasizes that this symbol's significance rests on the juxtaposition of the particulars that bring it into being. Her investigation is about what it is individuals create when they create a community. "An Atlas of the Difficult World" considers how the elements of community operate and, more particularly, what kind of relationships the framework of national belonging can allow.

In contrast to the work of juxtaposition in Rich's and Back's poems, Harjo's "The End" works metaphorically; the speaker's act of witness has a logic of substitution. Any evil leader can be substituted by another, because the poem supplants the details of the leadership with the label of evil. The focus is on the general prevalence of suffering, not on its particularity, although – given the informative blurb about Pol Pot's reign heading the poem – there is a sense that a witness would need to know the particulars in order to recognize the similarity. Enough information is provided for readers to understand that this speaker does know some particulars, though the poem does not bring readers to witness those particulars themselves. This poem does not depict compassion as a feeling but as an idea. While her poem, like Back's, features a personal perspective opening up into wide relevance, the individual experience does not lead convincingly into the broader statements.

To return to that matrix of generosity and waste which I see operating in each of these collections, we can understand these three poets to write different forms of generous compassion – generous in its openness beyond borders. Rich's girasol section suggests that it is in fact wasteful to consider generosity as something that might be wasted. With this understanding of generosity in mind, I offer these considerations in an effort to attend closely to some routes a compassionate impulse might take, to suggest how, outside of a circumscribed instance, a compassionate project might approach a conglomeration of detail, of comparison, of coinciding context.

I do not mean to privilege a certain mode of compassion over others. I am concerned, rather, with considering the implications of various ways of representing compassion. I find Harjo's poem to be the least compelling in terms of depicting compassion but, for that reason, the most compelling in terms of exploring compassion's operation. In an interview with Simmons Bunting, Harjo says,

Compassion doesn't depend on the reaction or response of others. It is, in its own right. I believe compassion gives the most overarching vision. Then, everything can fit, somehow. I'm trying to figure it out like everyone else. Art is a way to contribute to the figuring out. The artist bears witness, and can bring fresh vision into the world through art, to regenerate culture, to demand an accounting. (34)

It seems to me that Harjo is not speaking about the abstract through a collection of particulars (as Rich does). Harjo starts with the abstract, a compassion that just is, "in its own right." She indicates the necessity of particulars, but then leaves them out. The abstract is not tied to the particular, but tied to an idea (abstract itself) of the need for particularity. In "The End" the speaker's travel to Cambodia is invested with identification, a sense of shared suffering. The similarity of circumstances is denoted vaguely through the substitutability of one suffering for another within compassion's "overarching vision." Without the inclusion of the details legitimating the comparison, this similarity rests at a general level that sits oddly with the importance placed on the particular places of witness. Yet, to speak in the same vocabulary as this poetry, this generosity of compassion – the sharing of the compassion for suffering close at hand with suffering far away – is not wasted. This generality obfuscates the poem's approach – in that the project of witnessing and compassionate attention is depicted as a matter of fact but not in terms of its prospects for or routes to accomplishment – but also creates the conditions to examine issues that accompany compassion as a value. The poem "contributes to the figuring out" of compassion's relation to witness and accounting. How might one think through all the details of one's own and another place and find an "address" of compassion that speaks equally to both the near and far? How might one's compassion be tied to particularity while moving beyond the details of one's own experience? Does identification through similar experience contain compassion in its purview? How might one approach a balance between attention to difference and recognition of one's own location as a shaping force of one's perspective? Compassion can fall near to, be attended by, or become confused with feelings, conditions, or values that either are not compassion or inhibit it: ignorance, pity, identification, empathy, condescension. Poems, like Harjo's, which consider suffering across borders, investigate borders themselves, including what borders on the edges of compassion, and where these borders might lie.

Part Three

Witness in Social and
Artistic Structures

4

Accumulating Suffering: Waiting without End

In witness poetry, concerned as it is with social suffering and truth telling, reception is of special import. When the context of reception is modelled within a poem, there is an emphatic relation between speaker and reader, a contiguous relation created through the modelled metonymic strategies. In this chapter, I consider a metonymic approach to witness in poetry by Dionne Brand and Les Murray. My primary concern is the reader's position in this witness. I begin with Murray's poem "Letters to the Winner." This poem, from his collection *Learning Human* (2000), is a study in relationships of witness conducted through reading. "Letters to the Winner" and Brand's book-length poem *Inventory* (2006) use a similar poetic strategy of modelling metonymic relations in listed suffering. I argue that both poems too easily dismiss an idea of witness that includes in its purview a larger picture of life than proliferating suffering. However, Brand movingly evokes that larger life before dismissing it from the ethics of witnessing and Murray's dismissal may, I will show, be treated ironically.

Witness poetry positions its readers within relations premised on their reading as themselves, as people bringing their individual lives to the reading. My understanding of this poetry thus contrasts Helen Vendler's popular definition of the wider genre of lyric poetry: "we do not listen to him [the speaker]; we become him" in an "imaginative transformation of self" (qtd. in Izenberg 93n6). The objection to a universal application of such an understanding of lyric poetry is not uniquely relevant to witness poetry. In *Poetry's Touch: On Lyric Address*, for instance, William Waters argues for an alternative to "the prevailing critical approach to poetic address" in which address is "incidental to the real matter of a poem. Who (or what) gets addressed, when and how, will say little about the work's artistic or human concerns if all a poem's hailings are equally void of effect and therefore essentially interchangeable" (3). Yet the inhabitation interpretation is particularly harmful for witness poetry because this interpretation drastically alters the model of witness this poetry proposes. When the relationship between poetic witness and reader is understood through a vertical logic of metaphor, a reader's role is not to listen but to carry suffering onward.

I resist this model of knowledge-brings-feeling-brings-action in relation to both compassion and witness, proposing instead the alternative of with-ness as a contiguous space of attention and reflection. Consequently, I disagree with the conception of poetry of witness Harriet Davidson proposes in her article "Poetry, Witness, Feminism." For Davidson, poetry of witness is directed "toward the future as a warning, a call to action, an impetus to more poems or speech" and "creates a chain of witnesses each of whom receives this newly wrought history, charged with the affect which compels its retelling" (166). For Davidson, metonymy signifies this chain of witnesses. Thus, when she argues that this poetry's "primary trope would have to be metonymy – which figures so strongly in postmodern theory – that chain of speaking which can't ever speak the final word" (166), she does not share my understanding of metonymy's centrality to witness poetry as a form of with-ness. Indeed, the idea of metonymic rhetoric leading to a chain of witnesses is premised on the reader substituting for the poem's speaker, as Davidson demonstrates with her reading of a poem by Adrienne Rich, which ends "and I start to speak again" (170). For Davidson, "we, the readers, are lending that 'I' of the last line our historical time, while it gives us a vertiginous identity which must and will speak" (171). If no witness can ever have his or her own word, we merely have one word after another with no gathering of meaning or community. We have substitution without addition and action without unique or unified contribution. In a substitutive chain, each potential listener takes the place of the speaker, and there can be no conversation.

In contrast, in metonymic relation, identities are retained and witness poetry might be a collaboration through contiguity: a speaker implies a listener, and a reader enters the poem into this relationship. To overwrite the communicative aspect of witness poetry is to imagine a kind of verticality that is not neutral. An alignment of a reader with the speaker leaves little space for the straining of communication, the responsibilities of response, the translation between experience and its telling, and the partnership between telling and listening. I find reception to be built into witness poetry as a central concern through speakers' conceptual and affective approaches to the signs of suffering others. These poems model, I argue, a horizontal, contiguous mode of relation which suggests that responsibilities of reception are grounded in a metonymic approach.

Murray's work has a complicated relationship to metonymy. In much of his poetry and prose, Murray is concerned with creating an inclusive picture of Australia. As Steven Matthews sums up, "He has remained in conscious and contentious dialogue with debates about national emergence almost from the outset, bringing his own version of complex and distinctive nationalism to bear on what he sees as blindness, partiality, or cultural and class prejudice" (156). Such views are formed by the classist and anti-rural sentiment that he experienced growing up in an impoverished farming family.[1] In his *Paris Review* interview with Dennis O'Driscoll, Murray describes "being relegated and scorned, as a country bumpkin, an uncultured yahoo, all that sanctified anti-rural prejudice" (np). Matthews argues, "The complex denials, disadvantages, embarrassments and disinheritance amidst which he grew up led him to seek alliances, when imaginatively seeking to forge the conscience of his nation, with those in similar plights to his own" (4). In this way, Murray's witnessing tactic has often been based in identificatory strategies.

In particular, Matthews notes, Murray's early life has "contributed to his empathy with the Aboriginal plight, and to his contentious attempts to translate their culture – attempts correlative to those of an earlier poetic movement in Australia, the Jindyworobak – into wider contemporary national consciousness" (5). Ashok Bery considers more closely Murray's attempted fusion of Aboriginal people and poor rural white people in Australia into "a larger disadvantaged class" (53). Bery finds in Murray's corpus a strategy of "division and fusion" in which Australian identity (among other subjects his poetry engages through this strategy) "is divided into opposed terms, which are then made to merge" (51). Bery notes inconsistencies, omissions, and errors in Murray's attempts to consider these groups as one. In particular, he demonstrates that the problem lies in Murray's "claim that this feeling is *the same as* that of the Aborigines" (59). Thus, Murray approaches witness through the presumption of shared or shareable suffering and dispossession; he wants his witness to work through substitution. Yet, as Bery notes, Murray's poetic witness actually works through metonymy, in that the inconsistencies in his poetry show the differences in the sufferings so that one cannot substitute for the other. I will demonstrate a similar situation in "Letters to the Winner": this poem's speaker perceives witness as a process of identification while the poem overall shows witness to be metonymical.

Further, Murray's novel-in-verse *Fredy Neptune* works metonymically. *Fredy Neptune* is similar to Brand's *Inventory* in that both use a witness figure to list instances of global suffering. Murray's novel begins with Fredy losing his ability to feel (in the haptic sense) after witnessing the burning of a group of Armenian women. As Matthews puts it, the verse novel presents "a multitudinousness of narrated events, in which Fred is swept ... from one incident to the next" (133). The listing tactic is so predominant, in fact, that Matthews argues that the plot can feel "somewhat contrived, as though Fred's picaresque progress as a figure of early twentieth-century history must allow him to witness *all* of the century's oppressions" (141). Murray says, "My politics are best discovered by reading *Fredy Neptune*" (O'Driscoll). Thus, I read the contiguity of this listing strategy to be at the bottom of Murray's conception of witness, despite his (failed) use of identificatory strategies elsewhere.

"Letters to the Winner" models contiguous witness. This poem dramatizes and implicitly comments on the various positions of witness involved in witness poetry. The speaker narrates a story about "our neighbour" who "won the special lottery" (2). The lottery-winner receives a "fat" mailbag every mail day containing letters detailing the writers' suffering and requesting money (7–8). In reading these letters, the lottery-winner models the form of witness (witness through reading) that readers of witness poetry are engaged in. As will be the case in Brand's *Inventory*, we, as this poem's readers, witness witnessing. While the lottery-winner models a mode of witness through reading, the poem also comments on that reading through the speaker's perspective. Ultimately, I find the poem to undercut the speaker's way of witnessing by offering more than what seems to be there – more than the speaker recognizes is there – in the letter-reader's way of witnessing. "Letters to the Winner" finally proposes witness to involve an immanence metonymically indicating the intimate and long-lasting relationship between witnesses and what they witness.

The letter-reader witnesses the suffering of poverty through the letters he receives after winning the lottery. The poem's concern with poverty is clear from the speaker's opening explanation of the lottery winnings by way of what the amount would mean for two differently employed individuals:

> our neighbour won the special lottery,
> an amount then equal to fifteen years of a manager's
> salary at the bank, or fifty years' earnings by
> a marginal farmer fermenting his clothes in the black
> marinade of sweat, up in his mill-logging paddocks (2–6)

We know that the letter-reader is the farmer for whom the winnings mean more than three times as much as they might for another because he comes into his kitchen to read the letters after feeding his cows (11–13). Thus, much as we will see in Brand's *Inventory*, this witness suffers within the same larger system as those whose suffering he witnesses, except that he has been lucky enough to suffer less – as one of the letter-writers exhorts, "*remember you're only lucky*" (19). His "pausing at the door / to wash his hands" before he "came inside to read the letters" (12–13) suggests the "marinade of sweat" involved in his work but also his later "holding each page by its points" (30). His carefulness indicates his respectful hesitance despite "feeling an obligation / to read" (30–1). Further, he saves all the letters for "one day's reading" (44) and burns them once read (27–8). His clean hands and delicate touch, his cordoning of the letter-reading into one day, his immediate burning of the letters all suggest the letter-reader's attempt to keep the letters unsullied by his daily life, by his ongoing work, by his own suffering, by the fact that he is only lucky, not a saviour.

The letters' contents create in the poem a contiguous list of local suffering much like Brand's inventory of global suffering. In "Letters to the Winner," each line extracted from a letter ends with the poem's line breaks. The poem's lines differentiate one suffering from another while the illusion of enjambment, created by a lack of full sentences and punctuation, propels reading against grammar to complete one complaint or request with another. Through contiguous fragments, a sense of the district's poverty emerges. Formally, the letter-reader is positioned in contiguous relation to the letter-writers through the juxtaposition of lines from the letters with descriptions of his reading; despite his winnings, he is part of this district and its poverty. While witness represented through this contiguous logic suggests a set of relationships shaped by the larger capitalist system as well as by expectations of neighbouring and belonging that this man is a part of, the poem's speaker comes to describe the relationship between witness and witnessed through a logic of contagion. The notion of suffering's contagion is already apparent in the lottery-winner's careful and tentative treatment of the letters, but the poem's meaning will ultimately hinge on whether or not one trusts the speaker's account of the letter-reader's feelings while reading.

Readers outside of the poem witness the letter-reader along with the speaker. Importantly, we cannot read *as* the speaker. We are necessarily aware that this letter-reader is not "our" neighbour: we don't know anything about his life beyond what the speaker shares with us. Many readers will also be aware that they do not share this district's poverty. The speaker, as one who knows the man, the district, and the poverty, shows readers how to read the man's reading. Murray writes the poem from the speaker's perspective on the lottery-winner's experience rather than having the lottery-winner speak for himself. This choice makes the outcome of this poem's witnessing less certain since we have a report from a witness of a witness who reads reports of suffering. For example, readers are told that these letters are a punishment: "the Great Golden Letter / having come, now he was being punished for it" (22–3). It is not clear if these are the speaker's thoughts or the thoughts he imagines the lottery-winner to have. The lottery-winnings are figured as their own letter so that luck is "punished" in kind; this neat symmetry is suspect, and it points to the assumed symmetry between the speaker and the letter-reader.

Murray's speaker practices witness as identification (putting himself into the letter-reader's position and imagining his feelings) and represents the act of witness as identificatory (suggesting that the letter-reader's witness causes him to catch a contagious suffering).[2] Yet the speaker indicates that he does not know for certain what the lottery-winner is feeling: "That his one day's reading had a strong taste of what he and war / had made of his marriage *is likely*" (44–5, emphasis added). Because the lottery-winner's reading is flavoured by his own suffering, the speaker concludes that "he was not without sympathy" (45). The speaker implies that the letter-reader has sympathy because he has felt pain; the speaker's assumption that he knows what the lottery-winner feels as he reads the letters rests on the assumption that the lottery-winner also engages through identification (I know how you feel because I have suffered too). Yet the speaker has just explained that the lottery-winner's reading has him "fascinated by a further human range / not even war had taught him, nor literature glossed for him / since he never read literature" (40–2). A contradiction emerges between the speaker's assumption that the letter-reader can feel sympathy because he reads suffering he already knows and the indication that the letter-reader learns a greater range of suffering through witnessing what the letters communicate.

The speaker also characterizes what the man reads as "each crude rehearsed lie, each come-on, flat truth, extremity" (31). The word "extremity" contrasts the other descriptors and occupies the line's extremity, its far end. "Extremity" is the privileged term. The letters contain lies, but lies originating in true extremity. As the lottery-winner reads, "the white moraine kept slipping / its messages to him" (34–5).

A moraine is a "mound, ridge, or other feature consisting of debris that has been carried and deposited by a glacier or ice sheet, usually at its sides or extremity" (OED). The word "extremity" seems precisely the message that slips to the extremity of the line. Likewise, the letters are the debris deposited at the extremity of the district's mounded suffering. This depositing seems possibly fruitful when the letter-reader "husked them like cobs" (35). If opening the letters' envelopes might lead him to some fruit, some nutrition, there is a sense that the letters might be something aside from punishment.

Nevertheless, the poem's last line suggests that the lottery-winner has been tarnished by his winnings through the witness they demand: "he stopped reading, and sat blackened in his riches" (49). This tarnishing indicates that to witness suffering is to invite its happiness-destroying contagion. Formally, the poem reiterates this suggestion that the lottery-winner's riches are lessened through reading the letters. The first four stanzas initiate a steady pattern of alternating lengths of six and seven lines. The fifth stanza begins with the letter-reader burning the letters he has read. Unlike the self-contained stanzas preceding it, this stanza initiates a pattern of enjambment from one stanza to the next that continues for the poem's remainder. These stanzas bulge like the bags of letters that the lottery-winner burns to escape their excessiveness. However, burning the letters is what blackens his winnings; these two surpluses (the surplus of his own suffering through knowing others' suffering and the surplus of his lottery winnings) are tied to each other so that reducing the letters cannot reduce the suffering and the letters instead reduce the winnings (or their emotional value) in the end. The final stanza indicates this reduction: it has merely four lines. The poem's form suggests that the lottery-winner ends up with less than he had because his riches have burned up with the letters, or at least the goodness of his luck has with the guilt of the others' suffering.

However, the role of gravity and grace in Murray's work suggests a different reading of the poem and of witness in it. For Murray, grace is embodied. In "Gravity and Grace: Towards a Meta-Physics of Embodiment in the Poetry of Les Murray," Martin Leer explains, "gravity and grace is, as far as I can see, an expression of the Catholic theology

of the Incarnation, which tries to balance transcendence and immanence" (140). However, Leer argues that gravity and grace enter Murray's poetry "not just as abstract philosophical concepts, but as part of
the imaginative poetic process itself" (141); the "forces of *gravity* and
grace underlie the peculiar *meta*-physics, which is an important part
of Murray's poetics," a part Leer defines as a "physics with transcendental meaning, a physics by which the transcendent becomes immanent" (138). In "Letters to the Winner," actions of leaping, swirling,
and streaming upwards suggest a transcendent aspect to witness that
becomes immanent in the letter-reader in the poem's last line.

According to Leer, the figure of the "free fall" is one of "Murray's
seemingly endless metonymies for the transformation of gravity into
grace, for the diffusion of that collapse into chaos which in Murray's world appears not so much as a disintegration, but rather as a
concentration" (142). This poem suggests witness to involve weightlessness that leads to a concentration of grace in gravity. First, the
letters exhibit the pull of gravity: "Shaken out in a vast mound on
the kitchen table / they slid down, slithered to his fingers" (14–15).
After the lottery-winner reads them, he puts them in the stove and
"they clutched and streamed up" (28). Thus, he reads lines from the
letters in an experience of witness as weightlessness: "Black smuts
swirled weightless in the room *some good kind person* / like the nau-
sea of a novice free-falling in a deep mine's cage / *now I have lost his
pension* and formed a sticky nimbus round him" (37–9). The poem
ends as "he stopped reading, and sat blackened in his riches" (49).
The "black marinade of sweat" is the poverty the winnings alleviate,
but the burned letters blacken him anyway with their smuts. This
new marinade suggests that he has been tarnished through witness
by the contagion of suffering. Yet the ash is "a concentration of grace
in gravity" when it settles on him, in that the ash is a concentration of the letters. The suffering in the letters is concentrated into
the weightless transcendent. The letter-reader makes the accounts of
suffering that he witnesses weightless when he burns them (the heavy
bags of letters turn into floating smuts). This weightlessness is what
allows them to regain gravity through concentrating on him. When
the letter-reader is blackened, the letters of suffering are no longer

in bags across the room nor swirling above, but are now part of how the letter-reader as witness inhabits the world. At first, both the bagged letters and the swirling smuts, representing others' suffering, are physically apart from the witness. Finally, though, the witnessing process, begun when the letter-reader lets the letters slide down into his fingers, brings what transcends the witness's own experience into the gravity of his life. Witness is a transcendent response that finds immanence in a witness's embodied experience. This physical immanence is metonymical of a mode of witness in which witnesses carry what they witness, such that what they witness becomes part of how they live in the world.

The letter-reader achieves this state through his own momentary weightlessness. His "sympathy" is described as "his leap" (45, 46), and this sympathetic leap constitutes a new range of response. After his leap, he intimately carries what he witnessed. Witnessing involves this leap from the gravity of a life into engagement with other lives. But the leap is not only or finally the "novice free-falling" into a "cage." It is the mixture of immanence and transcendence that produces the grace that is this surplus of witness, the increased range of the witness and the addition to the witness's life through this extra he or she now carries. "Sticky nimbus" suggests grace, but a kind that the letter-reader can't avoid. The sticky obligation is the grace of witness, but it is carried without caging. It is surplus rather than confinement. The last stanza is not a shortened stanza but a surplus stanza that hits a boundary. The letter-reader "was not without sympathy, // but his leap had hit a wire through which the human is policed" (45–6). If he didn't hit a wire past that leap across the line break, he would be in free-fall; the wire is the return to gravity that is necessary for the immanent grace of witness. Grace is not in the free-fall of imagined identification – transcendence without gravity – because the grace of witness is the new weight to be carried through one's own life.

Grace is what comes of the letter-reader's witness. Witness is not the metaphor of contagious trauma but the metonymy of literal connection to suffering creating the grace (the something more) through that connection. The grace is what lets us differentiate witness from

merely watching or reading. The difference comes in his felt response
to these letters from his neighbours. He witnesses the letters rather
than reads them as they do not simply "gloss" suffering for him as
literature might have.

Thus, I read the poem's last line against what it initially seems to
mean. In "Irony, Identity and Les Murray's Poetic Voices," Penelope
Nelson argues that such turns at the end of Murray's poems are common: "I find it instructive to look at last lines. While these sometimes
encapsulate an argument or make a final rhetorical statement, they
are as often wry and ironic, marking a distinct change in tone and
undercutting the mood established elsewhere" (171–2). According
to Charles Lock in "*Fredy Neptune*: Metonymy and the Incarnate
Preposition," "not to recognize metaphor or metonymy" is "to be
taken in by the literal" (133–4). The metonymic in Murray's work is
the relation of weightlessness and embodiment to grace and gravity.
The literal, in this particular poem, is that the letter-reader is blackened by his proximity to the smuts. To be taken in by the literal in
this poem is to miss what the lottery-winner carries as an obligatory
surplus. Thus, to read this poem as its speaker does would be to misread witness – we, too, would be taken in by the literal. Instead, the
poem demands a relationship contiguous with the speaker so that we
can read the scene of witness against the idea of suffering as literally
contagious. "Letters to the Winner" is ultimately about readerly positioning and its importance for defining witness.

Dionne Brand's *Inventory* likewise takes readerly positioning as
a foundational consideration. *Inventory* (2006) is a long poem of
witness to a global condition in which "we mean each other / harm"
(42). Brand, Trinidadian-Canadian poet and novelist, creates this
list-like record of this century's violences from the perspective of a
solitary watcher. In her edition of Brand's excerpted poetry, *Fierce
Departures*, Leslie C. Sanders writes, "Brand's writing charts a complex history, a resolute politics, an ethics of witness, and the occa-
sional hopefulness wedded to deep despair. The long poem is Dionne
Brand's form" (ix). Brand's *Inventory* is a long list of suffering that
occasions an ethics of metonymical response. Though Brand lists
numbers and facts of suffering, a reader is not primarily engaged

in an epistemological project of transmitting information. Rather, a reader is engaged through a condition of being, an ontology of reading – that is, a kind of way of being as a reader – that is shaped through the poem.

A reader of this poem is, at a structural level, metonymically related to its speaker in the sense of contiguity. This poem positions readers as listening participants. As a listener, a reader is in a logical association with the speaker. The association is premised on this nearness rather than on a substitutability of reader as witness. *Inventory* presents not only a list of suffering, but also a speaker's experience of making such a list. In "'Nothing Soothing': Critical Perspectives on the Work of Dionne Brand," Leslie Sanders and Heather Smyth write, "Brand's great power lies in her revelation of how poetic image and structure can so precisely trace the emotive and political commitment of a compassionate ethics and political praxis" (4). Though the title makes the poem seem to be an accumulation of facts of suffering, *Inventory* primarily focuses on how the speaker is affected by the suffering she witnesses. The poem is not available to be read as only an inventory of suffering. Instead, it puts readers into relationship with the speaker as a witness and as the inventory's creator. The poem explores suffering through the lens of the speaker's own responding feelings; it attends to response and how that response might be communicated.

Brand's *Inventory* presents a woman inventorying the ongoing disasters and atrocities televised on the news. While the speaker witnesses the transmission of information through these news reports, the poem is not another mode of disseminating the events and statistics it references, but a space for their addition. *Inventory*, as an inventory, is a space in which "things, things add up" (52).[3] This poem makes available the juxtaposition of details, the spaces created between things put beside one another in the speaker's waiting through each "latest watchful hour" (23). What is for her an ongoing proliferation of suffering, requiring similarly ongoing attendance, is for the reader the act of waiting through reading the list the speaker has created.

To make an inventory is to take stock. Inventories list articles or goods, one's properties. In "'History's Pulse Measured with Another

Hand': Precarity Archives and Translocal Citizen Witness in Dionne Brand's *Inventory*," Brenda Carr Vellino reads Brand's "taking stock" to be "equivalent to moral reckoning based on an inventory of what is absent in dominant discourse" (250). Yet Brand's poem-as-inventory is as much a taking stock of the speaker's responses to suffering. A reader is similarly positioned to take stock of his or her own responses as the speaker's responses to suffering add up over the course of the long poem. The list form is necessarily contiguous (one thing after another) but also depends on the paradigmatic organizing similarity of a category (all items could be exchanged for others, so long as they all add up to global suffering). Yet the speaker emphasizes the process of addition, not the final sum. Since much of the poem is actually about the speaker's experience of creating this list, this space of waiting and addition is the space of reception. A reader's role is in relation to the space of waiting, to the list's creation even more than to its figures. Waiting is the primary element of the relationship between reader and speaker. Waiting is attendance to the relationship itself, the time of reading the poem in which the speaker and reader are connected.

Inventory's speaker "can't bear the waiting, / the metal, metal, metal of waiting, / she sits devoted, the pairing knife close / to a harvest of veins" (29). The repetition of the "metal, metal, metal" draws out this description of waiting, engaging the reader in his or her own wait; the speaker's evocation of waiting becomes, in the reading process, the felt experience of another waiting. The speaker's waiting through the news "each hour, each night" (29) is materialized in the metal that signifies it and the repetition that performs it. As both are made of metal, the waiting and the knife are linked. The knife threatens, but the waiting is already happening. In the speaker's wait through the news reports of ongoing suffering, she faces the threat of her own suffering in response, but the ongoing "metal of waiting" is the threat already made good. The speaker's compassionate attention is already to suffer in response to suffering; the waiting is not for response but is itself response. The knife is for "pairing" (joining together) rather than "paring" (cutting away). This re-labelling suggests that the self-threatening knife might also be a tool for shaping the relationship between a reader's waiting and the waiting the speaker depicts.[4] As witness, the speaker feels "the loosening clasp of affinities" (29). *Inventory* promotes the connection that the witness feels is wanting. Much as the speaker's waiting (watching the news through "the latest watchful hour" [23]) manifests in tangible, bodily pain, a reader's waiting (reading the long poem) comes through the manifestation of the poem's material conditions as language.

For Canadian and postcolonial literary scholar Diana Brydon, the speaker's "reading of the news enacts a model for our reading of her work" (995). She understands this model to follow Gayatri Spivak's idea of "critical intimacy" in which one "employ[s] both passion and reason while seeking understanding. One must enter the poem with all one's faculties while simultaneously maintaining a critical distance from it" (Brydon 995). As the reading of the news is sometimes reported directly by a speaking "I" and sometimes indirectly by a narrated "she," it seems to me that the poem might indeed remind its readers about the various distances that are a part of intimacy. Yet Brydon's suggestion about what the reader should enter the poem *with*, doesn't indicate *where* a reader does, in fact, enter this poem. *Inventory* involves a "you" that is sometimes present, sometimes absent, and sometimes seemingly another designation of the speaker – along with "we," "she," and "I."[5] *Inventory*'s "she" addresses "you," creating an unusual situation in which any of the following may be the case: the indirect "she" addresses the reader directly, the implied narrator that describes the "she" speaks around the speaker to the reader, the "she" is really all along the "I" that eventually takes over, or the "you" does not always indicate a direct address.

Thus, *Inventory*'s shifting pronouns complicate how an individual reader is positioned in relationship to the poem; it becomes unclear how the speaker and an addressed or implied reader might be paired. According to my reading, these shifting pronouns are about relationship. Vellino argues that Brand's "shifting dislocational pronoun use" creates "a post-identitarian ethical subject" (244) such that "Brand's speaker refuses the logic of individualistic lyric subjectivity" (243). In this project, I argue that lyric subjectivity is essential to witness poetry's compassion. Close attention to the self in the form of self-reflection is the key feature of the compassionate relationships this poetry models. Vellino notes that, in *Inventory*, "despite the speaker's ironic refusal of the homogenizing force of a 'we,' individualistic self-identification is also not an option" (245). While it is true that the speaker explicitly speaks against using "we," she does in fact use this pronoun. The poem refuses an uncomplicated approach to witness – indeed, Vellino notes the necessarily complicit nature of witnessing (246). While the poem's speaker does not avoid "we," there is similarly no sense that the speaker shifts into different individuals or presents a dislocated or unidentified individual through these shifting pronouns. Instead, in *Inventory*, it is relationships that shift. To work through compassionate responsibilities and to model such responsibilities for readers, the speaker presents a self who can occupy different contexts and positions in the poem. Brydon argues that "the poet employ[s] the range of pronouns, from 'I' through 'she' and 'you' to 'we,' to address or denote aspects of herself and her readers interchangeably. These pronouns invite readers to enter the text in various relations of critical intimacy, finding their own relation to this 'bristling list'" (1003). The problem I find with understanding the reader to be invited into all of these pronoun positions is that, if a reader situates him or herself inside the role of speaker, then the one to whom the speaker might be speaking has become absent. This reader takes over as speaker, precluding a dialogue in which he or she might respond as listener.

Moreover, these various pronouns, as I read them, often do not invite a reader's entrance. While "you" is most customarily assumed to be an address to the reader,[6] in *Inventory*, whom this "you" refers to changes without warning; of all the rotating pronouns in the poem, I find it to be the most ambiguous. To provide a point of comparison, *Inventory*'s "we" also, but more obviously, refers diversely. The "we" who are "doing the best we can with these people" – for "they hate our freedom, / they want the abominable food from our mouths" (27) – is not the same collective that appears a few pages later: "don't pray it only makes things worse, I know, / think instead of what we might do / and why, why are only the men in the streets, / all over the world" (34). Similarly, if less immediately apparent, the "you" of "what confidences would she tell you then, / what would possibly be safe in your hands" (23) does not seem like the same "you" of whom the speaker asks "what sound does the world make there, / the sound you must have heard / before these disasters" (34) or the "you" in "where you wonder did such men, ruddy with health / cultivate such wicked knowledge / then you realize [...] // they're traders, like anybody else these days, / in what's obvious" (44). While in the first instance the reader seems to be addressed as the one receiving the confidences of the inventory, the second "you" is more compellingly directed at those experiencing the disasters the speaker inventories and the third is arguably the speaker speaking to herself.

An important place of investigation for this use of "you" comes in part 3, at the shift from "she" to "I." It is here we are told that the speaker has "written a letter" (34). Brydon understands this letter to be addressed to the reader: "She has written a letter to an imagined reader, 'an account of her silence, / its destination all the streets / beginning with Al Kifah, Al Rashid' (14). The 'letter' concretizes the notion of poetic address" (992). Yet, as the quotation indicates, the letter's destination is these streets whose language is not this poem's, these streets the news reports show in disaster – not, it seems, a reader. It is after the speaker indicates that this letter provides "an account of her silence" that she speaks as an "I" (34). The letter is an "account" of the narration of a "she" rather than the direct speech of an "I" and the account seems to be an address to those at the destination of the letter, to those on streets where the speaker can ask about "the sound you must have heard / before these disasters, the sound / you must keep" (34). The account of her silence invites the self-representation of those experiencing what she has witnessed. The only response to this exchange of her silence for a description of sound is more silence: this address to those who endure these disasters cannot be answered within the poem and the "sound you must have heard" is not imagined here. That is, the speaker does not imagine a direct relationship with those whose suffering the poem inventories. As the speaker denies the possibility that she will speak for another, she might now speak as an "I" without engaging a fantasy of direct relation.

As the letter does not reach those to whom it is addressed, the "you" shifts at what appears to be the letter's end, just before the speaker is again called "she." This shift occurs at what I read as an invitation to the reader, creating now an account of the silence between speaker and reader: "if I say in this letter, I'm waiting / to step into another life, / will you come then and find me" (35). The reader is invited[7] to "find" the speaker's location of witness where she waits for "another life." But finding her would not open up this other life. Rather, finding her would mean additional waiting:

all I can offer you now though is my brooding hand,
my sodden eyelashes and the like,
these humble and particular things I know,
my eyes pinned to your face

understand, I will keep you alive like this (37)

The initial impulse in a poem about witnessing might be to imagine the witness's eyes to be pinned to a face that she witnesses, one of the sufferers from her inventory. Yet, if the "you" here refers to the reader, then we are back to the violent waiting that has been part of the inventory throughout the poem. To "keep you alive this way" would be to prolong – to "stay" – this position of reader through the continuation of the poem. The reader continues to wait with the speaker as long as the speaker keeps open this connection, this "pinned" communication.

The speaker offers her own feeling body – the hand metonymical of one's signature or writerly style, the wet eyelashes metonymical of sadness – in the writing of this letter. The speaker's description of her response is truncated as the list of these "humble particularities" ends after only two items with the vague "and the like," suggesting that her response is not modelled for a reader to replicate. The reader, forced out of a stable role or mode of address, has been continually placed back into his or her own individual responsiveness. Yet the "stay" in "Stay now, she's written a letter" (34) makes apparent the reader's role as one of waiting. This poem is the space of mutual waiting,

waiting which manifests for the speaker as an inventory of witnessed suffering and for the reader as reception. The form reception takes within the poem makes clear the division of duties, within a logic of waiting, between speaker and reader: "take this letter, put it on your tongue, / sleep while I keep watch, / know that I am your spy here, your terrorist, / find me" (37). The instruction given with the letter on the tongue to "sleep while I keep watch" demonstrates, through this distinction of actions (sleeping and watching), that the reader and speaker have different roles. Moreover, the speaker asks to be found: finding something or someone suggests an initial distance and a closure of that distance through discovery rather than assimilation.

To sleep under the watch of one's spy and terrorist indicates that the speaker's relation to the reader occurs within this waiting space of reception: the speaker is watching you to evoke your response to the terrible inventory she presents. Thus, the distance between the speaker and reader – the "desolate air between us" – is overcome by this "destin[y] to eat together": "the desolate air between us is no match / for the brittle orchids we are destined to eat together" (37). The shared if dissimilarly inhabited space of the witness poem ensures that both the speaker and the engaged reader take in – as with the letter on the tongue – the suffering witnessed through the inventory. In this inventory, the space between speaker and reader is a space of addition. The air between "is no match" because the two, once there is this "between," are in a relationship of addition or pairing.

Inventory repeats and reinvents actions of sharing and pairing throughout the poem, and, in doing so, displays its rhetorical strategies. Sharing and pairing is the work of rhetoric: in simile and the various forms of metaphor, pairing through similarity (and maintained difference) produces meaning shared across connection. When a comparison is implied in the work of metaphor, the connection is condensed in its articulation. In metonymy, a whole cultural or contextual understanding lies behind the logic of the common association that allows one thing to take the place of another. *Inventory* makes visible the work of its metonymical associations through their multiple repetitions. As metonymical modes of relation add up, the rhetorical work becomes increasingly apparent. One association, working inside a larger relationship, opens up the work of that containing relationship. That is, in a metonymical display which feeds into a larger metonymical structure, we know something about the internal workings of that larger association. As one example, the wet eyelashes (metonymical of sadness) and brooding hands (metonymical of poetic authorship) the speaker offers reveal the formation of the connection between speaker and reader. The speaker's body stands in for her affective and writerly response to suffering. It is this bodily response as witness she offers to readers. In the other direction, when she offers the letter (a written version of her response to witness), it is directed to a reader's body, to be received by the tongue.

Thus, a physical connection stands in for multiple aspects of poetic response and reception. This physical connection comes in the context of witness to physical suffering. The speaker constructs her relationship to suffering others through physical feeling (the pairing knife at her veins). We might consider these embodiments as I consider, in the previous chapter, Back's words of faith to bring back faith: the speaker articulates her positions in relation to sufferers (through her own bodily pain), readers (through her wet eyelashes and brooding hand as compassionate response), and poem (in its consistent materialization of language) in material terms that match what she witnesses (suffering bodies).[8] Though these images of materialization are an attempt to connect to the physical suffering the speaker witnesses, metonymical relationship also includes distance and difference in the attempt to connect like with like. The recurrent exploration of acts of sharing and pairing shows an investment in analyzing the mode of witness the poem performs.

The "brooding hand" which the speaker offers along with her pinning eyes is as much a part of this pairing as is the shared internalization of bitter things. While the "sodden eyelashes" offer a literal connection (the eyelashes being wetted by the tears that indicate sadness), the brooding hand holds symbolically the brooding the writer feels. Likewise, though, the "eyes pinned to your face" could only be pinned out of the emotional intensity of the person behind the look. Pinning indicates seeing but also establishes sight as a thing stuck to the other's face. As a kind of facial decoration, this seeing invites further looking. The eyes pinned to the face are a declaration of ongoing connection as well as a marking of that connection; the looked-at reader is marked as inhabiting a relation of sight with the speaker as witness.

The images of eyes and brooding hands are repeated: "Days, moored to the freight of this life, / the ordnances of her brooding hands, the / abacus of her eyelids" (38). The speaker's brooding hands as ordnances – as "implements of war"; "ammunition; missiles or bombs" (OED) – suggests violence in the hands' occupation of writing an inventory and a letter. If witnessing is a self-violence in the open waiting (time counted on "the / abacus of her eyelids") of attention to suffering, then the creation of a record of these attentions allows for others to take into themselves – like the letter on the tongue – the violence of this inventory.

Yet the dual meaning of brooding qualifies the aggressive or threatening occupation of these hands. While "dwell[ing] moodily upon a subject of thought" (OED) seems consistent with the idea of hands as ordnances of inventorying death and suffering, that which broods is also that which "cherishes (brood), hatches, or incubates" or, figuratively, that which "hovers closely around or overhangs (as a bird over her brood)." Brooding as a noun joins these two meanings: "A cherishing in the mind; moody mental contemplation." We might consider, then, the written account of witnessing as a weapon of cherishing and protecting.

Brooding's senses of dwelling on a subject and cherishing in the mind both connect it with waiting. Waiting, in this context, is ontological: waiting is a way of being in relation. Put into relationship with a speaker depicting the space of waiting that is an inventory, the responsibilities of reception here fall not to the facts of suffering, but to a way of being in relation to those facts. *Inventory* elsewhere explores such an ontological mode in an encounter between strangers that is not founded in coming to know but, rather, in a moment of engagement, a shared moment of ongoing not-knowing, a temporary nearness in space rather than the accumulation of knowledge through a common future. Brand's speaker – in an interlude from inventorying instances of suffering – encounters a stranger in a way that elicits another version of waiting: a collaborative moment of seeing alongside.

While visiting Cairo, the speaker finds herself in meaningful relationship with a stranger. She meets a storeowner who calls her "'Cousin," "that word" that "is more than father sister brother / mother, clasping what is foreign whole" (58, 59). Though the word "cousin" indicates a relation more genetically distant than "father sister brother / mother," this word "is more" than the others here. The speaker resignifies the distance between herself and the storeowner as a closeness operating through their mutual positioning as strangers. They share this word cousin: if I am your cousin, you are my cousin too (whereas if I am, say, your mother, you are my daughter).

The knowledge of the stranger is restricted to the moment of encounter. She "wanted to go back" (58) but "all the time nevertheless, / I left him to himself" (59), to

the time
you know, when something falls so perfectly
from your hands

I needed nothing from the market

after that, no scarves, no perfume bottles,
no nuts, no directions to all the gates of Cairo,
no souvenirs of ancient Egypt
other than the time we'd spent in some life,
before and since,
this charm of ours as I've said before

it meets you sometimes
on a hot mountain road or in a cool silver shop,
its startling purposes,
its imperishable beckoning grace,
so unexpected,
so merciful (59–60)

The speaker needed to take away from it "no directions" and "no souvenirs" – that is, no orienting of her future movement and no object of memory. She "left him to himself," suggesting that the importance of the encounter was "the time [...] when something falls so perfectly from your hands." Taken with the earlier "clasping what is foreign whole" in the work of the name "Cousin," this encounter is given its particular significance through the combined act of clasping into connection and letting that connection fall again from "your hands." The significance of this encounter is the experience of the moment itself; the truth of the nature of their relationship is not what is at stake in the moment and so need not be grasped. Indeed, the facts that could be ascertained about each other are so beyond the impact of the encounter that the man might have "never existed" (59). This time spent in "some life" does not continue in the trajectory of their individual lives, but is something set aside, something let fall. "Since" indicates a continuous action – not something "before" causing something "after" in a chain of events, but a moment to which one cannot return or have again because it is part of an ongoing condition. This encounter, evoking "some life, / before and since," approaches an ontological condition, bringing it into experiential or intellectual availability.

The name he calls her, "clasping what is foreign whole," suggests a way of encountering the foreign that does not require that it be undone by being brought into the realm of connection through shared attributes, twined lives, growing knowledge. Without reconciling their foreignness to each other, the charm comes to the hot mountain or to the cool silver now sold above the depth at which it once lived; these places for meeting charm are related through difference. The "charm" of the encounter has the "startling purposes" of "imperishable beckoning grace" – "favour or goodwill, in contradistinction to right or obligation" (OED) – and it is this beckoning that lives beyond the encounter itself. Grace – not a right or obligation – is non-essential. It is not a logical or moral necessity, but something superfluous or additional.[9] Here, deriving from a charm whose purposes startle, grace is also without foreseeable implications. This grace occurs, then, outside of teleology. This moment has charm, not because it creates a relationship that will progress into the future, but because it is an encounter that won't be repeated into the linearity of a shared, ongoing association. This non-teleological focus does not mean that the encounter is without connection to the future. Yet the shift in emphasis from that future onto the present makes clear that the grace the speaker feels is not so much the cause of a future effect as it is the ground of the meaning of a moment. Though I argue that the grace of this moment is not based in linear development or accumulated knowledge, it is not unconcerned with temporality or epistemology. This grace is "imperishable" – occurring before and since, not outside of considerations of time and continuation – and "beckoning" – calling not for cause and effect, as grace is not concerned with obligation or necessity, but for a gerund of attraction suggestive of ongoing response.

There is in "this time you know" and "this charm of ours" a syllabic and sonorous replication of sound. Although the speaker says, "this charm of ours as I've said before," she hasn't actually said it before; it seems that she is instead repeating the time that you know into a new vocabulary. The time and the charm are made structurally related but not equivalent, as the change of pronoun from "you" to "ours" moves from "speaking to" into the indication of something shared. The placement of "know" and "ours" offers a structural comparison of knowing with a condition of sharing. In their respective lines, knowing and sharing are differently associated. Knowing is related to time: knowing is within the spectrum of accumulation, of cause and effect (learning and coming to know), of linearity. The "ours" invoking sharing is related to charm: the attraction of an experience of collaboration which comes to meet you with startling purposes, unplanned and unknown.

The speaker rejects her impulse to extend the moment into the future:

I wanted to go back, take

his hand, eat from it, but,
that was, would be, another life,

and all our rumours would collide and
take that moment away from us when
he called me "Cousin," when cousin
came from both our mouths
and was a warning and a lie, and
a soft meeting and a love (58)

In contrast to the earlier image of letting something fall from the hand, returning to eat from his hand would be a form of holding on through consumption or internalization. For the speaker to go back would be to bring that moment from "another life" into an ongoing relationship. This move to return would be a push toward a future of knowing as the initiation of the process of getting to know one another, of letting their rumours collide by sharing and merging their stories. To act on this desire for knowledge would "take that moment away from us." As an ongoing relation, it would cease to be a connection existing before and since – rather than a moment that impacts all other temporalities, it would be part of a chain of moments connected across temporalities. The moment has its force in its separateness, in its special ontological character.

In that shared experience of asserting a genealogical relation – "when cousin / came from both our mouths" – the shared assertion is itself the experience of relation. The knowledge of the truth of that genetic relation is less important than the experience of relation more generally. But to go back would be to ignore the warning that the relation might be a lie. The experience of an ontological truth can impact the structuring of meaning at any point of one's existence while epistemological truth tests that truth against the other truths of one's life; it must fit into the structures of meaning already in existence or cause other knowledges to adjust to its factuality. To go back would be to fit him into the trajectory of her life where the nature of the relation (cousins or not) might matter more than the experience of it. The experience itself is valuable in a way that is not about knowledge (he might have been her cousin or he might have never existed; she needs no memorializing object or directions for her future navigation). Since an experience of grace (of more than what might be there in fact) makes this encounter meaningful, the encounter is about meaning, without necessarily involving knowing.

The earlier attention to eating and hands repeats in the speaker's desire "to go back, take his hand, eat from it," but this time in repudiation of the ongoing relation these actions suggest. The speaker wishes to find the facts of this man's life and to share in them as they impact the facts of her own life (if she finds him to be her cousin, she will have come to know herself as a cousin as well). The poem as a whole moves against this desire to grasp information, emphasizing instead ways of being in relation that are outside of an emphasis on knowing. The speaker and readers share such a relation: we do not know the information of witness in the sense of having lived the inventory's facts. The relationship structured between speaker and reader by facts of witness is outside of the sharing of these facts, the having or owning of them. The relationship is rather shaped by the shared attention to the information, by the waiting in relation to it.

Eve Kosofsky Sedgwick's account of the term "beside" provides a definition useful in thinking about reading witness poetry. For Sedgwick, the beside

> seems to offer some useful resistance to the ease with which *beneath* and *beyond* turn from spatial descriptors into implicit narratives of, respectively, origin and telos. Beside is an interesting preposition also because there's nothing very dualistic about it; a number of elements may lie alongside one another, though not an infinity of them. (8)

The before and since in witness poetry is something like Sedgwick's "beside," a way of thinking outside of a transaction from the present into the future of a chain of witnesses, each passing the knowledge of suffering onto the next. *Inventory*'s structure also operates in a way that resists origin and telos. I introduced this section set in Cairo as an interlude from the speaker's record of suffering. The poem is constructed of many sections of interlude. The poem as a whole can be read through each of these multiple smaller moments; it is arranged for continual deepening in its ongoing offering of different grounding possibilities for its reading. The Cairo section depicts grace (coming out of the collaborative moment) rather than the witness of suffering, and its impulses extend to the rest of the poem. The section's impact is before and since its place in the poem. This moment is not one of crisis, but the speaker's witnessing of crisis maintains the structure of this moment: the grace of her witness throughout the long poem is the offer of her own bodily, experiential response, her own suffering as collaboration, as the compassionate contiguity of feeling from nearby. Though "she sits devoted, the pairing knife close / to a harvest of veins" (29), it is from those all around her that "she'll gather the nerve endings / spilled on the streets" (30). Her own suffering is not the physical suffering of the killed or of the women from "battered kitchens" whose "passions" she also gathers (31), but the knife at her own veins symbolizes her own suffering in response. Her suffering is the "[s]omething else, more" of compassionate witnessing (56).

Brand's speaker says, "Something else, more happened there" (56) in the Cairo moment. She doesn't identify this "more," but recognizes its presence. The "more" and "else" that happened suggest an experience that, in its depth of meaning, cannot be immediately or easily reconciled with past experiences or with the future trajectory of currently held structures of understanding. In such a moment, then, one knows something through experience that one cannot know as facts or information. The speaker takes away no directions or souvenirs but rather the "startling purposes" of an "imperishable beckoning grace" that is both "unexpected" and "merciful." If the moment's difference from her current knowledge of the world (its unexpectedness) is a mercy, then this poem demonstrates value in a moment that is separate from, and competes with, coherent understanding. This moment cannot be reconciled to the trajectory of her life, the structure of meaning of that life, through a linear chain of memories of the past that lead to the meaning of the present and the navigation of the future.

This one moment becomes metonymical to the speaker's life. This significant encounter informs the speaker's life as a whole, before and since – that is, not as a juncture after which everything will change, but as an experience which impacts a whole way of understanding one's way of being in the world. This ability to stand in for a mode of living does not come through its similarity to other moments of the speaker's life, but through its dissimilarity. The before and since is another kind of pairing: this moment suddenly shares in the whole of the speaker's life. But it can only share in this way through the recognition of its difference, its unexpectedness in relation to everything else. The before and since is another way of understanding waiting as well. The moment's impact cannot be exhausted in the moment, but functions over an imperishable span of time.

Sophia Forster considers the function of inventory in Brand's earlier collection *Land to Light On*. As I do, she considers inventory's relationship to metonymy: "With this list, a set of facts that may all signify differently are metonymically linked to suggest a structure of domination impervious to the pockets of resistance" (np). However, what Forster calls metonymy is much more like metaphor; that is, Forster reads inventory as a substitutive strategy. Forster argues, "The use of inventory suggests not only that the items listed are connected (by the roles they play in a capitalist economic system) but that they are in fact interchangeable to a certain degree, since they are all reducible to the essence of 'harm.'" She suggests that Brand uses inventory as a strategy to demonstrate a "root connectedness of a series of oppressions geographically and historically dispersed to show that, at base, 'they're all the same.'" In contrast, I have suggested that *Inventory*'s speaker waits through witness even as there is more suffering than could ever be listed in its important particularity; here, Brand uses inventory to show that witnessing can never be up to the task of accounting for all the world's suffering.

Literary scholar Sara Murphy calls metonymy "the trope of deferral" (149) because it points from one thing to the next without ever creating a full picture. It is from within this deferral that Brand's *Inventory* asks its readers to respond.[10] In the deferral of a whole that might be grasped, a relationship is one of waiting rather than knowing, or of putting into conjunction various elements to create shifting configurations of meaningfulness. This is not to say that response to witnessing should not be about facts but, rather, that this poem structures another kind of response for its reader, one emphasizing a way of being over ways of disseminating knowledge. Knowing a fact is contrasted in *Inventory* with living that fact or living with the knowledge of that fact. Metonymy is both contiguous and deferring: it connects and leaves waiting. Like a knife that pairs (combines) and pares (cuts), *Inventory*'s metonymical strategies bring together and separate a speaker and reader, a witness and witnessed, and a graceful experience with the larger context of a life.

Inventory undertakes two simultaneous tasks: it creates a list of suffering and it forms a communicative space through which the speaker connects with readers. The poem's title makes obvious this additive mode in relation to the poem as list of suffering, but the additive mode is also a factor in the function of the poem as poem, that is, in how it structures response for itself. The list of suffering is a space in which "things, things add up" (52); similarly, the poem is an additive space between speaker and reader. Addition and pairing are conceptually linked terms, suggesting forming an inventory of suffering and forming relationship with readers as linked tasks. The speaker's pairing knife, as materialized tool of emotional work, is operative in both additions. Adding to her list is a kind of self-adding as well: every statistic of suffering is attached by and to the speaker's compassionate attention through her bodily emotional response. From the other side, a reader's engagement with the list of suffering comes through the speaker's selection and communication. It is in the connection between these two tasks that we can best consider the poem's overall work.

In the connection of reader to global suffering, the poem's work can be read as creating a kind of global community.[11] While this reading of *Inventory* is certainly available, and could be further established through my reading of its additive mode, I will focus on the more specifically enacted scale of a reading relationship. *Inventory* explores a psychic space between speaker and reader. One way in which a readerly relationship is modelled in the poem is through the moment between the speaker and the man in Cairo. Like this relationship depicted within the poem, the speaker-reader relationship is not one that extends beyond the moment of encounter (in that, the speaker and I, as reader, will not have an ongoing relationship that can have new moments outside of the encounter of the poem, even if I return to this moment through rereading or remembering). Rather than an idea of an ongoing community (which is similar to the idea of a chain of new witnesses), I see the poem forming a temporary association between speaker and reader. The poem's point, for me, is not to ask a reader to enact witness as part of a witnessing community, but to be affected by the compassion of another person as she communicates it. Rather than asking for an agreement to take on the task of witness the speaker performs, the poem makes space for readers to react personally to what another person feels.[12]

In contrast to my understanding of the poem's space for personal reaction, Cheryl Lousley's "Witness to the Body Count: Planetary Ethics in Dionne Brand's *Inventory*" argues that *Inventory* works through the impersonal. For Lousley, Brand's speaker, by occupying an impersonal position, "makes a communication network rather than shared humanity the basis for interpellation into an ethical relationship" (42) as the poem "dream[s] global ecological justice" (37). She argues, "the poem's lyrical voice is tempered with epic detachment to achieve a depersonalized testimony" (38).[13] In an interesting contradiction, Lousley also considers this depersonalized and detached speaker to be "a weepy, sentimental female spectator" (39). I bristle at this gendered characterization of the speaker's emotion. Not only does the label of weepy sentiment fall into a history of deflating women's emotional and artistic work through the charge of superficial, exaggerated emotion, but I do not see Brand's speaker invoking such terms with the emotion she expresses. Neither do I see her as depersonalized or detached. I argue that the speaker's fierce, harsh, aggressive, and steadfast voice is not detached but prominently seeks attachment, often – as when the speaker pins herself to the reader's face – in explicit content as well as tone.

Lousely recuperates the speaker's sentimentality, noting that though "sentimentalism assumes a universal humanity can be based on compassion for the suffering body" in contrast "*Inventory* transforms the weepy television viewer's sentimentalism into affective responsibility by marking the singularity of each death without recuperating lost voices or personal narratives" (52). I am interested in the transformation of the unfashionable "sentimentalism" into the currently more fashionable term "affect." Lousely uses the speaker's "bad" sentimentality and "good" affect to depersonalize the speaker's witness in either case: her sentimentality detachedly assumes compassion; her affect is impersonally responsible. According to Lousley, "Brand focuses on the impersonal position of being a witness without being present" (42). Being absent is not the same thing as being impersonal, and the speaker's affective responses – her sentimental attachments to readers, sufferers, and scenes – have as a primary goal showing global suffering as personal whether one knows those persons or not (that is, personal despite the lack of proximity to and knowledge of the intimate details of others' lives and deaths). The witness in her varying pronouns is not "anonymous and depersonalized" (45). Rather, as I have been arguing, her brooding witness models an emotional self-reflection inviting readers into a similar personal entrance to compassion. Compassion is not premised on a "universal humanity" but on a self-reflective awareness of relationship that is particularized by the awareness of an individual witness's unique points of connection. In my reading, Lousley's argument that *Inventory* suggests that "*anyone* could assume the ethical role of witness" is more universalizing than the speaker's sentimental insistence that witness occur through each individual witness's emotional response to suffering (45).

Inventory's last section works most explicitly within this relationship between speaker and reader and offers the best demonstration of my argument about how the poem structures its reception through this relationship. As the last section begins, the speaker acknowledges that "On reading this someone will say / God, is there no happiness then" (89). This "someone" responding "on reading this" is explicitly a future reader of this poem. The speaker here anticipates an expectation of the availability of certain forms of feeling in the poem. That is, the poem creates this expectation, structuring into the relationship it makes with its readers the idea that attention to happiness might be a part of that relationship. In a poem inventorying global suffering, it is not a given that readers would in fact understand a lack of happiness in the poem to suggest "no happiness" in general, or that they would have a complaint that a poem focused on suffering does not incorporate happiness into its interests.

In raising the idea, the poem implicates itself in a more whole rendering of the world. Its concerns extend beyond suffering. The speaker's response (to her own statement ventriloquized as a reader's) brings the poem to depict experience more broadly, experience that "of course" (89) includes happiness. The speaker's affirmation that "of course" there is happiness initiates a new list. The presence of this list of happy things proposes a view of witnessing aligning with philosopher Kelly Oliver's belief that "witnessing is the essential dynamic of all subjectivity, its constitutive event and process. While trauma undermines subjectivity and witnessing restores it, the process of witnessing is not reduced to the testimony to trauma. So, too, subjectivity is not reduced to the effects of trauma" (7). *Inventory* is about testimony and trauma, but it is also about human relation and experience more broadly.

The speaker's question and response indicates a sense of responsibility, a need to answer to a reader. While recording suffering is the speaker's explicitly stated responsibility, this new list is the structure for and occasion of a responsibility less available on the surface of the poem and more specifically poetic. This responsibility is for the communicative space it structures and offers. The speaker assumes (and, in assuming, creates the conditions through which the assumption might be correct) that a reader will ask questions about what a lack of happiness in this inventory means for the world the poem engages, the world in which readers live. That is, this last section explicitly raises questions about the way the inventory of suffering is related to its readers as people.

Though the speaker earlier tells us "nothing personal is recorded here" (22), this last section is a personal account of how the world affects this speaker. Yet her earlier claim alerts us to the fact that perhaps this personal sharing is not the point: this last section is not for us to better know the speaker and her love of music, "the whole of it" (95), or her affection for "one woman / Marlene" (98). These personal facts are less important in what they tell us about the person offering them than they are in what they mean for the relationship between the speaker and the readers with whom she shares these details.[14] The speaker's responsibility to answer to a wish for happiness comes in relation to her poetic responsibility. This last section, in which the speaker's attention returns again and again to her own creation of this list, most explicitly engages with *Inventory* as a poem. She first speaks of the list in the passive voice, as though it is self-generating: "were / the dancehalls mentioned before" (92); "the many times that rain is mentioned here" (96). Yet the voice becomes active when she resists making the list: "ask them / about happiness, not me, why should / I know how to dance and sing in the middle of it all, / okay, okay this list is not so exhausted yet" (94). Though she decides to go on, the speaker's interjections continue throughout, as if in conversation with the readers to whom she answers with such phrases as "ask them / about happiness, not me" (94), "let's leave" (96), "how can we" (96), and "you have to" (97). While this section questions the poem's turn to happiness at all, more significantly, it measures its overall role as a form of art in global witness. *Inventory* attends to its own creation in order to account for its poetic responsibility. Earlier, as she lists deaths, the speaker asks "why does that alliterate on its own, why / does she observe the budding of that consonant" (38). The speaker denies agency over the aesthetics of the inventory, but in the final section engages the poetic form that structures the possibility and particular reception of the budding of alliteration and other attentions to language and style.

The poem's communicative process itself is a part of the list. While rain is given as happy, so are "the many times that rain is mentioned here" (96). The poetic repetition is itself a thing of happiness. Even more explicitly about communication is the speaker's thought on words: "some words can make you weep, / when they're uttered, the light rap of their / destinations, their thud as if on peace, as if on cloth, / on air, they break all places intended and known // soft travellers" (99). The emphasis on reception is apparent in "the light rap of their destinations," a description of the words' arrival which omits the moment they hit; the words don't rap, their destinations do. The destinations themselves make a sound in anticipation of the "thud" the words will make. This poem contains its readers' anticipation, the "rap" of our waiting through this reading, insofar as its poetic tactics are aligned toward the task of suggesting for us the sort of rap we will make, the sort of destinations it would like for us to be. The thud of the words themselves follows, "as if on peace, as if on cloth, / on air": the effect of a reception of "some words" is first abstract, then tangible, and finally something in between – concrete, but invisible, permeable. The thud "on air" loses its "as if" as though the correct level of concreteness to describe the move of words from utter to thud has been reached. The description of reception as words hitting air is suggestive of the mode of being I find the poem to propose. A word received by air is not received into an abstract, conceptual realm of peace. Nor is it received by cloth, a synonym of material (as woven fabric), that might, as a particular example, stand in for the material realm. Materiality has throughout the poem been associated with reading (as waiting through the poem and listening to the speaker). These words are received, not in the abstract and not in the material conditions of the reading alone, but into the atmosphere through which we live. To be received by air is to be received into the very substance of existence, the invisible environment that contains our everyday experiences. This reception is one in which readers integrate these words into their being in the world.

These words break "all places intended and known" in this poem whose recipients are unknown and cannot be specifically intended. As it is in the Cairo section, mutual strangerness is important here. The speaker is not inventing an ideal reader or a particular life for these words to impact. This is a relationship built entirely by this poetic moment for anyone entering into it, built by "some words" which work to suggest a manner for their own reception.[15] The words' "soft travelling" plays a role in this response. The offer of aesthetic pleasure builds a certain relationship with a reader. *Inventory*'s unpleasant facts are not delivered unpleasantly. *Inventory* is not a cacophonous breakdown of meaning, it is not particularly fragmented, it does not use unsettling language or evoke graphically upsetting images. This poem is not made difficult in the aesthetic ways prevalent in both modern and postmodern endeavours. Rather, *Inventory* is a list of suffering made beautiful in its telling. In relation to its subject matter, that

beauty becomes particularly meaningful. The poem's style is necessary
for my point that *Inventory* solicits readers as listeners to a communication of compassion. Further, though, the poem tackles beauty as its
own topic. In fact, the speaker's list of happiness in the world is less
about happiness, I argue, than it is about beauty. She never does say
that these are happy things. Though introduced after a question about
happiness, the list has only vague identifications of its topic, as in the
vague pronoun reference in the line, "sleep is infinitely this" (93).

In contrast to this vagueness, the speaker discusses beauty specifically. In one item, men waiting "to go do some mindless work" are
"willing the truck to arrive or meet / with catastrophe, let this be the
morning of the end / of the world, they pray, / there's something of a
beauty there" (91). If this wish for catastrophe can be something of
beauty, it is not clear why it should be included in a list dealing with
happiness. Similarly, the speaker lists "the irregular weather of hurri-
canes, / tsunamis, floods, sunlight on any given day, / anywhere, however disastrous at least magnificent" (89). It is arguable that there
is implicit here an idea that beauty or magnificence brings a sort of
happiness. Yet I'm not sure happy is the thing beauty makes us. The
above examples of natural disaster and desire for catastrophe hardly
seem to imply happiness. More specifically, I would suggest that
"beauty" or "magnificence" be aligned with the earlier invocation
of grace as "imperishable beckoning." If I were to account for the
beauty of "the end" it would be in this sense of imperishable beckoning. Beauty that, like grace, beckons imperishably[16] is a condition
of intrigue, or curiosity, or inclination, or seeking that can never be
fulfilled or satisfied. The beauty is in the imperishable beckoning, a
state aligning with that of waiting. This section of the poem is not to
make you happy, or even really to address a concern that happiness
be present, but to beckon you into engagement. The state the poem
creates for its readers is akin to this imperishable beckoning.

Yet, in the end, the speaker undermines this relationship and this
beckoning. If this poem proposes an act of witness that broadens its
scope to include more than trauma, the speaker finally reinscribes its
borders. She expresses this limit to her witness as though it is an ethical enforcement. On the poem's last page, the dates of "the bloodiest

days in one year, / in one place" break into the list. Throughout the list as a whole, the speaker is frequently distracted back to suffering, and finally declares that "happiness is not the point really, it's a marvel, / an accusation in our time" (100). The conclusion states a responsibility for ongoing attendance: "I have nothing soothing to tell you, / that's not my job, / my job is to revise and revise this bristling list, / hourly" (100). The speaker replaces a grace-like imperishable beckoning with a "job," something no longer outside of right or obligation. The nature of the responsibility to others has shifted to the task of this particular witness from one of an essential witnessing which we, by virtue of existing in a shared air of possible reception, owe to each other.

Like Harjo's speaker, who, I argue in chapter 3, asserted her witnessing as a special ability, *Inventory*'s speaker, in the face of the inclusivity of the witnessing so recently constructed, concludes with the particularity of her task. Readers do not share this job: if it is not her job to tell us soothing things, we are the listening unsoothed. While we have always been aligned in such alternate points of a conversation – her writing her list, us reading it – our readerly role as destinations for the "soft travellers" of her words depended on a widened definition of witnessing. We are not witnessing suffering. We are witnessing a poem about a speaker watching the news about suffering. When the poem tried to deal with its own mediated position, its own distance, its own aesthetic being, it did so by proposing the effectiveness of a poem, its ability to draw readers in with its beauty, its aesthetic communicative powers. In this last page, the speaker undoes the work she has put into validating a poetic response to suffering. It is not her "job" to do what she was doing in this concluding section (which is not, on that note, all soothing, as we saw through its evocations of catastrophe and disaster). It is her job to "revise this bristling list," to attend to suffering, to write its facts. At the last hour, the speaker backs away from the privilege she has accorded an ontological mode of witness and turns to an epistemological mode. This epistemological mode seems to me to be the easier of these two as ethical tasks. I do not disagree with there being an obligation to know the facts, to be politically aware, to be informed. Seeking out information which does not directly affect our own lives can be a moral action. Yet more challenging, I think, is the suggestion that we must not simply witness the facts, but feel that witness, or live it.

This final assertion of the speaker's "job" drastically restructures the relationship between speaker and reader. Now that her job is not to tell us something soothing, but to revise her list, there is a suggestion that her job is not to tell us anything at all. The speaker's job is "to revise and revise this bristling list, / hourly." As the poem ends here with this suggestion of the speaker's task ongoing through time, a reader's job is left unclear. The speaker's task has been addition and pairing: the logic of the poem, and the logic of lists, suggests that her job would be to add to this list, to continue tracking the world's suffering. To revise is not to add but to "improve"; "alter ... after reconsideration"; "reread or relearn"; "see again or repeatedly" (OED). If the job is to maintain engagement with the list in order to continue to learn from it, ought not a reader to hold this job too? If the speaker instead refers to improving or altering the list, must she not be referring to its poetic elements rather than its factual ones? In this shift from adding to revising, the speaker moves into a solitary, non-communicative, non-witnessing position which clashes with the spirit of her statement here as well as with everything about her act of witness which has come before. This position leaves readers unhinged from the poem and from a sense of responsibility or possibility for continuing engagement.

When I first read this conclusion, I felt betrayed by the poem. Yet I assumed I was culpable for my feeling as the intended reaction to the poem's charge. Happiness might not be the point, but the speaker includes it anyway, includes it so that it might become "an accusation." Though the speaker accuses herself as well, it is the reading "someone" that makes her give this list in the first place. The reader is responsible for wanting happiness and further responsible for being soothed by finding it exists here, in this inventory meant to list suffering. And so I assumed my emotional reaction to the end of the poem was a result of this accusation, of finding myself at fault for wanting to be distracted from my implication in a global condition of suffering. My reaction was just the one the poem had positioned me to feel, I thought.

Brydon likewise notes her struggle with this conclusion:

> Even happiness, granted a section of its own, becomes, in the end, "not the point really, it's a marvel, / an accusation in our time" (100). When I first read this line, I found it entirely bleak, seeing even the ability to enjoy happiness as suggesting insensitivity to the horrors recorded here. On reflection, however, it is the potential ambivalence in these lines that strikes me. Without abandoning that first interpretation, I can also see how it might be read otherwise. As a marvel, and a joy, happiness works as a potent accusation, presenting a powerful alternative to both the status quo and the poet's despair. (996)

Brydon's reading tries to make sense of this ending as an ethically effective suggestion. Yet these lines cannot be read as an alternative to the status quo because the examples engaging happiness and beauty are not given as imagined possibilities but as actualities of the world as it is. The items of this list are as much the status quo as are the items of the inventory of suffering. Moreover, as I've mentioned, many of the items are not at all hopeful or contrary to despair. The list deals more often with the beauty of a wish for the world to end and the magnificence of disaster – or with the qualified positivity of "barrios and slums, crazy, crazy places" where "happiness is a light post, a scar" (97), "drunk recrimination" because "at least it's an examination / of things past" (94), or "a wrecked and wretched boat" that "still has all the possibilities of moving" (92) – than it does with anything obviously better or different from suffering.

There was surplus in the pairing of speaker and reader and in the space of addition between them. The grace is the surplus of the pairing, and the speaker models and invites embodied relationship earlier in the poem with her "brooding hand," "pairing knife," and her witness "pinned to your face." By then closing witness off as a solitary obligation, she betrays witness's surplus aspect – the aspect that, in this poem, readers were earlier asked to bring into their own embodied lives. In an interview with E. Martin Nolan for *The Puritan*, Brand's comments about this poem suggest that she may also disagree with her speaker's concluding thoughts:

> If the woman in *Inventory* had gone to bed, she wouldn't have made the list and something would have been erased. She couldn't live with that. She wouldn't have a happy life if she did. To see is to be. There is not unhappiness is [*sic*] seeing. There can't be *too* much that you know, that would be the woman in *Inventory*. As to me, to some extent – there can't be *too* much that I know. That I do not know that something exists does not make me any richer.

That not knowing does not make one richer is precisely the lesson I find in Murray's "Letters to the Winner." When Brand's interviewer continues the thought, "And knowing that it exists doesn't make you any – " and Brand interjects, "Poorer," it is clear that, in Brand's view, witnessing means more than suffering the knowledge of suffering because becoming poorer in happiness cannot be understood to be witnessing's essential consequence.

But the poem's final accusation of happiness abandons one sense of responsibility (the poetic one) to turn to a more obvious sense of responsibility (mindfulness of suffering). To build this relationship of responsibility with readers through the medium of a poem, an aesthetic use of language, only to accuse them of being affected by the beauty, the budding consonants, the soft travellers of words, is, however, to betray that relationship, and to betray the work the poem has done. On the surface, it seems more ethical to return to a remembrance of suffering and the task of its witness. Yet, if the listing of facts were the primary task of this poem, then there would be no reason for it to be a poem. Its deeper task is to do something with words and to do something with the communicative possibilities of a reading relationship.

We can consider the kind of responsibility which the speaker first structures in this poem, and from which she finally backs away, in relation to Mikhail Bakhtin's sense of responsibility in "Art and Accountability":

I have to answer with my own life for what I have experienced
and understood in art, so that everything I have experienced
and understood would not remain ineffectual in my life. But
answerability entails guilt, or liability to blame. It is not only
mutual answerability that art and life must assume, but also
mutual liability to blame. The poet must remember that it is his
poetry which bears the guilt for the vulgar prose of life, whereas
the man of everyday life ought to know that the fruitlessness of
art is due to his willingness to be unexacting and to the unseri-
ousness of the concerns in his life. The individual must become
answerable through and through: all of his constituent moments
must not only fit next to each other in the temporal sequence of
his life, but must also interpenetrate each other in the unity of
guilt and answerability ... Art and life are not one, but they must
become united in myself – in the unity of answerability. (1–2)

The speaker[17] answers with her own life by denying the artfulness of
her art, by assuming that this artfulness entails guilt. This position is
in contrast to the mutual answerability which Bakhtin suggests, in
which the art must answer to the same ethical demands of the life,
and the life to the demands of the art. This answerability means that
if a life can meet with beauty – and a life really must, especially by
the terms the speaker proposes for beauty, in which beauty can be a
part even of catastrophe – then a work of art must likewise account
for its own beauty, not dismiss it as a guilty soothing pleasure. The
speaker has abandoned this difficult beauty for "the vulgar prose of
life" which she determines to be ethical only insofar as it is concerned
with suffering. An ethics concerned only with ethical failure (with
the proofs that "we mean each other harm") is likewise self-limiting.
This kind of answerability to life is not exacting. Though it seems
utterly responsible, it is a responsibility that – following the hard
rule that it is hardship that must be seen – does not demand active
thought: the moral law is in place and one need only follow it. Of
course we should attend to the suffering of others. A more difficult
question is how to make that attention matter. I think this mattering

is only possible through the inclusion of the fullness of life in our attentions.[18]

At the centre of the last page of the poem, the speaker declares that "there are atomic openings in my chest / to hold the wounded" (100). The heart of the page holds this idea of holding the wounded. But the top of the page – its intellect, so to speak – has evacuated readers from the poem which had up to that point been open to them. In this way, the poem ends up grounded in only the personal ethical account-ability of its own speaker to do her job. Her words – separated from a social, communicative function and from the speaker's life outside of this job – can only circle her own wound. If we all carry within us the woundedness of others, but cannot hold those wounds open to the wholeness of the life holding them, then this attention is a form of navel-gazing with a slightly raised point of vision. Witnessing one's own painful openness is less compelling as an ethical dictum or a job than is the witnessing *Inventory* earlier invokes as an unsatisfiable inclination toward being in relation.

5

Signing Skeletons: Relational Structures of the Actual and Artistic

In this final chapter, I examine the structural relationships of witness poems. In my previous chapter, I considered witness poetry's metonymical strategy for positioning readers. Here, I consider witness poems' metonymical connections to the poets who write them. Much as my third chapter builds on and expands my second chapter's notion of compassionate relationship within community by considering that relationship within broader contexts, here I build on my fourth chapter's consideration of the metonymical relationship expressed between speaker and reader through the broader context of the structural relationship among a poet, a poem's content, and the people, events, and feelings that the poem is about.

How do poets sign their poems? That is, how is the poet's relationship to what was witnessed evident within the poem? These questions emerge through this chapter's account of structures of witness. I begin by exploring skeletons as imagery through which witness poems navigate the structural relations to the events, conditions, and people – including the poets – the poems exist within. I consider this skeleton imagery in poetry by Seamus Heaney, Antjie Krog, Dionne Brand, and Derek Walcott. Because the exposed skeleton incites the shock of visible structural matter, this imagery brings out the process of witness as an explicit topic. Correspondingly, ekphrasis emerges as an important strategy in these skeleton poems. The focus on the visible relationships within a poem, including the focus on where we

can see the poet's signature, brings me to consider a short film set in
an ossuary. Jan Švankmajer's *Kostnice* (1970) features bones turned
into art (and used to form a literal artist's signature). The soundtrack
to the ossuary visuals is a sung lyric poem taking as its topic the
relationship between art and artists. This film, alongside Shoshana
Felman's comments on film and Frank Chipasula's conception of
witness as song in Heaney's poetry, brings me to this chapter's final
section. There I conclude my reflection on the relationship between
poet and witness poem through an exploration of poetic dedication
as a form of signature.

Through images of skeletons, the poetry I arrange in the following
chapter investigates structure as it pertains to witnessing relationships and the intersections of individual and community. We might
often imagine a connection as a straight line between two elements,
but there is no reason for that line to be straight, or singular. Skeletons are the contiguity of bones (the knee-bone is connected to the
thigh bone), but the skeletal structure is not linear. Tracing the points
of connection in a skeleton involves backtracking, retracing, moving sideways and in circles. This multiple and non-teleological connectivity emphasizes connectivity itself. Witnessing in the poetry I
study here is not a chain leading somewhere, but an investigation of
the mess of proximate relationships in any context. A skeleton, as
emblematic of human mortality, suggests vulnerability while it also
functions as the durable record of human life. This memorializing
role is one aspect of witness. As the invisible structure of the individual human body, a skeleton made visible and touchable also suggests intimacy and proximate relationship. Yet, dissociated from the
memory of a particular person, skeletons become generic, stripped of
the visual qualities that mark personal distinction. Witness poetry's
skeletal images suggest a complex structure to relation and commemoration as established by acts of witness.

In witness poetry, I find an artistic and ethical concern with structural connection expressed through recurring images of skeletons and
ossuaries. In "Bone Dreams," a poem from Seamus Heaney's collection
North that I consider in my first chapter, the speaker encounters a bone
that turns into a bone-woman who turns into part of a national land-

scape in Northern Ireland. South African poet Antjie Krog translates poetry from the original Afrikaans for her first collection to appear in English, *Down to My Last Skin* (2000). This collection suggests the speaker's stripped condition, with the poem "Country of grief and grace" depicting the "decrowned skeletons" of apartheid (c. 9). In the long poem *Ossuaries* (2010), Dionne Brand portrays a woman's struggle through a painful life in which her own bodily structure is metaphorically dismantled into the ossuary of a global system of human misuse of humans. In Derek Walcott's "Ruins of a Great House" (*In a Green Night* 1962), Walcott finds a bone in the grounds of a Caribbean plantation house during his meditation on the social and cultural structures of colonization. What is the significance of the rhetorical skeleton? If these skeletons and bone-houses stand in for a concept of structure, how do these images shift in valence between the synecdochal (personal) and the metaphoric (societal) operations?

I

In Heaney's "Bone Dreams," the speaker finds an individual bone which becomes a "Bone-house" (II.1) of the languages of a land's history (II, III).[1] Through this history and in the speaker's embrace, the bone becomes a skeleton-woman and, simultaneously, a part of the landscape. The bone is the material remnant of an individual human, the signifier of a linguistic cultural history, and a point of access for the speaker to the contemporary geography. Within these multiple significations, "Bone Dreams" creates a reciprocal relationship between the speaker/holder and the held/witnessed:

> I hold my lady's head
> like a crystal
>
> and ossify myself
> by gazing (IV.7–10)

Gazing at this skull, the speaker too becomes as bone, but "to ossify" is also "to become rigid or fixed" (OED); to ossify himself is a commitment to the gaze that creates the ossification. This feed-back loop suggests witness as a self-perpetuating holding. Heaney presents this witness as a mutual relationship in which "we end up / cradling each other" (V.1–2). In this cradling, witness and witnessed are both held and holding. Here, he holds the skull like "a crystal," which, ambiguously, might refer to a crystal ball or a crystal stone. This gazing, then, involves seeing either time (the future through the crystal ball) or space (the world's many facets through a crystal's prisms) more fully. Since the speaker becomes ossified like the object he holds, this intensified gazing becomes a held position.

The speaker has a second interaction with a dead head. After finding a dead mole the speaker

> was told, 'Blow,
> blow back the fur on his head.
> Those little points
> were the eyes. [...]' (VI.9–12)

Much as gazing at the skull ossified the speaker into a common condition of holding and being held, when he blows back the fur to see the mole's eyes, the mole holds the speaker's gaze. Though the dead mole cannot see, the speaker blows life into the mole just as he touches life into the bone. Yet in both cases, bone and mole, the speaker has the solitary responsibility for communication, even if he imagines a mutual gaze. First, he reads the skull as a crystal for its meaning. Next, he blows back the mole's fur in a kind of oral witness, a communication of sight. Though he physically animates the bone-lady and the mole, neither live outside of their relation to his interest. The bone he finds is part of language's bone-house: the container for language but not its agent. This aspect of the poem indicates the essential privilege and responsibility of the speaking witness. *North* is controversial in just this respect; critics cannot agree on the ethics of the collection's exploration of the voyeuristic privilege *North*'s speakers take. Yet, as much as the speaker in "Bone Dreams" brings these dead remnants into the service of his witness, the vulnerability of engagement is depicted here as mutual. As Heaney's Medusa-like bone-woman ossifies her witness, the speaker, too, is vulnerable to the gaze he imagines into life, and it is precisely this vulnerability that makes him hold his position of witness.

Heaney's poem takes as a topic the significant fact that, when making art out of social suffering, the artist's voice is, either implicitly or explicitly, the arranging or creating force. I will return to Heaney later in this chapter. For now, I turn to how the polyphony in Krog's account of the South African Truth and Reconciliation Commission likewise addresses this concern about the artist's dominant voice. Krog's mixed-genre narrative *Country of My Skull* holds, in its collection of voices,[2] intersections of individual and communal scales. While the title points to the dominant or overarching perspective of the artist, the text indicates its structure as skeletal, not in the sense of bare bones, but in the sense of exposed connectivity. This text focuses on the multiplicity and tangling of relationship. Poet and literary critic Meira Cook argues of *Country of My Skull* that "the title of [Krog's] memoir implies that what occurs between the covers of this book has taken place primarily within the confines of the narrator's skull" (np). Cook critiques this focus as "claustrophobic" and "narcissistic." The title suggests to me quite the contrary: an interrogation of art's structure as it relates to witness.

In "Global Resonance, Local Amplification: Antjie Krog on a World Stage," Anthea Garman examines Krog's witness celebrity. Garman argues that "Krog is emblematic of a new type of representative public person who is no longer afforded a hearing just because of the excellence of their ideas, writing or speech, but who also embodies pain, suffering and affectedness" (187). One of the factors allowing Krog to speak from this position is her identity as a politically engaged poet:

> what we see in Krog, with her roots in poetry and her many
> years of performance as both poet and political dissident, is
> someone who brings into public discourse the appeal to respond
> with feeling, guilt and contrition. This type of public figure is
> no longer the emblematic enlightenment subject of the nation
> state, but an affected, implicated *human being* with the potential

to reach across state boundaries to connect with all similarly
affected humans. (198)

For Garman, this authority through affect is connected to "the nature of
the post-apartheid public sphere" that is "permeated by performances
of affect which are used to surface issues and experiences that cannot
be captured by the 'logos-centred rationales for deliberative democracy'" (Michael Huspek qtd. in Garman 198). Thus, the "narcissistic"
focus on the self is part of a form of responsibility. Exercising this
responsibility, one privileged (for multiple coinciding reasons) self can
bring into conversation otherwise marginalized issues and experiences
by recognizing and articulating her feelings on the public stage. While
her "roots in poetry" are part of what makes Krog a "public person"
who "embodies pain, suffering and affectedness," it is precisely her
role as a public figure that complicates an easy conflation of Krog the
"implicated *human being*," the affected speakers in her poems, and
Krog the emblem. Indeed, as a "representative public person," Krog
does not bring to public discourse simply human affect but, indeed,
the representation of it. Neither her poetry nor her public performance
can be understood merely within the bounds of the personal (or the
narcissistic). Whether it is the representation of suffering in her poetic
speaker or the representativeness of suffering in her public person, that
suffering and its relation to "affected humans" must be considered in
terms of the "performances of affect" and the forms of authority they
have in their political, cultural, and social contexts.

Skull images hold Krog's concern about the relationship of her
literary art to her witness. She explores the seizure and violent shaping involved in turning her country's suffering into poetry. "Country
of grief and grace" (included in *Country of My Skull* as well as in
Krog's collection *Down to My Last Skin*) depicts the speaker "seizing
the surge of language by its soft bare skull" (b.8). This seizing seems
preventative, a stop to the surge of words. Indeed, seizure suggests a
violent, appropriative holding, particularly in relation to the vulnerable malleability of the "soft bare skull."

Cook locates in *Country of My Skull* Krog's "fear that she will
not find an adequate literary structure for these traumatic narra-

tives" (np). I see a similar concern with structure and communication in "Country of grief and grace" when the speaker posits "a line which says: from this point onwards / it is going to sound differently / because all our words lie next to one another on the table now" (h.20–2). Given the future tense, this posited line, presumably, is not the line we actually get here that says that everything will sound differently; indeed, the poem does not promise that everything will sound differently but that there will be a line that will say so. The change in sound is premised on moving "onwards" from the stationary proximity of words that "lie next to one another." "Now," words lay on the table so that in the future there can be the line that speaks change. Thus, the poem's earlier violence of seizure is replaced by metonymical proximity, but this proximity is not the final structure. The poem speaks to a structure of poetic witness that differs from the structure of poetic proclamation. Contiguity, as deferral, is the cause of future change. Moving into healing, South Africa, the poem suggests, is only beginning a long process.

This contiguity develops over the course of the poem. At its start, the connective space must be travelled:

how long does it take
for a voice
to reach another

in this country held bleeding between us (a.12–15)

The voice must reach across a space created by the bleeding country and demonstrated visually by the line break. Held between, the country occupies a vulnerable position. Like the visible skeleton, there is here an externalization of relationships that should be foundational. The voice reaching calls to mind arms reaching to hold the country, thus emphasizing the breadth of the space "between us." But by the end of the poem, the country moves inside its citizens: "because of you / this country no longer lies / between us but within" (f.1–3). Like the mutual cradling in Heaney's "Bone Dreams," the speaker, holding her country "in the cradle of my skull" (f.7), moves toward a less vulnerable intimacy, toward a deepening of the contiguity that will let things sound differently one day. Voice is metonymical of the body and reaches out of the body to communicate across space. The country becomes akin to a shared voice as it is held inside but communicated outward to connect individuals.

In Brand's *Ossuaries*, too, questions of vulnerability arise through voice and perspective. *Ossuaries'* sections alternate perspective between the first and third person. The speaker/character, then, sometimes speaks for herself but is at other times the subject of an implied narration, as the perspective of a character must implicitly include a narrator, someone to see and tell. This shifting perspective in a poem concerned with ethical witnessing raises questions about how this poem holds its story. Are the character and narrator contiguously or hierarchically arranged? With what sort of representation of this speaker's suffering is the reader in relationship? *Ossuaries* contains a structural engagement of issues of speaking and being spoken for.

I read the split in narration in *Ossuaries* as the difference between a narrated character and a character speaking for herself. An implied narrator gives, in the past tense, Yasmine's story. Yasmine, as speaker, speaks in the present tense from a temporal point after the recounted history. In my reading, *Ossuaries* separates Yasmine's past from her present, her linear biography from her non-linear reflections and emotions, her story from her living. These separations suggest her disarticulation from herself. However, the "I" sections in *Ossuaries* can alternatively be read as the voice of a poetic speaker, as Yasmine's narrator speaking, not about Yasmine, but about herself. In this reading, we can understand the "I" as the voice of a poet, a reading permitted by references to this communication as poetry, as "the dim-lit ambiguous approaches of these stanzas" (35). From this perspective, the relationship between speaker (speaker-poet-within-the-poem) and character is one that explores the situation of telling another's story of suffering. This second reading would need to account for the similarities between the lives of speaker and character (for one small instance, the speaking "I" "had so many languages" (50) and Yasmine is "a polyglot" [54]). Yet, in this second reading, these coincidental alignments suggest that suffering is built into social structures such that this poem is not only the story of one unhappy life; the poet is privileged (because she can speak where Yasmine cannot), but her life holds this suffering as well.

My preferred reading of a speaking character and a narrated character is consistent with Brand's own account of these two voices in an interview with E. Martin Nolan: "But you know there are a couple voices or narrators, an intertwining of narrators in *Ossuaries*. It's not just Yasmine all the way, and it isn't the other voice all the way either … there are certain synergies between the two … so it's Yasmine and some consciousness and a movement toward a unified voice but still keeping a kind of magnetic – mis-attraction between the two" (np). When Nolan asks if the narrator is omniscient, Brand responds, "But not unengaged, so not omniscient really. In fact, it's very in there." For me, the "intertwining of narrators" most compellingly suggests Yasmine as her own narrator and then another implied narrator who, since focalized through a third-person Yasmine, is indeed "a movement toward a unified voice" while "still keeping a … mis-attraction between the two."

My reading intervenes in a scholarly trend to read the "I" in "Ossuaries" as Brand herself. Paul Watkins, for example, writes of the "metaphoric constituencies (between Brand and Yasmine)" (130), between "the narrator (who is very possibly a version of Brand herself) and Yasmine, who take turns soloing over each 'Ossuary'" (127). But in this reading, Yasmine, narrated in the third person, does not get a turn soloing. Nolan tries to pursue the same reading for both *Ossuaries* and *Inventory* in his interview with Brand. As Nolan explains, Brand's characters are frequently considered to be "extensions or hyperboles" of herself. Brand responds to this suggestion with "are you kidding?" In reaction to Brand's incredulous reply, Nolan must conclude that, though so many readers "have assumed a closer connection," this assumption must be "some fallacy."

Though I will contrast our stances on *Ossuaries'* overall affective outcome, Anne Quema gives a reading closer to my own in terms of *Ossuaries'* dual perspective. For her, the split between "I" and "she" is the split between subject and object caused by the force of trauma

(np). But, in the third-person narrative, she argues, "we are not dealing with a subject somatically enacting a verbally unrepresentable
trauma. Instead, we are dealing with the verbalization of a political
urgency whereby the trope of hysteria signifies the distress of the body
politic." Quema comes to contrast this trauma and trope of hysteria
with calmness. I will return to Quema's argument later, but will note
immediately that *Ossuaries* does not propose calmness as the valued
opposite to trauma, hysteria, or systemic distress. The poem examines
societal structures, "the invisible architecture" in which Yasmine and
her friends "tried to be calm" (12). There is no sense that being calm
would be a desirable response to this system. The first pages of *Ossuaries* detail Yasmine's experience of a life in which her "every waking
was incarcerated" (10). Later, Yasmine describes her acceptance of her
vulnerability: "I must confess, I must, that early on / it was nothing
to me, believe me, / you could dip your dingy hand in my chest" (47).
The social holding as incarceration is linked to the opened body that
holds the intimate intrusion. The attempt "to be calm" involves making intrusion "nothing." Yasmine "confess[es]" this early emotion as a
troubling one; contrary to Quema's position, I believe that, in *Ossuaries*, it is calm that most urgently signifies distress.

   Brand's long poem examines the interrelation of an imprisoning
social structure, the vulnerable structures of individual bodies, and
the structure of witness. Yasmine experiences a sense of the generalization of her person, depicted through the stripping of her body to a
depersonalized structure:

   here I am,
   down to the last organ and happy to be there,
   tired with it, exhausted to be there, bone dry

   without walls, without embrasures, no height at all,
   scatter bones, losing all relation to myself,
   reified, common really, common the powdery skulls (48)

Relation emerges as a central concern through the poem's depiction of
social and bodily structures. The dismantling of the skeletal structure

"without walls, without embrasures" (no enclosure and no opening) is a loss of self-relation. This lack of relation is "reified," made concrete, made into an actual lived structure that is as "common" as the skulls broken to powder within it. Though "here I am" asserts presence, the lack of walls and the scattered bones indicate displacement, as does the division implicit in the disjunct between "*here* I am" and "happy to be *there*." Yasmine's deictic self-assertion is countered by her displacement from herself into the skeletal social structure. She suggests that because she has been stripped to her last organ – truncated with no height, dry with no blood and flesh – she has been reduced to that common structure. She knows that her skeleton is not her own because she can see it holding up this social system.

As in Krog's "Country of grief and grace" and Heaney's "Bone Dreams," Brand's *Ossuaries* understands this relational system by way of language and articulation. For Yasmine, "each bone has its lost dialect now, / untranslatable though I had so many languages" (50). A wandering character with many literal languages, Yasmine feels speechless at this foundational bone-level in her dislocation from community, or more accurately, her sense of community as dislocation: "I was waiting to throw my limbs on the pile, / the mounds of disarticulated femurs and radii" (49). While this disarticulation refers to the disjointed body, it also suggests a speaker who finds herself speechless, a condition represented in a poem whose structure requires that it articulates Yasmine in the third person as often as she speaks for herself.

At the same time, the vulnerably displayed bones speak a language, testifying to the violence of a society that breaks down its internal relationships:

who would mistake these wounds,
who call these declarations nothing,
these tender anatomies

love should meet them, nothing short,
these broken heads and propitiatory arms,
clean love should meet them (85)

As in Krog's "Country of grief and grace," voice – "these declarations" – moves across connective space. Across the same space, affect, as "clean love" – a love somehow uncontaminated by the structure it moves in – "should meet them" without falling "short." *Ossuaries* calls for the intersection of affect, voice, and wound; as in Krog's poem, it imagines witness as physical contiguity and imagines a future structure that might emerge through the contiguity of affect and voice in witnessing. The "broken heads" recall the skull Heaney's speaker holds and the mole's head he blows on, while the "propitiatory arms" recall the way Krog's "we" must hold their bleeding country between them while feeling, as Garman puts it, "guilt and contrition" (198). In Heaney's, Krog's, and Brand's poems there are these "tender anatomies," the unwrapped skeletons, whose "wounds" call for "nothing short" of the space of communication of the witness poem across which love can "meet" the disarticulated.

II

Each section of Brand's collection is titled as a numbered "Ossuary." While this title gives a sense, through the idea of the skeletal, of the structural focus I have been considering, "ossuary" can also signify figuratively as "a mental or spiritual charnel house" (OED). In this sense, the title suggests commemoration. Commemoration is another kind of meeting: remembering through public celebration brings individuals together while bringing the significance of the past into the present's meaning. Quema reads *Ossuaries* to be "poised between carnage and commemoration." Brand's lines about clean love come from Ossuary XI, a section dedicated to the ekphrastic reading of African-American artist Jacob Lawrence's *War Series*. Quema connects love and commemoration in her reading of the ekphrastic inclusion of Lawrence's paintings: "In a mythopoetic gesture, Yasmine attributes the origins of Lawrence's art to Venus, planet of love: 'he lifts these paintings from their ultraviolet vats, / from the Venusian winds that blow only west' (81)." Yet these lines seem to refer not to the mythic idea of love but to the literal planet and its sulphuric acid-whipping winds. This literal reading of the Venusian winds aligns with Ossuary XI's "dense clouds of carbon" (82) and "wind whiffing through / ribs" (84).

For Quema, though, this Ossuary's ekphrasis is "the occasion for a history of affect that creates a sense of commemoration and a soft hope for release from gravity," a difference from other sections of the long poem that is "conveyed by the fluidity and calm of the tercets." Quema's reading of commemoration is more optimistic than *Ossuaries* allows. Being met by love would not be an escape; clean love is merely that which does not "call these declarations nothing." Commemoration and love are forms of witness, and witness is not a solution to pain and suffering (as much as it is an essential first step to any possible solution). Getting off Earth to Venus is not an escape from gravity and painful reality, but a realization of the universality of the painful chemical winds. I do not find the calm Quema references in this Ossuary's barbed wire imagery (87), in its "povertous dowries" and "scapegoat necklaces" (86), in the "last gushes" and the "gauze and blood" (85), or in the cacophony of its arm "electrified and supplicant, spiked" (85). Quema concludes that "Ossuary XI is suspended beyond the time of necropolitical trauma and the space of gravity" in a "mythopoeic time for reprieve." Yet "a body out of time" is a body "'reported missing' again" (86). Being out of time is no mythopoeic reprieve; it is to be "moving at a constant angle" (86) in "flights impossible to correct" in "reports" that "reach no one" (87). Thus, the "hope behind this wire" that "gravity must give up its hold on us" is only the hope of going missing (88). Indeed, this gravity would "unhook our hearts" and leave "us [...] beyond the punishments [...] of our own skeletons" (88); the hope is only to go missing from the body in the way Yasmine is disarticulated from her own story. Moreover, this Ossuary's final hope is for a disappearance from predators effected by their own bodies in the "here," not the beyond (or for the disappearance of the predators themselves):

here we morph as twig and ice and bark
and butterfly, weed and spider, vespids,
hoping against predators

convergent mimesis, all means,
stand still and hope it passes, the diatonic,
ragged plumage of our disappearances (89)

What they hope passes is ambiguous: "it" might be the predators or
their disappearances. Either way, disappearing is a function of preda-
tion, and disappearing into the line break is the best hope that they
have. With the "diatonic" plumage, no notes come from outside of this
scale: this morphing is no escape into something new. The morphing
into small creatures that mimic natural elements to blend into their
surroundings is not mythic hope, but the desperate hope for survival.[3]

While Quema argues that the "mythopoeic time for reprieve" is
made possible through ekphrasis, I argue that ekphrasis does not
bring a reprieve from reality but instead brings a surplus of meaning
equal to a surplus of affect. For Quema, *Ossuaries* offers a "poetics
of rupture" in which

> the tercets hurtle with the velocity of what Sara Ahmed describes
> as a surplus of affect (45). While language is used to upstage
> the violence of biometrics and its necropolitical effects, it is also
> caught in the vortex of this political violence whose intensity
> and power derive from an economy of exchange among bodies,
> nature, texts, and readers. Manifesting a necropolitical uncon-
> scious, hysteria is this surplus of affect.

For Quema, hysteria is the surplus of affect deriving from a system
of political violence that the language both reflects and "upstage[s]"
with its own "velocity." Since the hysterical speed of the poetic lines
is fuelled by this systemic violence, Quema argues that it is only when
the hysteria is calmed through ekphrasis that there is a reprieve in
the poem. This reading depends on a negative reading of *Ossuaries'*
surplus affect. Quema writes,

> A statement such as "you will discover, as I, / that verbs are a
> tragedy, a bleeding cliffside, explosions" (14) makes violence a
> trope of poetic address and hits at the very core of the belief in

redemption through poetry. Thus, circulating among the tercets, between the "I" and the "she" sections, bodies and things, and Yasmine and readers, necropolitical violence accumulates surplus.

There is no need to disbelieve the power of poetry if "verbs are a tragedy" because verbs alone do not comprise poetry. I read this line to suggest instead that action is tragedy, doing anything, including writing poetry, is tragedy; for Yasmine, living itself is tragic. Further, Yasmine's account of her own experience does not necessarily add to the surplus of violence in the world simply because she does not believe her own actions will be redemptive. Yasmine's surplus affect is not equivalent to (the same as) the violence she reacts to, even if it is equivalent to (comparable to) it in vigour. I find a dangerous slippage in reading affect that does not redeem violence as affect that contributes to that violence. Quema undermines Yasmine's survival when she writes that "each Ossuary undergoes the tension between the pressure of trauma and the mere metonymic push to the next line in search of meaning." In fact, the metonymic push onward might be a significant reaction to violence (not a "mere" continuance). Yasmine's living despite the tragedy of it is not "mere." It is precisely the surplus affect that is Yasmine's response to the systems of meaningless violence she lives within, and to mistake that as the "mere" push onwards is to "call these declarations nothing." The surplus affect is itself meaningful.

Thus, Quema's privileging of calmness comes through the depreciation of surplus affect. Yet ekphrasis seems to me aligned with surplus; the power of ekphrasis is in the surplus between the original and the re-creation in a new form. Ossuary V ends with Yasmine's reflection on Jose Villegas Cordero's "Lucia Monti." For Yasmine, the painting works by "summing up // the black ages before her, / gleaming beyond / the aesthetic of sin and purgatory" (51). The painting breaks its aesthetic structure and tells history. The appositive connection between these ideas makes it unclear if the one causes the other, but there is at least a relationship between aesthetic structures and historical records. Ekphrasis is "gleaming beyond" one structure to say again the meaning. Yasmine's last lines in this Ossuary ask, "will my bones glitter beyond these ages, / will they burn beyond the photographs' / crude economy" (51). She looks for the surplus of the photograph, an aesthetic of her age. She looks to ekphrasis to hope for her own commemorative potential; she does not hope to save her bones, but to have them glitter in order to produce surplus in new aesthetic structures in the future. The hope of ekphrastic commemoration is that new, alternative, or additional aesthetic structures might bring opportunities for further affect that keeps alive the memory of past pain.

In *Ossuaries*, witnessing means the creation of commemorative relationships. Considering Lawrence's paintings, Yasmine says:

> if we could return through this war, any war,
> as if it were we who needed redemption,
> instead of this big world, our ossuary
>
> so brightly clad, almost heroic, almost dead,
> the celebratory waiting, the waiting,
> the smell of wounds (82)

Yasmine expresses the witnessing relationship between viewer and commemorative artwork as "celebratory waiting." As both "a calling to remembrance" and a "public celebration" (OED), "commemoration" captures the making-public involved in celebration as well as the individual mental state of waiting with memories. Commemoration incorporates public attention to affective relationships and personal time for remembering one's place within them. Witness poetry and commemoration are about "the celebratory waiting" and "the smell of wounds"; these poems are ossuaries because they are spaces for response to unredeemed violence.

In *Ossuaries*, Yasmine's witness is commemorative representation, much like the painting to which it alludes. This commemoration is associated with the skeletal in *Ossuaries'* last lines:

> so here we lie in our bare arms,
> here the ribs for a good basket, a cage,
> the imperishable mandible, the rhetorical metatarsals

the hip's alertness, the skull's electricity
firing, the lit cigarette tip of the backbone
leans for its toxic caresses

here we lie in folds, collected stones
in the museum of spectacles,
our limbs displayed, fract and soluble

were this a painting, it would combust canvases,
this lunate pebble, this splintered phalanx,
I can hardly hold their sincere explosions (124)

The "ribs for a good basket" sound like a container that holds safe; the condition of lying "in our bare arms" takes on a positive intimate quality. But these ribs are also "a cage" that recalls the vulnerable lives Yasmine describes in terms of imprisonment. The condition of being within is ambiguous in this passage. Yasmine's assertion that "here we lie in folds" adds to the uncertain meaning of these images. Folds could mean the ground, pens for domestic animals, or the bent and entwined bodies of the vulnerable. As "the dwelling-place" that is the surface of the earth (OED), "folds" indicates a multiple and global foundation of relationality. In contrast, lying in animal pens suggests the earlier-invoked images of an imprisoning depersonalization. These meanings come together in the bending together of bodies, of bodies making their own folds, an intimate entwining premised on mutual vulnerability to "toxic caresses." Yet, despite the toxicity of the condition, the descriptions of the itemized pieces of skeleton suggest continuance. In "Bone Memory in Dionne Brand's *Ossuaries*," Tanis MacDonald writes, "The metatarsal bones are the bones of the foot that are most anatomically disposed to be broken in what is known in medical discourse as a stress fracture" (106). Here, the stressed-out bone is "rhetorical," suggesting some power to articulate the potential and actual fractures. Perhaps there is some hope in these last lines that the declarations will not be nothing. Or perhaps these ossuaries put stress on rhetorical structures that mistake the wounds. The "fract and soluble" seems aligned here with bones that are "imperishable," with bones' "alertness" and their "electricity firing." These bones are "in the museum of spectacles" but the "sincere explosions" might break or dissolve that structure, not themselves.

These explosions recall Cordero's painting that gets outside of its own aesthetic, ideological, and thematic system. In these final lines, it is only a conditional scenario – "were this a painting" – in which they would break the representational form of spectacle by "combust[ing] canvases." But the fact that these individuals leading vulnerable lives would explode their structures if those structures were artistic suggests an ekphrastic hope for new structures of witnessing. Replicating the shifting speaker position at the level of the poem as a whole, Yasmine shifts perspectives from the inside ("we") to a position of external witness ("their") and, as witness, Yasmine "can hardly hold their sincere explosions." Yasmine's state of hardly holding suggests that "they" continue to carry their own meaning in excess of how they are represented. The lack of final punctuation leaves their "sincere explosions" unheld and leaves readers with questions about what varieties of holding, hardly holding, and not holding occur in witness and ekphrastic witness.

In her acknowledgments for *A Map to the Door of No Return*, Brand lists Derek Walcott as one of the poets to whom she is "particularly indebted." Brand's ekphrastic engagement with the legacies of colonisation and slavery might be usefully considered in relation to the ekphrastic techniques Walcott uses to explore artistic and historical structures in "Ruins of a Great House." In "A Trans-Atlantic Vandal: Omeros and the Ekphrastic Counter-monument," Renae L. Mitchell argues that in *Omeros* Walcott uses ekphrasis to create a poetic counter-monument opposing colonial buildings. Mitchell explains, "The grandiose monument (and all it represents) is, in *Omeros*, reduced to the 'sum of its parts'" (158). In contrast, in Walcott's ubiquitously anthologized "Ruins of a Great House," the manor, already reduced to parts by time, is explored as *more* than the sum of its parts. Indeed, it is the main thrust of the poem that the manor's parts add up to a house that is in turn only a single part of the "leprosy of Empire" (10). In a similar sense, while the manor's skeleton, "[s]tones only" (1), are the parts, the "bone / Of some dead animal or human thing" cannot be merely counted among the "disjecta membra" to add up again to the house (16–17, 1).

Indeed, the contiguity of the ruins add up to one house, to the violence it authorized, to the larger system of slavery and colonization, and to the nation of England with its historical cultural output. Thus, the ruins occur as part of the speaker's exploration of the metonymic connection of the empire's literary achievement to its colonial violence. In "Metaphor and Metonymy in Derek Walcott's Poetry," Roberta Cimarosti finds a metonymic strategy across Walcott's work which, she explains, promotes a sense of expression as arbitrary and decentred: "Metonymy is contiguity, difference and continual diachronic shifts of ideological 'centres', whose ideals and momentary absolutes are conceived as continually 'displaced' within the enormous, multi-dimensional, multi-cultural human existence" (153). The metonymical displacements Cimarosti finds in Walcott's corpus are a different expression of the line by Donne ending Walcott's poem: "'as well as if a manor of thy friend's'" (51). The violence of colonization and slavery affects all of humankind; a loss somewhere reduces all everywhere. By the same logic, any achievement is part of the "enormous" (to use Cimarosti's word) human condition. The speaker can feel compassion for the colonial power because "Albion too was once / A colony like ours" (44–5), and, at the same time, he need not dismiss Britain's literary creations as merely products of violence.

Though "[a]ll in compassion ends," this conclusion arrives "[s]o differently from what the heart arranged" (49–50). The speaker's compassion is surplus to the structure of feeling that history had built in him. He finds this surplus feeling by exploring the great house's landscape to find more than what is there; he adds the empire's poetry to the ruins' lawn. The fragments of literature create a kind of montage: the metaphoric "green fields" and "happy groves" of William Blake's "Night" as well as the "[p]art of the continent, piece of the main" and the other manor of John Donne's "Meditation XVII" become pieced together as a whole that also is more than the sum of these parts. Jean Antoine-Dunne considers filmic montage in work by Caribbean poets, including Walcott, who have "made clear statements about their affiliation to filmmaking" (592) because film "is at the centre of twentieth-century debates about the ideological power of the visual" (592). Montage works through contiguity. For Antoine-Dunne, "Fragmentation becomes both an ideological tool and an aesthetic practice" (594). Walcott's use of ekphrastic montage to describe the ruins and their yard not only serves his critique of empire but also his concluding compassion: the metonymic movement between the ruins, the bone, and the pieces of poetry lead to the surplus of compassion.

"Ruins of a Great House" commemorates a particular historical violence and its ongoing effects without rooting Caribbean culture in or limiting it to that violence. The poem participates in the surplus of humanity or the web of cultural interrelations that Cimarosti argues Walcott evokes through his metonymical strategies. It is the metonymical chain connecting his speaker's experience of living with the history of enslavement into the larger experience of being human that allows his speaker the surplus of compassion. In his *Paris Review* interview with Edward Hirsh, Walcott explains, "what I am saying is to take in the fact of slavery, if you're capable of it, without bitterness, because bitterness is going to lead to the fatality of thinking in terms of revenge" (np). He continues, "It is not because one wishes to forget; on the contrary, you accept it as much as anybody accepts a wound as being a part of his body. But this doesn't mean that you nurse it all your life." Though the speaker in "Ruins of a Great House" is "[a]baze with rage" (41), it is not all-consuming; the "coal of my compassion" can still fight to be its own fire (43).

Walcott's poem aligns well with the previously mentioned image in the final lines of Brand's *Ossuaries*: "here we lie in our bare arms." We are a tangle of mutual, if inequitably distributed, vulnerability. Like the empire's ruins ekphrastically registered in "Ruins of a Great House," Brand's "toxic caresses" would – if they were a painting, if this poem could, in an act of reverse-ekphrasis, create the painting – "combust canvases." It is the possibility that these toxic caresses might exceed their structure that allows "sincere explosions." Sincerity is a structural surplus somewhat equivalent to Walcott's coal of compassion. Both compassion and sincerity come through surplus in their respective poems. Both reactions contain the possibility of burning, but only the possibility: the sincerity is conditional ("were this a painting") and, unlike the ablaze rage, compassion is the fuel for a fire still fighting to ignite. Though the end of Walcott's poem, which stresses compassion's potential, is more optimistic than Brand's poem's conditionally explosive sincerity, even *Ossuaries* suggests the possibility that a form of compassion is inherent in entangled vulnerability. Certainly, this is no idealized compassion and it, perhaps more than that in "Ruins of a Great House," finds use for bitterness. Yet *Ossuaries'* conclusion offers compassion stripped to its most basic skeleton: feeling along with another, as well as if a bone of thy friend's.

We can continue exploring the relationship between witness and ekphrasis by returning to Heaney. In *Poetry and Responsibility*, Neil Corcoran considers ekphrasis's significant presence in Heaney's work. Corcoran provides a summative analysis of Heaney's ekphrastic poems, including the "Two Poems in Dedication" that open *North* (120–4), a collection that is ekphrastic on the whole as the poems "scrutinize various objects into the precisions of an appropriately spare language" (121). These objects are often human skeletons, and it is presumably the sparseness of that object that warrants a bone-thin language. Corcoran reads this skeletal ekphrasis as Heaney's engagement with his position as a witnessing poet:

> The ekphrastic moments of *North* all put their weight on Heaney's figuration of himself as an "artful voyeur" in "Punishment"; and, beyond its immediate context in that poem, the phrase may do duty for the ethical awkwardness inevitable in some forms of ekphrasis too. The varied critical reception of the bog poems strongly suggests that these poems give rise, of their very nature, to awkward ethical issues. These are continuous, in fact, with those raised by the agonistic relationship between writing and image in ekphrasis more generally. (122)

Such a relationship is central to "The Digging Skeleton *After Baudelaire*." Like "Bone Dreams," this poem appears in *North*, a collection

Brian Donnelly describes as "concerned primarily with understanding imaginatively the North of Ireland in relation to the bloody, violent history of northern Europe" (246). The poem is a remake – "to remake" is Heaney's term for what he does in his English versions of poems originally in other languages (Donnelley 254n3) – of Baudelaire's "Le Squelette Laboureur," an ekphrastic meditation on anatomical plates. Donnelly finds one difference between the original poem and Heaney's version: "For Baudelaire these skeletons are images of an existential horror upon which he gazes in quizzical fascination; for Heaney they are exemplary figures of dispossession. They are the mute sufferers – 'my patient ones' – and he is their witness" (248). Heaney's poem imagines the skeletons' perspective: "Some traitor breath / Revives our clay" (II.16–17). Though the skeletons ostensibly speak from the anatomical plate, their words appear within this poem; the "traitor breath" that makes them suffer again in death may be the poet's. Ekphrasis takes the image – static, stuck in time – and gives it motion and life through words; these skeletons may have been painfully revived by poetic description. Heaney's poem considers the poet's writing in relation to the skeletons' digging. This is a comparison he famously makes in his early poem "Digging," but here the involuntary digging is not made equivalent to an art-form. "The Digging Skeleton" explores the power relations witness poetry involves, and it suggests that the form has intrusive elements that cannot be ignored.

This poem implicitly considers the poet's role, separately from the speaker's role, in poetic witnessing. Donnelly argues that, though "The Digging Skeleton" is "a poem not much noticed by readers" (246), "its nightmare vision and its rhetoric of pity" (249) make it significant for understanding Heaney's "need to bear witness" (251). For Donnelly, the poem "may be read as a signature piece that reveals ways of seeing and feeling that characterize some of the more celebrated lyrics in *North*" and is indeed "informed by the emotional and moral pressures that lie behind much of the poetry that he wrote during the 1970s" (247). Yet this "signature piece" is a version of a poem by Baudelaire. Heaney's "signature" here follows another's form, image, and idea. Thus, a poem characteristic of Heaney's witness derives from another's "quizzical fascination" – that is, from a different context of looking. What is the significance of the surplus of ekphrasis itself (re-imagining what has already been imagined)? What is the additional significance of the surplus of the doubled ekphrasis between Baudelaire's and Heaney's poems? Moreover, what is the significance of the expanded surplus of the "very rich socializing of the lyric voice" Corcoran finds connecting Heaney to other artists in his ekphrastic poetry (120)? This socializing connectivity counters the impulse to collapse speaker and poet. With these varying artistic contexts at play, witness poetry is more clearly an aesthetic process not fully accounted for by a poet's direct relationship to the object under study.

Heaney's jacket image – a portrait of Heaney painted by Edward McGuire – included in *North* raises this issue of the poet's relationship to the poetry. Corcoran recounts the unusual situation of *North*'s inclusion of an author portrait since the publisher, Faber, had until that time "never featured author photographs or jacket art" (Heaney qtd. in Corcoran 122). Corcoran explains that Edward McGuire's "now well-known image seems exceptionally well attuned to the poetic persona implicit in the volume's many uses of the first person singular, although it was presumably completed before the poems were actually written" (122). Even further, Corcoran argues, "McGuire's portrait is, superbly, a representation of Seamus Heaney as one of his own *North* poems" (123) and "makes its subject an icon" (123).

Yet, in a later poem, Heaney troubles this collapse of portrait, person, and poem. Corcoran explains, "In 'A Basket of Chestnuts' in *Seeing Things* Heaney revisits the portrait" (123), considering a basket of chestnuts that was present at the sitting for the painting but not finally included. For Corcoran, this poem is

a very peculiar form of ekphrasis. "A Basket of Chestnuts" is both an ekphrastic poem by a poet on his own portrait and a poem about a painting that does not exist. Summoning the idea of an alternative composition, the poem holds the relationship between writing and painting in an admiring but almost awkward tension.

It has, in a way endemic to ekphrasis, both a genuine complementarity and a competitive edge. The poem is tribute and displacement; and since it is a self-representation that is being displaced, the competition is not only with the painter but with an earlier self and poet too. (124)

I argue, however, that the competitive edge is not with this earlier self; rather, the competition is with the earlier self-as-icon that has become symbolic of the poet as he is collapsed into his own speakers.

The poem opens on the speaker describing "a giddy strange assistance / That happens when you swing a loaded basket" (1–2): "The lightness of the thing seems to diminish / The actual weight of what's being hoisted in it" (3–4). The loaded basket becomes "the thing," an imprecise word that, in the context of this poem's precision, emphasizes the basket as a symbol that can be replaced by other meaning. The assistance of the swinging basket seems akin to the speaker's imaginative engagement with the bone in "Bone Dreams": "I wind it in // the sling of mind" (I.12–13). Given the ekphrastic situation of "A Basket of Chestnuts," the swinging suggests this imaginative engagement as the writing of what was seen. In the "sling of mind," the thing loses its actual weight as it becomes held by art.

Yet it is the weight, not the lightness, that validates the holder and artist:

For a split second your hands feel unburdened,
Outstripped, dismayed, passed through.
Then just as unexpectedly comes rebound –
Downthrust and comeback ratifying you. (5–8)

Holding the thing's full burden is confirming. The poem suggests that the strange assistance of imagination and artistic representation requires the comeback, a reminder that the artist continues to hold what has been unburdened into art. The literal return of the swinging basket is the "return to a condition, to the memory" or "return to consciousness" that is remaining in relationship to the thing after it has been made art ("come back" OED). When the speaker "recollect[s] this basket full of chestnuts" (9), he remembers the chestnuts but also collects them again to be weighty in his mind. Since this portrait has become an icon of *North*'s witnessing speaker, Heaney's ability to continue to hold what has been made art is a way of not being "outstripped, dismayed, passed through" by the unburdening of artistic representation; as a witness that goes on existing beyond that collection, the speaker in "A Basket of Chestnuts" disrupts the static image and its identification with *North*. Being ratified by the comeback of the basket of chestnuts that was not in the portrait extends the ongoing relationship between the person in the portrait and future witnessing speakers.

In terms of witness poetry, this continued holding of the burden confirms the witness as witness. The witness does not merely represent suffering in poetry and leave the burden behind; turning witness into art may be unburdening but witness entails an ongoing obligation. The "downthrust" of this weight evokes the writing and digging through which suffering in *North* appears and recalls the ethical problem that emerges in "The Digging Skeleton." The poet's writing must be an obligation akin to the skeletons' eternal digging to avoid partaking of artistic practice as an unburdening. Though art helps hold the burden of witness, this help dismays the witness by "seem[ing] to diminish / The actual weight" of what is represented.

These reflections in "A Basket of Chestnuts" on weight and gravity are not isolated in Heaney's career. In *In Gratitude for All the Gifts: Seamus Heaney and Eastern Europe*, Magdalena Kay explains that, for Heaney, "gravity is involuntary yet positive, connected to a sense of mission or artistry, motivated by devotion more than compulsion" (130). He articulates his idea of poetry's ethical valence through this term; Kay notes that Heaney interprets Simone Weil on gravity and grace "so that her idea of balancing these two forces is made comparable to Heaney's notion of redress, 'tilting the scales of reality towards some transcendent equilibrium'" (187). Considering Heaney's Eastern European poetic influences, Kay argues, "what reading Eastern European poets teaches him is that poetry's soteriological function comes about through its discovery of grace even where we were convinced the force of gravity held us in thrall" (201).

Yet, in "A Basket of Chestnuts," this soteriological function seems to come about in quite the opposite way: poetry saves by refusing to unburden us simply because it carries the weight of witness. Witness poetry keeps us in gravity's thrall.

Of course, this gravity is not without grace. The contrast between heavy and light, gravity and grace, recurs throughout the poem. There is an implicit punning in which weightiness enters into relationship with lightness in the senses of brightness and lack of heaviness. The basket holds a "really solid gather-up, all drag / And lustre, opulent and gravid / And golden-bowelled as a moneybag" (10–12). Weight is suggested in "solid," "gravid," "drag," and "golden-bowelled as a moneybag." The reflected light involved in "golden" and "lustre" comes with the heavy plumpness and abundance of "opulent." The chestnuts were present for the painting because they might have been used "[a]s a decoy or a coffer for the light" (22). Thus, the chestnuts represent that which were meant to catch or fake the light. If they had been painted, they would have been holding the light. With the basket, lightness (lack of weight) is "shadow-boost[ing]" (1). More literally meaning an unseen boost helping to hold the chestnuts, "shadow" also suggests the light the chestnuts would have caught; lightness represents lightness. If the chestnuts had been painted, their purpose would be to be light in both senses; their representation would be the helpful boost that unburdens the artist.

The basket of chestnuts, however, was not in the painting, and thus the chestnuts represent a relationship not created in art, something seen in real life but not illustrated. "A Basket of Chestnuts" ultimately suggests that it is representing what was witnessed that creates the ongoing relationship of obligation. What is in the painting is the confirming weight; the absent chestnuts dismayingly unburden the painter:

> What's there is comeback, especially for him.
> In oils and brushwork we are ratified.
> And the basket shines and foxfire chestnuts gleam
> Where he passed through, unburdened and dismayed. (25–8)

It is not making the artistic record of witness that leaves the witness outstripped. Thus, the suggestion in "The Digging Skeleton" that the poet's breath may have culpably revived suffering and made it eternal is countered here by the suggestion that witnessing without some form of testimony to what has been witnessed is also culpable. *North*'s voyeurism, then, produces a heavy burden that, however eased by its onloading into poetry, is an ongoing weight for the voyeur. This weight is the heaviness of ethical responsibility.

In terms of this poem as an ekphrastic mediation on Heaney's portrait, the conclusion further suggests that the painting's static finality may also dismay and unburden Heaney by turning him into a final product, an icon, that can replace the living individual in his relationship with his speakers. While witness must keep going beyond its unburdening into art, Heaney's relationship to his art cannot be encapsulated by the art's "shadow-boost." The basket of chestnuts "wasn't in the picture and is not" (24). This specification that the basket still "is not" in the picture emphasizes the static nature of the portrait as compared to the dynamic change this poem features in the swinging of the basket. There is something missing from the portrait that has come to stand in for Heaney, particularly Heaney as witness. What is missing is the dynamism that allows the portrait to present a person in ongoing relationship with his poems rather than an icon that is equivalent to his poems. This poem's ekphrastic engagement reintroduces that dynamism.

III

This discussion has thus far made three things clear: (1) skeletons feature significantly in witness poetry to represent structural connections between art and its subjects; (2) these skeletal explorations, because they concern the structure of the poem and its points of connection to the outside world, sometimes offer ways to respond to the collapse of speaker and poet so problematic in witness poetry's reception; and (3) ekphrasis is one strategy by which poets use skeletons as an image of witness and an image of structural exploration. Ekphrastic reflection on human skeletons – as suffering or dead people, depicted in art or as actual remains – raises questions about the ethics of looking at and telling about other peoples' deaths. To consider such questions further, I turn to a short film which features bones literally becoming art: Jan Švankmajer's 1970 short film *Kostnice (The Ossuary)*. As Jan Uhde explains in "The Bare Bones of Horror," *Kostnice* documents the Sedlec Ossuary. In 1870, František Rint completed his decade-long project: using the ossuary's thousands of skeletons to create "fascinating displays of shapes and objects, including skull pyramids, crosses, a monstrance and a chandelier containing every bone of the human body" (np). While *Kostnice* is not, as is witness poetry, engaged with suffering,[4] it does address artistic response to human vulnerability. As the official website states, "The Sedlec Ossuary is artistically decorated by more than 40,000 human skeletons" (np). Rint "was appointed to place the bones in order" (np). As these decorations speak to art's role in organizing the world into comprehensible forms, the arrangements of these bones operate as reflections on human meaning. But putting "bones in order" signifies differently than making bones into decorations or "fascinating artistic works" (np). The solemnity attached to human remains makes the decorations in *Kostnice* particularly suited to an interrogation of the process of turning life (or death) into art.

The film represents this bone art in an ekphrastic-proximate approach by pairing its visuals with a poem that speaks to the ethics of the aesthetic situation. While the film considers witness and art through a similar strategy to the ekphrasis I have been discussing in witness poetry, it also works through the metonymic logic I have been considering in this book. Ernesto Laclau includes a consideration of filmic metonymy in "Articulation and the Limits of Metaphor": "[Joan] Copjec, in her film studies, has shown how close-ups are not a part within the whole, but a part that functions as the very condition of the whole, as its name, leading to that contamination between particularity and totality that, as we have seen, is at the heart of all tropological movement" (66). Švankmajer's film uses an individual skull in a repeated close-up to suggest that witnessing this skeleton head has something to do with witnessing in art more broadly; the skull clearly does not stand for all the bones as one whole since they come from multiple dead bodies, but instead suggests that this insistent and intrusive encounter with the single skull is associated with the condition of witnessing. This skull makes the same demand as the arrangements of bones do – the response of the witness – but it makes that demand through the reminder of the particular death within the larger framework of artistic representation.

In this chapter, I have been considering witness poetry's skeletal images as they signify an interest in relationship, primarily between speakers as witnesses and those whom they witness. I have also been considering the relationship between poetry and its poets. In the film, the poem is made analogous to the crypt, and Jacques Prévert's poem, sung over the images of bones made art, works as a re-presentation of the crypt-as-art, bringing to the fore the question of the artist's role in making art. My study of skeletons and crypts as relational images is also a study of encryption as it pertains to indexical relationships between artists and their art.

I can return, then, to Shoshana Felman's comments about Claude Lanzmann's *Shoah* to explore her idea of the artist's signature in relation to *Kostnice*'s engagement with signatures in the crypt and the poem. In Felman's commentary on Lanzmann's *Shoah*, she obscures Lanzmann's shaping role as artist by considering his signature to be a voiceless foundation for other voices to speak from without his artistic mediation. She understands Lanzmann through three roles,

> as the *narrator* of the film (and the signatory – the first person – of the script), as the *interviewer* of the witnesses (the solicitor and receiver of the testimonies) and as the *inquirer* (the artist as the subject of a quest concerning what the testimonies testify to; the figure of the witness as a questioner, and of the asker not merely as the factual investigator but as the bearer of the film's philosophical address and inquiry). (216)

Strangely, Felman understands the film to be signed not by the artist – "the figure of the witness" who is concerned with deeper meaning and who bears responsibility for the film's address and inquiry – but by the narrator. Lanzmann, "the 'I' of the narrator, of the signatory of the film, has no voice: the opening is projected on the screen as the silent text of a mute script, as the narrative voice-over of a *writing with no voice*" (217). This assumption, that the first person of the text is the signatory, mirrors the assumption that the speaker is the signatory of the lyric poem. It is through such an understanding that Felman can argue, as I discuss in my first chapter, that Simon Srebnik's voice signs itself such that the witness's voice can be valorized at the expense of the witness himself. Whether with Srebnik or with Lanzmann, Felman seeks for the film to be signed by silence.

Moreover, she understands film itself to be literally witnessing in a way that obscures the actual function of film as art. Lanzmann's project, Felman argues, is "to bring the darkness of the inside to the physical light of the outside. to [*sic*] literally and effectively *narrate the Holocaust in light*" (239). Since the darkness that the film's light would be penetrating is metaphorical, it seems unnecessary to emphasize the light's physical, literal nature. Felman is referring, as her footnote explains, to the film's medium: "The expression is alluding to George Wilson's description of the very art of film" (239n20). She argues that the film's "heart of darkness is revealed as utterly unknown and perhaps unknowable. The film's role, however, is to physically *shed light*" (239n19). Felman seems to suggest that the metaphorical dark can only be dispelled by the literal light of this particular material form. Is "the very art of film" the only art that can truly witness? Though Felman's other contributions to *Testimony* (focusing mainly on literary texts) do not suggest so, this privileging of the film's materiality mirrors the privileging of literal traces in witness poetry.

In her chapter, Felman privileges film's ability to witness over "writing's impossibility": "Film would thus seem to be the very medium which accommodates the simultaneous multiplicity of levels and directions, a medium that can visually *inscribe* – and cinematically bear witness to – *the very impossibility of writing*. The film is not merely an overcoming of an actual impossibility, but specifically, a testimony to it" (248). Yet the proof she offers for writing's impossibility is that Lanzmann was not able to complete a book on the subject, an inability he does not, in the quotation she cites, attribute to the medium: "The questions which are unresolved in the book are solved in the film, but not on the same level ... I had to grow up and there are questions that ... become meaningless in the course of life ... You give the answers, but on another level" (248). Lanzmann attributes this other level to his personal maturation, not to the artistic form. Regardless of such evidence, Felman is committed throughout her text to literality, materiality, and concrete actuality that nevertheless demonstrate silence, impossibility, and absence. This is the approach through which art can be understood as signed by literal traces of trauma rather than by an artist. In contrast, *Kostnice* explores what it means to be a witness through literal human remains – the traces the dead leave – and through artfulness – what happens when literal material remains are turned into art.

Švankmajer's film is initially concerned with movement into relationship. The opening scene moves down a road of interlocked stones. Contrasting this forward motion, the camera focuses on the circling of bicycle pedals. Of course, this circling is also in forward motion itself and is the cause of that motion. When the ossuary eventually appears, its relationship to viewers has been determined as multi-connected through the contiguity of the road's stones, the implied bi-directionality of a road, the forward momentum of the bike, the causal circularity of the pedals. The camera brings us into the ossuary, but only through erratic flicking between shots, and after a revolving shot of the stationary church. The disruptions to direction require viewers to resituate themselves in relation to the connections between the images depicted, to consider the linear as it derives from the circular or the static as it exists unnoticeably in the rapidly shifting. The camera moves similarly inside the ossuary; as Uhde explains, "The film-maker employs elaborate, contrast-rich editing, alternating static images and leisurely camera pans with bursts of rapid-montage, swish-pans and tilts" (np). In these techniques, Švankmajer foregrounds the film's changeful relational structure.

The opening scenes further invoke relationship texturally. Many shots begin from afar and zoom into textured detail, demonstrating the shift in significance existing at different degrees of proximity. The film's images of collection work similarly. Before entering the ossuary, the film shows buttons in jars, piles of shells, and doll pieces. These collections suggest the interaction of fragmentation and collectivity, and foreshadow the collection of human bones. These initial collections – the skeletons of underwater creatures and the broken bodies of toys made in the human image – prime viewers to consider the individual elements in the collective, to see each bone in the ossuary as a fragment of an individual. The buttons, a symbol of connection, prepare viewers to understand the bones also in recombination as an artistic collectivity. In the shifting relationships of direction and focus, *Kostnice* privileges the intersections of registers of meaning.

Švankmajer's inclusion of Jacques Prévert's poem "Pour faire le portrait d'un oiseau" ("To Paint the Portrait of a Bird") connects artistic creation to the film's concern with relationship. As the title suggests, the poem provides instructions for creating a work of art. To make a painting of a bird, "Paint first a cage / with the door open" (1–2). The creator's agency is in making this structure. In contrast, for the bird to arrive, one must "say nothing / don't move" (14–15) and "wait / wait years if need be" (20–1). The creator has control over the cage – the arrangement that holds the subject – but not over whether its subject exists within it. In relation to the bone-ornaments with which this poem is paired, these instructions suggest how to navigate art that is also witness to human vulnerability. For witness-art, the carrying over of meaning occurs through the index-ical witnessing that connects the artwork to the world. It is in the relationship between carrying (from world to poem) and holding (the awareness of art's structures) that something meaningful exists. If the bird sings, the painted cage holds artistic expression and spirit:

> wait until the bird decides to sing
> If the bird does not sing
> that's a bad sign
> A sign the painting is no good
> but if it sings that's a good sign
> a sign you can sign (40–5)

"Sign" here is a mark of significance as well as the mark of the artist.[5] In *Kostnice*, Rint's signature is built out of bones into the ossuary wall. This official signature is juxtaposed with vandals' signatures on the bones themselves. *Kostnice* suggests that the two sorts of signing – authoritative and subversive – are aligned: both are the signing of a name to another's body. Art that expresses an intimacy with another's vulnerability risks exploitation. The artist's signature indicates that he speaks through the material remnants of others' deaths.

It is the indexical relationship between artist and creation that is potentially concealed or encrypted in art (or concealed by certain readings of art). This cause and effect connection is implicit in the fact of art (an art-object exists because someone made it). But the precise nature of this relationship may be less obvious. In poems dedicated to a family member, the poet's relationship to his or her poem is to some extent incorporated openly into that poem. In the creation of a painting in Prévert's poem and in Rint's bone-decorations, the relationships between the art and the artist are hidden or rearranged. In the poem, the painted-out cage is the relationship between bird (the spirit of the art) and artist. The cage is the artist's way of holding the bird. As a sign of that relation, the cage indexically links the painting to the painter's waiting for the bird to arrive. Painted out, the conditions of artistic production are erased; the cage that depicted the artist's waiting relationship to the art's meaningfulness is no longer clearly available in the painting. The painter's signature, and the conditions under which he could sign the painting, becomes of significance beyond marking the painting as his own, or, rather, marking the painting as his own becomes significant for how the painting might mean. In witness-art, this relationship has ethical significance. It is the artist's relationship to witness that underpins and shapes an artwork's function as witness. A primary task of reading witness poetry, then, is to establish the poet's relationship to witness insofar as this relationship is evidenced within the poem.

In his collection *O Earth, Wait for Me* (1984), Frank Chipasula investigates such a relationship in Heaney's poetry in a poem he dedicates to Heaney. "Double Song: *for Seamus Heaney*" has two side-by-side columns, the first directing "you" (presumably Heaney) to enter the forest and the second directing "you" to leave the forest. When the poet enters the forest, "A little birdsong / threatens / to burst out / of your heart / caged as a bird" (I.3–7). In the next column, when the poet leaves the forest, "A little river / struggles / to break out / of the barbed trees / whose roots drink blood / and / flow like a bulbous / song" (II.3–10). If the forest is the reality the poet witnesses, the birdsong (the heart's song) is the responding art that seeks to be uncaged "and / flow like a deep / river" (I.8–10). Indeed, the river in the second column leaves the forest flowing like song.

Thus, Chipasula's poem emphasizes the mutual relationship between witness and art: the song of response to the forest becomes the river of art that flows like the song of response. Since the poet wishes for his art to be like song, the art that he makes is signed by its songlike quality. In this way, the art evidences the poet's relationship to what he witnessed: the essential quality of his witness (its songlikeness) is reflected in the art. A single column centred beneath the first two ends with "[y]our words are very close / to what is happening" (III.4–5). Heaney's words are not what is happening, but are close to it; "Double Song" explores the process of achieving that closeness through response and re-creation of response in art. For Chipasula, Heaney signs his poems at the level of the poem. Heaney's signature can be found in his poetry as the song of his response made into art that responds.

Likewise, Rint's signature, made of rearranged human bones, is not encrypted (except literally, in that it is located within a crypt). His name, coded by bones, is made consistent with the art it signs; his name as sign of the indexical connection between art and artist is complicated by the closeness of its relationship with the art it signs. On the other hand, the bones themselves retain their indexical connections to the bodies that they demonstrate had lived. This memorializing connection is made prominent. Yet, while they are these durable remains of human existence, these bones are also generic; they lack the individuality of living humans. Further, the skeletons are rearranged out of the human shape. The skeletons' direct connections to human life – as remnants of it – are disrupted. Rint's role is putting "in order" the human remnants in an ossuary. In this new order, what relation do his creations bear to human life? If this relation is commemorative, as is suggested by the context of the ossuary, how does that memorializing relation alter when the bones shape the artist's name?

IV

I have been considering poems whose speakers exist within the same contexts as the poets writing them. While I have been careful to distinguish speaker from poet, in witness poetry the two are often closely related. It would be incongruous for me to ignore the relationship between poet and poem since I have argued that compassionate witness is a mode of reading and being in the world, that these speakers model such a disposition, and that I, as a reader, model it again. I will examine this relationship here through ideas of signature and encryption. The poet's signature is the carrier of his or her identity. As the signifier of witness outside of the poem, this signature is the indexical connection between a poem and its contexts. A strong likeness between poet and speaker lends itself to a total identification between the two. Yet to read the speaker as the poet is to carry away a poem's hermeneutic meaning. In contrast, I find the poetry in my corpus to hold the relationship between speaker and poet at a distance that allows for the interplay of the metaphoric and metonymic, the symbolic and indexical, the hermeneutic and the heuristic.

One method by which my poets sign their witness is through dedication. Peter Balakian's dedication of the poem "The Oriental Rug" to his daughter inscribes himself within his poem as a living poet and as a father. His speaker works within a context of intergenerational memory. Similarly, the map in Joy Harjo's poem is passed on from generation to generation; her dedication of "A Map to the Next World" to her daughter positions her poem as an actual inheritance. These dedications put the poets into indexical relation with their poems. These poems function literally to communicate inside of these family relationships at the same time as they are addressed to unknown readers. That is, readers are put into a relationship with the poem that is explicitly different from the way the poem is already in relation to the dedicatee. This is not to say that the poem is not for unknown readers (it is not a private document), but that the poem emphasizes that there exist various levels of intimacy through which the poem will be engaged. A reader's position is filtered through the announcement that the poem tells a family story and makes family connections through or across the suffering it engages.

Adrienne Rich's hermeneutic dedications involve a more distanced intimacy. The section "(Dedications)" in "An Atlas of the Difficult World" addresses the poem to various imagined readers and to a series of "you"s that can designate any reader. These dedications form a hermeneutic framework of relationships rather than a heuristic connection between particular elements. In contrast, the section directly before "(Dedications")") is "(For M.)" (XII). The poem for M. involves the intimacy of a dedication to a particular person but presents for readers a sign rather than a name; readers lack the full name or other identifying information for the person who presumably exists outside of the poem. The dedication encodes a message, indicating intimacy but leaving readers outside of it.

This poem for M. is concerned with signs. M., the mark within the poem, stands for a person keen to identify or record: "impatient to mark what's possible, impatient to mark / what's lost" (XII.11–12). The dedication is, through M.'s characteristics, associated with witness as marking. M.'s marking privileges the indexical or actual, the tied to life, as her "back arched against all icons, simulations, dead letters" (XII.13). This resistance to the not actual suggests that the poem's connection to M. indicates actual relationship. In other words, this mark forms a living, not a dead or simulated, letter. Before the poem's hermeneutic dedications, then, is this heuristic (in that it is a sign that points to the real person), particularized mark of Rich's actual relationship. In the poem for M., readers find a sign of intimacy from which readers are partially excluded – we can still read the poem, we just cannot fully know at whom it is aimed. We are made aware of this actual intimacy that is indicated in the poem but not delivered to us. In contrast, in "(Dedications)," all readers are presumed to be in intimate relation with the poem, even though the poem does not know who they are. These different forms of intimacy demonstrate the intersections of the heuristic and hermeneutic as I consider them in my second chapter in terms of intimate and distanced knowledge.

Brand's *Inventory* brings readers into intimate relation with the personal and public memory of a person. Brand dedicates one section of *Inventory*'s fourth part to activist Marlene Green.[6] The speaker wishes for the deceased woman to return to tell her mourners how to

> mount demonstrations against
> your death,
> will you send word
> in letters, in goldenrod leaflets [...]
> till then Marlene,
> we will fix petals of you to our eyes (62)

This mourning witnesses Marlene through the "petals of you," but also witnesses the world through Marlene. To "fix" what amounts to rose-coloured glasses "to our eyes" suggests that it is through Marlene that "we" will see. Marlene is also a synecdoche for her social and political achievements, so that witnessing Marlene is also witnessing the world as she has left her mark on it. This section draws readers into a view of the world that is shaped by Marlene's work. The section begins, "We should carry you" (62) and indeed carries Marlene into poetic relationship through which to "demonstrat[e] against / your death." While the speaker asks Marlene to "send word" "in letters," in "leaflets," the poem itself is a way of sending word. The poem holds Marlene within commemorative relationship that is achieved through the carrying of Marlene from actual relationship into poetic mourning.

Brand's work more broadly is concerned with mourning. In *Ossuaries*, Yasmine notes the "branded bones" (36) of those living in "the waiting rooms of existence" (38), for whom "to love is an impediment to this hard business / of living" (34). Branded bones are marked not only by the destruction this long poem witnesses, but by that witness. The poem touches on the intimate engagement of that doubled vulnerability (to suffer and to be shown suffering) in the later suggestion that

it's always in the lyric

the harsh fast threatening gobble,
the clipped sharp knifing, it's always,
in the lyric (108)

The extended lyric of the long poem is not outside of the "presumptive cruelties" (108) that are "always in the lyric" but also "always, in the lyric" (108): always existing and always existing in the poetry. Art's intrusions are a reaction to and also a part of the cruelties already existing (cruelties represented here in references to eating and cutting used throughout *Inventory* as it expresses its concern for taking global suffering into the witnessing self and for the connections and detachments involved in this form of relationship-building).

The violence that is always in the lyric matches the temporality of the bones: the branding of poetry (labelling violence in the world, holding its own violence) matches the longevity of branded bones as memorializing objects. The attunement to loving affect and the waiting of commemoration I discussed earlier are shown here in connection to the violence implicit in branded bones. In relation to the shifting of Yasmine's voice between "she" and "I," we can think of these branded bones as a kind of author-inscription in the "speaking for" in which such a poem partakes. Imagining Yasmine's life, the poem puts forward a character's suffering in relation to actual suffering in the world, but not a suffering that is the poet's own.

I read the last poem in Rachel Tzvia Back's collection to include an encryption of the poet's name. The alliteration in "Bringing the Buffalo Back Home" calls attention to this title in which the inclusion of the poet's last name in the carrying home of the buffalo is suggestive of the poet's self-insertion. I read this line as "I brought the buffalo Back" in relation to the account of this bringing back home: the buffalo "kept // me company / until // one day / she was gone – // I had no choice: / alone // I brought her / home" (40–8). If Back is alone (the buffalo "was gone"), the buffalo can only come home into – as a part of – Back herself. Thus, when the speaker says the buffalo has returned – "I brought the buffalo back / home" (1–2) – what could we imagine it saying but an ambiguous "I'm back?" The section "After five years of writing buffalo poems" suggests this relationship between Back and the buffalo, as the buffalo, described in relation to a pregnant woman, becomes aligned retrospectively with the pregnant speaker of the collection's first section. The significant consideration in witness poetry is perhaps not whether the witness poem has traces of a poet's actual suffering, but instead how the poem contains artistic indications of its relationship to its creation and its contexts. That is, what I find significant is the manner in which a poem shows its particular intimacy or distance to the suffering it engages. This is the idea Chipasula suggests in his poem dedicated to Heaney: Heaney's poetry stays close to what it witnesses by showing the relationship between song, forest, and river – that is, between the experience of witness, the experience of response, and the art emerging from that witness and response. Deciding whether Back primarily presents her own suffering (living in a violent context) or the suffering of others (depicting those more subject to violence than herself as well as depicting another context – American colonization – through which she has not lived) seems less pressing than considering how her poem works through the idiosyncratic collision of violent contexts in one person's life. Not only witness poetry, but all poetry has indexical connections to the world; any poem is created in relation to and because of elements of a poet's life or a poem's social, historical, and geographic location. In witness poetry, the markers of those connections are of special significance not only to how the poem means but to how it offers itself for ongoing connection. The forms of witness established or depicted shape the relational forms it might establish with readers, through whom the poem finds its continuing connections to the world.

I consider carrying and holding by way of surplus. What the poem holds of a poet's life is carried over into celebratory waiting: personal commemoration carries an exhortation to communality. Something a poet holds (dear, close) is carried in poetry to be held anew by readers. The waiting that is involved in art's holding for the surplus of public commemoration seeks the unpredictable surplus of each new holder of the poem and waiter in witness. The commemoration is the surplus of the memory. Readers, belonging to a commemoration of memories that do not belong to them, participate in a communication based less on knowing and more on charm or grace, to use Brand's words for the unexpected drawing into collaboration for unfathomable purposes or unfathomable participants. The charm of encryption is this leading through discreet personal inclusion, the surplus of the poem as the crypt that buries memories for the possibility of commemoration.

This chapter's two related topics – (1) skeletons and ossuaries indicating a concern with relationship and connection and (2) the encryption of poetic signature – are indicative of a larger concern with relational structures. Not all of the poetry I investigate in this project has a preoccupation with the skeletal, but the coincidence of encryption and crypt does draw out the relationship between carrying and holding that is established in all the examples I consider. Cryptic poems make speakers, and ask readers to be, ossuaries, holding-containers of compassion and commemoration. Remembering together (com-memoration) seems a particularly appropriate response to suffering along with another (com-passion). My consideration of compassion as a mode of being appears to emphasize the scale of the individual but it is ultimately compassion across individuals that I reach for in this book. Art is communal in form; witness art investigates that form as an invitation (or exhortation) for communal compassion.

Conclusion

Poetry is a source of genuine power. Yet poetry's discussants routinely undermine this power by attributing extraordinary abilities to the form. The idea that trauma literally inheres in a poem – to create witness and thus action – is essentially a faith in poetry that fails to accord much power to a poem's actual strategies. In this book, poetry appears as the words of real individuals whose selves and experiences are nevertheless unavailable in the poetry, and these words communicate as words do, no more and no less. Poetry is a particular context of interpersonal interaction. Poetry is an art form, with all the mediation and distance that form implies.

In terms of witness and compassion, poetry's power is that a poem can distill a set of relationships. The positions a poem holds open for readers make claims on them. A poem's invitation has particular responsibilities attached that are relevant to the wider situation of being a person interacting with other texts, systems, and people. These positions and their attendant responsibilities, however, are only clear if we read poetry for what it offers.

The view of trauma studies that literature is a privileged location to pass trauma from an author to a reader, fashioning readers into a chain of witnesses as it moves, functions as a claim to be applied to any individual poem. The idea that witness poetry can serve as evidence because it carries trauma's literal traces never has to enter a poem; that claim can rest in the connection between a poet's biography and the fact of a poem's existence. The notion that a poem carries its poet's trauma is an abstract claim because it functions as an assumed rule and, as I have shown, poems that do not serve that rule can be dismissed, misread, or chastised for misrepresenting that trauma. Indeed, though trauma studies seems to make the most concrete of claims – that traces of trauma are literally available in the poem's broken language – it can only find that concrete evidence through a lens under which all witness poetry looks abstractly alike.

To make space for any individual poem, my claims for poetry rest on continuums. Metonymy may be my privileged term, but it is inseparable from metaphor. Compassion and identification form the extremes of a range of possible response to suffering. Poetry engages with emotional and historical truths through the mediation of art, but it also creates or contributes to actual interpersonal relationship. It is thus not surprising that, although this book's first chapter challenges the assumption that a poet's suffering inheres in a witness poem as indexical traces, its last chapter searches for traces of a poet's signing, or signs of the relationship between poet and poem.

The reason I am drawn to the side of the continuum that I am – the same reason that I propose so much witness poetry ends up here – is that these terms have continuums built into them. That is, the commitments I find in witness poetry allow for a strategy of surplus. Metonymy is a trope of association that works from pre-existing connections to build vast networks of meaning. Metonymy is the trope for turning actual relationships into new systems. I associate carrying with metonymy, and it is carrying connections across new ground that constitutes metonymy's surplus. Formally, metonymy mirrors compassion's surplus. When I feel compassion, I feel with you. When I feel with you, my feelings are added to yours; they are surplus feelings in that they do not collapse into your suffering by imaginatively becoming it. My surplus feelings join us in relationship. If instead of compassion I felt empathy, I would imagine that I felt your feelings. Through identification, I would claim your feelings as my feelings. As a consequence, there would not be two positions between which a relationship could form. In compassionate response to a poem, a reader feels with a speaker rather than as the speaker. It is this response that contributes to a network of care extending beyond the poem. Actual relationships between readers and speakers can metonymically become part of a system of compassionate response when readers feel their own feelings in response to poems' speakers. Thus, though I say that I read witness poetry for what is actually in it, some of what is actually in a witness poem is an invitation for specifically surplus feeling, for feeling that necessarily exceeds what is in the poem.

We can see this surplus in many of the strategies or preoccupations I have explored in this poetry. Dionne Brand, Rachel Tzvia Back, and Adrienne Rich each prominently use shifting pronouns to suggest networks of potential relationships. Seamus Heaney, Derek Walcott, Joy Harjo, Elizabeth Bishop, and Peter Balakian, as well as Brand and Rich, use ekphrastic strategies to produce relationships of significance between written and visual texts and between showing and telling. The surplus of diegesis, telling what the poem is doing, in poetry by Antjie Krog, Harjo, and Rich is a form of metafiction that makes the poem exceed itself as its own commentary. Moreover, Rich, Brand, Bishop, and Krog use a variety of formal elements – such as images of waiting and waiting rooms, a long poem, or temporal markers – to produce or suggest a temporal surplus. This temporal surplus is necessary for the creating of witnessing relationships that are not based in chains of quick successions, but in a long-term production of individual connection.

This "more than is there" that I find in witness poetry, this surplus, may also be articulated as hope. For example, Jack Mapanje, another Malawian poet to whom Frank Chipasula dedicates several poems, was imprisoned in Malawi for four years without trial. His poem "Skipping without Rope," in his collection *Skipping without Ropes*, repeats "I will skip without your rope" as the speaker's response to his denied request to borrow a skipping rope so that he might exercise while imprisoned (1, 3–4, 7, 34). The poem is a defiant declaration that he will use more than he has: "I will create my own rope, my own / Hope" (7–8). "I will, will skip with my forged hope" (12). The surplus of hope – more than what is there – may well be a forgery. Hope, though, is a forgery that creates itself. In this case, the poet's signature is a genuine hope that forges the conditions it can exist in. The event in the poem is not signed by the actual, but it is signed by hope that creates itself in the signing.

Along with hope, surplus has several possible analogues in the
poetry appearing in this book. Of these analogues, grace is the most
prominent. Whether grace was previously named by the poem itself
or by critics, I have shown poems by Les Murray, Heaney, and Brand
to feature grace as surplus. Krog's "Country of grief and grace," as
the title suggests, concerns a grace I have not yet discussed. In Krog's
poem, grace, though not named as such in the poem proper, appears
as the opposite to the grief that "comes so lonely" (g.5). Indeed, grace
emerges through community:

> you cut me loose
>
> into light – lovelier, lighter and braver than song
> may I hold you my sister
> in this warm fragile unfolding of the word humane (g.9–12)

Grace is achieved through the help of "my sister," presumably the
"you whom I have wronged" from the poem's previous section (f.16).
It is "because of you" that "this country no longer lies / between us
but within" (f.1–3); South Africa lies "in the cradle of my skull" (f.7),
the speaker explains, because when she begs forgiveness of those
wronged in Apartheid (f.13–15), when she begs, "please / take me //
with you" (f.16–18), she is indeed carried across this gap of the line
break into the fragility of the unfolding word "humane." She is not
cut loose into a new humaneness – a new state of "feeling or showing
compassion" (OED). Rather, she travels only into the existence of the
word because this is a poem about how "this country belongs to the
voices of those who live in it" (b.12). The poem considers specifically
how acts of language might work toward a new future for the country. Earlier, the "speechless" speaker asks, "whence will words now
come? / for us the doers" (c.1–3). The poem's final section indicates
that communal belonging in a state of compassion is not possible "if
the old is not guilty / does not confess" (i.1–2). It is confession that
moves "the doers" across the lonely gap of speechlessness and into
the grace of humaneness. The "hold[ing]" together in the "unfolding of the word" is the poem's surplus. Indeed, the holding within

the word exceeds the word and the poem: it is "lovelier, lighter and braver than song."

Grace also features as surplus in Harjo's poem "Grace" from her collection *In Mad Love and War*. The speaker, in "a town that never / wanted us," is in an "epic search for grace" (6–7). In this "year we had nothing to lose," the speaker recalls, "the cold froze / imaginary buffalo on the stuffed horizon of snowbanks" (1–3). But "one morning […] / […] in a truck stop […] we found grace" (10–11): "I could say grace was a woman with time on her hands, or a white buffalo escaped from / memory" (12–13). The untaken time that might characterize grace for the speaker suggests the waiting so important to witness and compassion. The white buffalo recalls the frozen imaginary buffalo from the poem's first stanza; it also recalls the buffalo hunted into memory by colonizers. Indeed, this imaginary or merely remembered buffalo recalls the buffalo image escaped from the speaker's heart in Back's buffalo poems. Harjo's images, like Back's images of her speaker's heart's buffalo are not of grace directly. Rather, Harjo tells us what the speaker might say grace is. Like Harjo's deictic explanation in *A Map to the Next World* that "I wished to make a map" (1) that ends with "You must make your own map" (51), this speaker's description evokes grace without presenting it to readers. Instead, grace is a promise: "in that dingy light it was a promise of balance" (13). There is more in the truck stop's dingy light than is there. It is the promise of balance that allows the surplus of time or of imaginary buffalo. The poem ends, "I know there is something larger than / the memory of a dispossessed people. We have seen it" (17–18). The imaginary buffalo they saw balances the memory of actual buffalo. In that balancing, "something larger than the memory" is produced, as this surplus is produced in the woman with time on her hands: time balances memory, and a woman possessing time balances the memory of a dispossessed people. Grace as the promise of balance, like Krog's country held within the cradle of a skull, is the position between holding and carrying, between confession and change, between memory and more.

Holding and carrying are pieces of the same movement, a movement I consider in terms of the cradling that comes up more than once in this book. When Heaney's speaker and his bone-woman cradle each other or when Krog's speaker cradles her country in her skull, I imagine this cradling as the rocking one uses in cradling a baby because this rocking moves between stationary holding and the changeful motion of carrying. Like the soothing to which I compare it, this rocking is the easing into a position in relation to a poem, one's life, and the larger world of other lives. It is the easing into a relation between one's life and another's. Or, to try again, this holding and carrying is like the speaker's walking into witness in "An Atlas of the Difficult World": "These are not the roads / you knew me by" (I.75–6) but "this is where I live now" (I.60). Compassionate relation is the opening of new roads between where one knows and is known, and where one's life might expand into new engagement.

Carrying and holding each has its own surplus signification. Though never fully separable, holding and carrying are structurally nearly analogous to metaphor and metonymy. While holding involves a relationship between two terms that is suppressed in its expression, carrying involves relational space, a space having to do with relationship as such. But carrying and holding each have an additional sense. In this book, I also consider holding as the work of a symbol (as meaning-making within art) and carrying as the indexical connection between art and the contexts of its creation (as meaning carried within this network of relationships). Thus, holding and carrying operate at two different levels, one within the poem and one in the space between the poem and its contexts. It is how meaning operates in the simultaneity of these two levels that is the surplus of poetry. Thus, while I distinguish between carrying and holding, they are part of the same motion. Cradling becomes the important term indicating this relationship between carrying and holding, a relationship that underpins my examination of witness and its contingent terms. Cradling is the surplus of meaning in the union of carrying and holding.

Commemoration, belonging, compassion – the feelings and conditions I consider in their relationship with witness – occur between one individual and another, or between an individual and community or public life. Meaning, residing in the spaces between things, comes as a surplus, uncontainable through extending relationships. Commemoration is individually held in memory and also carried into the public realm. This poetry considers commemoration as it unsettles memory into movement. Belonging, too, takes the space between being behooved (carrying/carried) and being moored (holding/held). Belonging in community involves upholding that community, being held in its boundaries, and also carrying belonging past those boundaries towards those not yet held. National belonging is addressed through surplus significations resulting from various and shifting entanglements of body, landscape, and map. Such belonging is nowhere arrested – belonging as it is imagined in these poems is not the belonging set down in law, though it could inform those stabilized forms – but is evoked as a complex set of relationships in which people actually exist.

Compassion likewise does not fully reside in myself, but in the space of relation between another's suffering and my feelings as they are shaped by that suffering. It is this surplus that this poetry depicts when it imagines compassion to occur in the waiting through relationship. Witness poetry's tendency toward diegesis is suggestive of this temporality of attention as waiting. The emphasis on telling – as opposed to showing a meaning already existent – involves the reader as present listener and indicates ongoing relationships of response. Compassion that does not come through attentive relation could not be compassion as I, through these poems, understand it. This relational quality of compassion is also why I come to consider it as a disposition rather than a feeling: the ongoing relationship (even if it is a one-sided relationship of my mindful presence to unknown others) may involve many feelings of varying intensities. Compassion, as a way of living attentively in relationship, opens space for these other feelings to attend it. This surplus is likewise evident in Brand's use of "before and since": a moment of compassion might extend non-teleologically to adjust an entire life to its demand. Much as I said that carrying and holding form the cradle that is the foundation for witness, I could say that reflection and waiting form compassion in the surplus space of relationship. The relational work that involves both reflection and waiting is the dynamic of compassion, community, and commemoration – the "withs" of witness.

Notes

INTRODUCTION

1 Nussbaum's discussion elucidates my concern. In her analysis of a poem by Walt Whitman, Nussbaum writes, "the ability to imagine vividly, and then to assess judicially, another person's pain, to participate in it and then to ask about its significance, is a powerful way of learning what the human facts are" (91). How accurately might we imagine another person's pain if it is truly foreign from our own? Does reading experiences-not-our-own prepare us for this assessment? Are readers equipped to assume the right to make assessments about the significance of another's pain as though we have participated in it? Nussbaum uses the following example to make her point: "if one cannot imagine what women suffer from sexual harassment on the job, one won't have a vivid sense of that offense as a serious social infringement that the law should remedy," but "the judicious spectator" does not "stop with the experience of the other person's pain: one must then ask, from the spectatorial viewpoint, whether that pain is appropriate to its target, whether it is such pain, or anger, or fear, as a reasonable person would feel in those circumstances" (91). What a dangerous argument for a model of reading, it seems to me, to suggest that a spectator – let's say, a man in a position of power – can, having heard a woman's story of sexual harassment, assume that he has experienced her pain such that he can now judge if the pain she expresses in her story is appropriate (or, in other words, if her pain is, by his judgment, equal to what a reasonable person would feel).

2 A cultural emphasis on identification is summed up in Purdue University's Online Writing Lab's explanation of the contemporary understanding of rhetoric ("Rhetorical Situation"). This source is particularly appropriate for noting a broad trend since the site seeks to represent a generalized

consensus for non-experts. As a trustworthy resource from which students might learn foundational information, it is a useful marker of basic ideas underpinning current thinking. Citing Kenneth Burke's *A Rhetoric of Motives*, this resource suggests that rhetoric has ceased to be defined by persuasion and has evolved to mean identification: "rhetoric is the set of methods people use to *identify* with each other – to encourage each other to understand things from one another's perspectives (see Burke 25)." More broadly, common sayings like "walk in someone else's shoes" or "I feel your pain" also point to an emphasis on identification. Since colloquial phrases exist through their use by many people to conceptualize and articulate their thoughts and feelings, they point meaningfully to prominent concepts in a culture.

3 Despite the emphasis on empathy, there may be a growing space for a focus on compassion in fields like Feminist Love Studies or in approaches to the contemporary cultural moment based in the New Sincerity ethos. Interestingly, compassion currently has a prominent place in health studies. For example, the Associated Medical Services' Project Phoenix, initiated in 2011, takes as its tagline "Bringing compassion to healthcare." Compassion is, of course, an active term in Buddhism and some of its popularized practices.

4 For a detailed consideration of engagement with another's pain, see Sara Ahmed's *The Cultural Politics of Emotion*. For Ahmed, "the ethical demand is that I must act about that which I cannot know, rather than act insofar as I know. I am moved by what does not belong to me. If I acted on her behalf only insofar as I knew how she felt, then I would act only insofar as I would appropriate her pain as my pain, that is, appropriate that which I cannot feel" (31).

5 Despite my emphasis on consciously enacting compassion, I do not mean to say that compassion cannot happen spontaneously. While engaged attention can be sustained without intention, it is the situations in which attention does not come (or continue) spontaneously that lead me to say that identification cannot be the only available approach.

6 It is not because engagement based solely in identification is a response that does not move beyond the pre-existing knowledge of the self that I consider it a fallacy. There are many occasions of engagement in which the hard-hitting impact on the self warrants primary or exclusive attention, or in which lack of other knowledge, great emotional involvement, or brevity of encounter makes another sort of engagement unlikely. What I mean by the

fallacy of identification here is an approach that proceeds from a sense that what the poem asks for or offers is only to find oneself in the difference depicted.

7 Radstone makes this critique at greater length to suggest that the subject matter restricts discussion in the forums where that discussion may normally best occur: "Though there is much that remains to be debated concerning every aspect of trauma analysis, the open debate of trauma analysis's grounding theories, and of the readings that it produces are hindered by the nature of the material itself and the contexts – particularly in conferences – within which it is discussed. Criticism and debate can easily appear callous, or even unethical, in a context where an audience is being asked to bear witness to unspeakable sufferings. This can lead, however, to a silencing of discussion which leaves hanging any number of questions about the continuingly problematic nature of academic discussion of trauma" (Radstone 22).

8 In a review of *Literature in the Ashes of History* for *Parallax*, Ryan Topper defends Caruth's choice to ignore critique: "Put simply, Caruth may not care about the debates surrounding her work. For some readers, most likely those actively engaged in trauma studies, this lack of response will be seen as a weakness. I, however, disagree. The strength of Caruth's latest work is precisely that which has made her previous work remain a topic of debate: staying true to her de Manian, Yale-School roots, Caruth provides insightful, beautifully articulated close readings of literary and theoretical texts" (np). Of course, the fact of "staying true" to one's perspective does not make the content of that perspective irrelevant. This defence that Caruth need not recognize claims she is doing harmful or inadequate work because she is so committed to that work makes the troubling suggestion that total conviction brooks no correction, and shouldn't. Though Topper indicates that criticisms to Caruth's work are focused on the ethical and political shortcomings of trauma theory, he concludes that Caruth's new book "is not a direct response to the political debates surrounding trauma theory, but a work of comparative literary criticism grounded in the traditions of psychoanalysis and deconstruction – and a good one at that." Skill at doing something politically and ethically faulty seems an odd quality to celebrate, but it is perhaps even odder that Caruth's reception is characterized by the claim, made by Topper here, that "her strength always was, and continues to be, her close reading." As many scholars have argued of *Unclaimed Experience*, and as I will demonstrate in *Literature in the Ashes of History*, Caruth's close reading is often selective or flawed.

9 This is not to say that no reader could be traumatized by reading these poems or that that reader's response would be inappropriate, but only that it is not a readerly duty to respond as though traumatized, or as though one has received the poet's unconscious trauma, particularly if one's experiences, disposition, reading situation, and other factors do not make a relationship to the subject likely to produce a traumatized reaction.

10 In the following, I do not mean to imply that attention to biography is unimportant or misguided. As Peter Balakian writes in a defence of Forché's anthology, "Poetry of witness, she argues, engages us in bibliographic context, for poets whose lives have been in some way directly affected by political catastrophe force us to consider how those events may surface in the imagination" (189). This consideration is certainly an important one. My argument is that this consideration is dominating the field and has had the peculiar effect of overshadowing the poetic aspects of poetry of witness in some readings.

11 For another discussion of testimony and indexicality, see James Berger's chapter "Representing the Holocaust," specifically pages 72–6. For Berger, the "view of testimony as direct transmission of the inconceivable event is ultimately more theological than empirical" (73–4).

12 For an idea of how emphasized this biographical authority is, consider this explanation Forché provides of the arrangement of her anthology which explains the importance of the poets' biographical experiences again in every sentence: "Within each section, poets appear in chronological order by date of birth, with biographical notes to illuminate the experience of extremity for each poet, and a selection of poetry from available works in the English originals or in translation. The criteria for inclusion were these: poets must have personally endured such conditions; they must be considered important to their national literatures; and their work, if not in English, must be available in a quality translation. The necessarily brief biographies included here provide information relevant to the poets' experience of extremity" (30).

13 "Articulation and the Limits of Metaphor" comes within Laclau's *The Rhetorical Foundations of Society*. Laclau includes Jakobson's work to show that metaphor and metonymy "are not just some figures among many, but the two fundamental matrices around which all other figures and tropes should be ordered" (60). Further, he understands the role of rhetoric as "ontologically constitutive" (66). He shows that all other tropes can be reduced to the metaphor/metonymy matrix, that the operations along this

continuum are essential to signification, and that "the tensions that we have detected along the metaphor-metonymy continuum can be seen as fully operating in the structuration of political spaces" (67). His central purpose in this discussion – to explain the operation of hegemony through this matrix – is aside from my project.

14 Take Adrienne Rich as an example. Sylvia Henneberg, in "The Self-Categorization, Self-Canonization, and Self-Periodization of Adrienne Rich," argues that Rich's prose has supplanted close analysis of her poetry. Henneberg's investigation of the body of criticism surrounding Rich's poetry shows that scholars "have welcomed the politics set forth in Rich's prose as a means to assess and label her poetry" (270). As a result, "criticism of her work is to this day suspiciously uniform and predictable; many readings of her poetry appear to be collective shortcuts through her strongly politicized prose of the 1970s and 1980s, ultimately compromising her art" (276). More recently, Emily Taylor Merriman makes a similar point: "Under the influence of Rich's own most clearly and frequently stated values, her critics have tended to concentrate on the content of the poetry: *what* the poems are doing rather than precisely *how* they are doing it" (8).

15 Representativeness is particularly impossible for this project since I choose to pursue some lines of influence and conversation, thus giving space to certain contexts over others.

16 There is an added incentive to begin with Chipasula rather than with a very well-known author like, say, Adrienne Rich. With Rich, I would need to vigorously contextualize the poem within her corpus and my reading within the many readings by other scholars. Because Chipasula is less studied and less well known than many of the other poets included here, I can approach his poem with more directness. While this directness serves an introduction well, I also begin with Chipasula because I will turn to another Malawian poet, Jack Mapanje, in my conclusion's reflections on hope and grace. I like the parallel created by including a Malawian poet in both the introduction and the conclusion because the shared context between the two poets at opposite ends of the manuscript suggests key terms and concepts that will arise over the next chapters: the connection and distance in Brand's "pairing knife"; poetry's mediation of literal connections (as, for instance, in Chipasula's habit of poetic dedications, frequently to Mapanje); the surplus of waiting; the surplus of carrying and holding; and the surplus that comes through community and registers in these poems as the grace or hope about which Mapanje writes. I like the parallel between Chipasula's

focus on art's witness and Mapanje's focus on forged hope (hope that is nonetheless real for being forged) because this book's organization suggests that these poems have the capacity to write hope into existence.

17 In Chipasula's *Whispers in the Wings*, the lines appear as I have described them. In the poem's publication online, "metaphors" has been brought into the previous line (15). In this version, the line, longer than the others, seems to come to a point that makes the line itself a sharp metaphor that can pierce.

CHAPTER ONE

1 In his article "Speak, Trauma: Toward a Revised Understanding of Literary Trauma Theory," Joshua Pederson uses Leys's critique and updates it with reference to Richard McNally's 2003 review of new clinical research, a review that challenges the idea of trauma as unspeakable, unknowable, and unrepresentable. Pederson critiques Caruth's work to propose a new way to use trauma theory in literary study. Yet, since Pederson takes a trauma studies approach to literature (treating literary texts as unconscious performances of trauma rather than as crafted and deliberate artistic communication), he reproduces the model with different rules, asking readers to look for the author's trauma in the text by identifying its qualities by McNally's criteria rather than by Caruth's.

2 For example, along with her more general comments, Leys critiques Caruth's reading of Tancred and Clorinda (292–7), as does LaCapra (WH 181–4). Pederson notes the errors in Caruth's analysis of *Hiroshima Mon Amour* (344–7), as does Amy Hungerford (84–5).

3 The full passage emphasizes this nobility and its relationship to material comfort: "In reclaiming his creature comforts, he recovered his old martial elegance. He stood very straight. His face, solemn and mysterious, marked by happiness and hope, seemed rejuvenated and fuller. He no more resembled the Chabert of the old greatcoat than an old sou resembles a newly minted forty-franc gold piece. Looking at him, anyone could easily have recognized one of the noble remnants of our former army, one of those heroic men who reflect our national glory" (69).

4 A non-exhaustive list of these scholars includes LaCapra, Hungerford, Catherine Wake, and Geoffrey Hartman.

5 Kalaidjian does critique Gubar's understanding of the critic's empathic position, quoting her by way of example for this claim that "not only poets but literary critics of Holocaust verse are likewise susceptible to symptoms of trauma stemming from the event insofar as they disavow critical judgment in the name of empathic identification with the Holocaust's victims" (67).

6 Hungerford similarly criticizes the way critics have created what is acceptable in the genre of Holocaust memoir (68). Brenda Vellino, though she does not "disput[e] the insight that an aesthetics of rupture may evoke an ethical connection to the uncanny and haunting aftermath" and "traces of trauma in poetry" (153), suggests a "shift beyond" trauma theory to "expand the frame of who counts as a witness and what counts as witness poetry when read through a human rights lens" ("Beyond the Trauma Aesthetic" 148). Vellino argues that expanding the critical focus beyond primary witnesses and beyond lyric poetry "enables us to engage poems with documentary, activist, and interventionist priorities that help us move beyond traumatized and victimized subject positions to consideration of human rights poetic subjects as political actors and interveners" (153).

7 The interaction of body, land, and nation recurs significantly in the witness poetry genre. I will return to this trilogy of concerns throughout this book.

8 For Margaret Bedrosian, "The rug is one of the richest symbols in Balakian's work, operating at many levels as an affirmative image that contains and orders strands of history into patterns" (201). Kalaidjian's focus on loss downplays the richness of this symbol, as well as its affirmation of meaning.

9 Though I refer to the speaker as "he," it is important to remember that the poem is written from the perspective of an I. This perspective is significant in terms of the speaker/sufferer/reader positions outlined by the poem.

10 Note the difference between reading the poem as an index of suffering and reading an element of the poem as a figurative index which remains nonetheless explicitly metonymical to the suffering itself. Within the poem, the rug's material connection to the land offers the speaker a direct link to the context or setting of suffering, but still not to the suffering itself.

CHAPTER TWO

1 This language of "mindful presence" resonates with that of Buddhism. Eve Kosofsky Sedgwick's account of the Buddhist idea of realization describes

forms of attention and consideration in contrast to a kind of attention ending in knowledge. Sedgwick distinguishes "between knowing something – even knowing it to be true – and realizing it, taking it as real" (208).

2 For more on Rich's relationship to ekphrasis more broadly, see Elizabeth Bergmann Loizeaux's "Women Looking: The Feminist Ekphrasis of Marianne Moore and Adrienne Rich." For Harjo's comments on the interplay of forms in her poetry, see her interview "Becoming the Thing Itself" collected in *Soul Talk, Song Language*. She discusses in this interview the "fusion of the oral and written" in *A Map to the Next World* particularly. Here and elsewhere in the collection, Harjo comments on her poetry's relationship to painting and to music. The collection's introduction sets up these concerns and also discusses the illustrated children's books Harjo has written.

3 "In the early 19th century, the United States Indian policy focused on the removal of the Muscogee and the other Southeastern tribes to areas beyond the Mississippi River. In the removal treaty of 1832, Muscogee leadership exchanged the last of the cherished Muscogee ancestral homelands for new lands in Indian Territory (Oklahoma). Many of the Lower Muscogee (Creek) had settled in the new homeland after the treaty of Washington in 1827. But for the majority of Muscogee people the process of severing ties to a land they felt so much a part of proved impossible. The U.S. Army enforced the removal of more than 20,000 Muscogee (Creeks) to Indian Territory in 1836 and 37" (Muscogee (Creek) Nation).

4 While Harjo's poetry includes these specific Creek elements, Craig S. Womack points out that the she also works within a pan-tribal tradition: "Harjo's Creek grounding strengthens her pan-tribal vision" (225). In "A Map to the Next World" specifically, take as example of this pan-tribal vision its first lines – "I wished to make a map for / those who would climb through the hole in the sky" (1–2) – which refer to an element of creation stories that is common among many indigenous groups in North America.

5 According to Robert Warrior, "the overt reference is to Hopi beliefs in this being a fourth incarnation of the world that will sometime soon emerge into a fifth incarnation" (344).

6 The "language of suns" suggests the significance the sun holds in Creek cultural understanding: "The fire supplied heat and light for both the households and the community ceremonies, as the sun supplied these things so that all life forms might flourish and continue. For the Mvskoke people, the

sun and the sacred fire within the ceremonial ring (pasko'fv) are the same" (Muskoke (Creek) Nation). See also note 110.

7 The complex shifting of literality here is comparable to the function of the rug in Peter Balakian's "The Oriental Rug" where the rug is literally and figuratively connected to the land that is a part of the Armenian nation but also sometimes stands in entirely for the nation and its people.

8 Balakian explains in his commentary on this poem, available on his personal website, that "in the Near East, in Armenian culture in my case, rugs are complex and unique things. They are, in some sense, the equivalents of oil paintings in Europe – a high mode of visual art" (np).

9 I focus on similarities between Rich's and Bishop's use of maps in these two poems. For a useful study contrasting these poets' approaches to the poetic representation of knowledge through metaphorical maps, see Roger Gilbert's "Framing Water: Historical Knowledge in Elizabeth Bishop and Adrienne Rich."

10 Considering Bishop's descriptions of objects more broadly, Zachariah Pickard writes, "The central goal of her poetry is not so much to relate an emotional experience (though it may) as to trigger one in the reader ... Her intensive poetics is organized around controlling the reader's imagination directly rather than inspiring it to vibrate sympathetically in the Romantic style. Intensive imagery is an essentially rhetorical process" (35). Thus, Bishop's poetic goal aligns with the poetic goal I find in witness poetry: to encourage self-reflection in readers rather than to pass on the speaker's feeling to them (Pickard has reasons to focus on control in Bishop's poetry, but the difference between controlling the imagination and encouraging self-reflection is important for my study).

11 A "reverence for sun and fire" is tied, Womack suggests, to the Creek migration story explained as "a search for the sun" (Womack, *Red on Red* 55). See also note 6.

12 However, Rich also has moments when the map is inside the body (VII.14–15), so this is not a case of divergent tactics, but of the simultaneous existence of multiple ways of understanding the relationship of the individual to the community.

13 In section 5, the lines appear in the following manner:

> Where are we moored?   What
> are the bindings?   What be-
> hooves us?

Section 11 ends with the lines as follows:

> Where are we moored?
> What are the bindings?
> What behooves us?

14 In contrast, Hedley reads this address to readers as "disturbingly personal" (14) and focuses her analysis on the fact that her own "situation has not been captured in any of [Rich's] descriptions" (15). I find this assumption of readerly identification limiting. Hedley argues that the line "'I know you are reading this poem' is an apostrophe: an address to hypothetical readers that 'turns away from' the reader who is actually present" (15). But just because Hedley's situation has not been captured does not mean that no actual reader's situation has been. Hedley's response generalizes her experience as "the" reader's experience. The point in "Dedications" is that how this section speaks will differ among readers.

15 While this idea in Rich scholarship is sometimes stated as an accepted truth, some articles make the argument more particularly. Both Gilbert and Hedley compare Rich's earlier poem "Rape" and the later "Frame" to demonstrate what Rich learns after her earlier failure to poetically negotiate experiences not her own.

16 Useful here is Allen Grossman's essay "Whitman's 'Whoever You Are Holding Me Now in Hand': Remarks on the Endlessly Repeated Rediscovery of the Incommensurability of the Person," in which he argues that the "originality of Whitman consists of a poetic discourse which presents itself as none other than the speech of the principle of representation" (118). He reads Whitman's poem as "the reinvention of representation through the overcoming of representation with the intention of producing by poetic means a 'human form' that is truly human because free" (118). Free, that is, from the representational law that "visibility is *commensurability*" because "there is no image of the incommensurable, as there is no actual social formation characterized by equality" (114). It is, then, only through the words as they struggle to overcome the inequalities of representation that they might produce the "acknowledgment which has been made free (or as free as poetic originality can make it …)" (119).

CHAPTER THREE

1 For Jakobson, "the metaphoric step" is "based on association by similarity" as compared to the metonymic "association by contiguity" (128). He calls metonymy and metaphor "two radically different tropes that are both

artistic transformations – the former of contiguity and the latter of similarity" (129). Similarity works through "selection (the paradigmatic axis)" while contiguity works through "combination (the syntagmatic axis)" (130). As I note through Ernesto Laclau in my introduction, subsequent theories compete with Jakobson's placement of metonymy and metaphor on separate axes. Jakobson's theory allows me to consider the (primarily) contiguous strategy I find in witness poetry in contrast to the (primarily) substitutive strategy operating in the discourse surrounding witness poetry. My study emphasizes this separation although, in fact, substitution and contiguity cannot operate in isolation from one another.

2 "The capacity of two words to replace one another is an instance of positional similarity, and, in addition, all these responses are linked to the stimulus by semantic similarity (or contrast). Metonymical responses ... combine and contrast the positional similarity with semantic contiguity" (Jakobson and Halle 77). See "Two Aspects of Language" for the use of "Combination" and "Selection" (60).

3 While we might not immediately think of feeling as something we intend, the idea is particularly appropriate for considering poems which develop a sense of compassion as a mode of being. In this poetry, compassion is a feeling that one intends to promote in oneself.

4 Maureen Garvie explains in a news article about Maracle that "it was the custom for a carver on the West Coast to honor a woman in his life – mother, lover, wife – by making her a 'bent box.' Used to store precious things in, like ornaments, or medicines, it was made out of a single straight piece of wood, somehow transformed by its maker's special skill and magic into a square box" (1). According to Garvie, "the idea of taking something linear – like a log, or a story – and crafting it with the artist's special skill into something new and marvellous is an image Lee Maracle frequently comes back to when she talks about what she does as a writer" (1). In Maracle's words, "I take things out of context. I drop things in out of context and let everyone swim around them a little bit" (1). These observations are suggestive in relation to Maracle's compassion across borders.

5 Maracle's interest in compassion across borders is not limited to this collection. When asked about her perspective on the term "transnationalism," Maracle answers that Indigenous peoples "must look beyond our borders at the whole world, the conditions of our relatives everywhere, and include them in our sense of justice" (162).

6 In *Facing Up to Modernity: Excursions in Society, Politics, and Religion*,
   Peter L. Berger explains that "the broadest definition of patriotism would
   be *loving one's own*: This is my place, these are my people, and in this place
   and with these people I am most myself" (118). Berger also provides discussion on the ethical capacities of patriotism in relation to the suspicion it
   garners as an ideological force (124–5). It is further noteworthy, in thinking
   about particularity and abstraction, that Berger defines patriotism through
   the relationship between its communal or face-to-face aspect and a sense of
   belonging in the abstract (120–1).

7 The soul in section 5 of Whitman's *Leaves of Grass* has material presence.
   But the speaker addresses his individual, already completed soul: "I believe
   in you, my Soul" (22.1). It is "peace and knowledge" of God (25.1–4) that
   produces the soul as well as its community with other souls: "And I know
   that the spirit of God is the brother of my own; / And that all the men ever
   born are also my brothers" (25.3–4). In this example, a belief in a transcendent whole creates wholeness in the individual, rather than individuals
   coming together to form a whole and a transcendent surplus through that
   communal spirit. In both cases, though, a communal sense arises from a
   shared belief in community. Despite this depiction of the tangible individual
   soul, the community of souls depends on God's "promise," "spirit," and
   "love" (2, 3, 5).

8 As I will demonstrate, this metonymical relation of individual to community is much the same as that between reader and poem. Poetic community
   does not exist simply because individuals read the same poem, but it might
   exist if that group believes the poem to address readers meaningfully as a
   group. That is, poetic community occurs if a poem is successful in structuring a belief in readers about how the poem wishes to affect them.

9 Similarly, for Gwiazda, Rich asks if poetry is "capable of creating a common bond between people of different ethnic and social backgrounds"
   (179).

10 The girasol's standing in for more than the parts of the country as the additional binding element is evident in the flower's naming. While "sunflower"
   would indicate a direct connection between the plant and its source of life,
   girasol – "*gira-re* to turn + *sole* the sun" (OED) – shows the work of connection, the turning involved in building the relationship between the flower and
   what it faces.

11 "1866 J. LINDLEY & T. MOORE *Treasury Bot.* I. 575/1 The name of
   Jerusalem Artichoke is considered to be a corruption of the Italian *Girasole*

Articocco, or Sunflower Artichoke, under which name it is said to have been originally distributed from the Farnese garden at Rome soon after its introduction to Europe in 1617" (qtd. in OED, "artichoke").

12   This compassion across distance is a significant presence in Harjo's work more broadly. As Angelique V. Nixon notes, "Joy Harjo's poetry engages in the complex social and political issues of not only Native Americans but also other marginalized and oppressed peoples" (1).

13   In an interview with *Triplopia* collected in *Soul Talk, Song Language*, Harjo addresses another such move across contexts in "Returning from the Enemy," also from *A Map to the Next World*. She ends this poem with reference to a woman who sang as she was raped and killed in a massacre in El Salvador. Harjo questions this ending: "To take what was meant to destroy her and turn it into a song is one of the most powerful acts I have been witness to, and I was witness to it in a story that was printed in the *New Yorker* … And in the context of my poem/story sequence, which references a historical span of much degradation, killing, and theft, it made sense. It does make quite a leap, in the context, and that could, in the end, be an inherent weakness in the sequence" (12).

14   This collection uses several numbering systems, and I replicate these systems in my referencing. The first two parts of *On Ruins & Return* have numbered sections. I identify the parts by name and use Arabic numerals to identify the sections. The third part has named sections that are unnumbered. When referencing sections from this third part of the collection, I use the section titles. The fourth part also uses titles. The fifth and final part is a single titled poem.

15   The two quotations are: "*canst thou bind the buffalo with his band / in the furrow? or will he harrow / the valleys after thee*" (12–15) and "*who / hath, as it were / the strength / of the buffalo?*" (41–4); from Job 39:10 and Numbers 24:22, respectively (101).

16   We can compare this withholding to Harjo's withholdings. Unlike Harjo's poem, this withholding of the buffalo's name seems mobilized by the poem's logic: the speaker indicates a layered absence of the buffalo as it is for her the memory of what was a personal experience of the world, while for readers, it is the evocation of its presence, subsequent world-absence, and new memory-presence. For us, the buffalo itself was never present nor absent and withholding her name suggests that, even more for us than for the speaker, it is not ours to hold.

CHAPTER FOUR

1 Poverty, class, and capitalism are central concerns for both Murray and Brand in the poems I consider in this chapter as well as more generally. Gary Clark begins his article considering the role of Australia's history and ecology in Murray's corpus with an account of "the extent of the poverty" Murray grew up in (27), arguing that "the experience of poverty as a youngster seems to have grafted in him a heightened awareness of the hardships endured by the underprivileged. Being a poor rural child, it is no surprise that the natural world and issues of class, poverty, and economic centralization, became two of his main concerns as a poet" (28). A similar concern underpins Brand's *Inventory*. Cara Fabre argues that *Inventory* is concerned with "imaginative and concrete circuitries of capital within urban and global diasporas" and is part of Brand's "resistance work" against "the capitalist ideology that informs contemporary forms of colonization" (104–5).

2 The poem does not explain how the speaker witnesses the scene in the first place. The vagueness of the witnessing situation adds to the evidence that the speaker might tell more than he could know, that he moves beyond contiguity into identification. Even if the speaker imagines the entire situation, the contradictions in this imagining are telling in terms of how we might understand witness and compassion in the poem.

3 In *On the Edge of Genre: The Contemporary Canadian Long Poem*, Smaro Kamboureli describes such an "inscription of excess" as integral to the long poem (85). In an interview with Pauline Butling, Brand says that she prefers the long poem for this extra space: "I was starting to figure out how to do this fulsome and expressive thing and also this longer thing. But I wanted to figure out how I could do them both together ... I just don't like short poems. I don't think they're sufficient. I mean they can be, when people who can do it well do it well. But I wanted much more speech ... There is so much space to fill up and spill over and over and out and out" (79).

4 As Kamboureli notes, "The long poem ... makes itself felt through its discontinuities, its absences, and its deferrals by foregrounding both its writing process and our reading act" (xiv). This interest in "the materiality of language" (xiv) works, in relation to waiting here, with the long poem form, whose length makes the reading process indeed a kind of waiting. In this particular context, the materiality of language works to structure readers in relation to the speaker's modelling of response. The speaker's felt response to suffering is depicted as a physical pain of waiting. A reader is positioned

to encounter the poem as an experience of waiting, a felt response reaching outside of the poem to individual readers.

5 Pauline Butling, interviewing Brand, says that "it's very interesting as a writing position, to be addressing 'you' instead of speaking as 'I,' even though the 'you' may be the 'I.' And the 'you' can also include someone else" (80). Brand's response suggests the care with which she uses the 'you' in her poetry: "Yes, I'm very wary about using the 'you' because it's easy to sound accusatory. And that tone reveals that you're not taking any responsibility in the poem. Somebody else is always doing something. So it's very tricky to use it" (80).

6 When I speak of "the reader" I do not mean a monolithic conception of readerly experience, but, rather, the reader position which the poem structures and into which individual readers enter.

7 This invitation is conditional, offered only "if" the speaker were to say these things. Yet the conditional form of this offer invokes the "before and since" which I discuss later in this chapter: the offer is being made only potentially but, in being included in the poem, the speaker has already said what she says she might say. This offer, then, seems always to be in process, always potentially about to be offered and already offered. Like the state of waiting, this offer is less something that can ever be enacted than it is a mode of relation to the reader.

8 Note that the materializations in this poem are different from the sense of suffering's traces often understood to exist within witness poetry. In the discourse surrounding poetry representing the experience of atrocity or violence, there is an idea that another's suffering is touchable in the texture of poetry. This idea – paradoxically – combines with the conception that suffering cannot be adequately communicated, creating the sense that poetry overcomes its own (lacking) words to materialize the suffering it otherwise could not adequately express. To engage with Renu Bora's definitions of texture and texxture, critics sometimes take the "surface resonance" (98) of the poetry (the texture of fragmented lines and harsh sounds) as the "stuffness" (99) of the poet's material and historical experience (the texxture of suffering). In contrast, I see Brand's poem to make use of a connection between tangibility and emotion. Eve Kosofsky Sedgwick explores this connection in *Touching Feeling*. Sedgwick (also citing Bora in this introduction) indicates that her title "records the intuition that a particular intimacy seems to subsist between textures and emotions. But the same double meaning, tactile plus emotional, is already there in the single word 'touching'; equally it's internal

to the word 'feeling.' I am also encouraged in this association by the dubious epithet 'touchy-feely,' with its implication that even to talk about affect virtually amounts to cutaneous contact" (17).

9 I read *Inventory's* conception of grace to be outside of religious tradition. Theology enters the poem, but by way of the speaker's lack of faith (see pages 34, 70, 84). Yet, in relation to non-belief, the speaker asserts, "That's not a revolution you want, ever, to win, / the theory of nothing, theories of nothing in return" (48). The speaker's recoil from theories of nothing suggests to me her secular grace as a theory of something, that is, of meaningfulness, something in which one might believe in answer to its "imperishable beckoning."

10 Though Cheryl Lousley writes that "the complete perspective implied by inventory is impossible," she argues that this impossibility derives merely from the timing of the inventory, the speaker's "undertaking such a task at the beginning of the century" it inventories (37). On the contrary, I think it is important that *Inventory* suggests a list of a century's suffering could never be complete or completely understood.

11 Brydon understands Brand's poem to create "global intimacies" and "affective citizenship," terms which her article develops in relation to other current theories of intimacy in a global setting: "The implication of each in the other poses human relations in terms of complex entanglements that twine and cut in multiple directions … Edouard Glissant's 'poetics of relation' and Kamau Brathwaite's 'tidalectics' (Brathwaite, Dalleo, Reckin) move closer to characterizing the emotional geographies of Brand's social philosophy. These Caribbean-based theories mesh well with current theorizations of 'the new hybrid intercultures of the oceanic zone' (Ogborn), global flows (Appadurai), and rhizomatics (Deleuze and Guattari), and with the recent renewal of interest in affect (Brennan), especially subaltern affect (Beasley-Murray and Moreiras), and to some extent, in trauma theory (Johnson)" (998).

12 This distinction might seem unnecessary. Wouldn't a reader feeling a part of this witnessing community after reading this poem necessarily be affected by the speaker? Wouldn't a reader being affected by the speaker feel a kind of community with other imagined readers feeling similarly affected? Yet a poem depicting suffering has the potential to draw readers into a sense of duty to witness that comes precisely from this acknowledgement of duty, from an idea of moral conduct more than from emotion. Or, this desire to be part of such a community might come less from compassion than from the guilt of feeling implicated in these facts of suffering. In this poem titled

as an inventory, it is possible to minimize the role of the speaker outside of her witnessing relationship to suffering others. My reading emphasizes the import of the speaker as a depicted person and of the poetic relationship into which readers are positioned. I do not wish to negate the possibility of a wider community, but I am concerned with considering particularly the means by which this poem might go about creating that community.

13 Lousley is not alone in this perspective. Franca Bernabei comments on *Inventory*'s depersonalized speaker in her article on *Ossuaries*, "Shaking Up the Subject in *Ossuaries*: Dionne Brand's Lyrical Anti-Lyric" (206).

14 Brydon similarly understands the poem to privilege relationality: "*Inventory* shifts the terrain from the personal (with its focus on the autonomous individual as separate from others) to the intimate (that is, to the co-constitutions of subjectivity, image, word, and world and to a self developing through relation). Two models of autonomy are at stake here: the first developing from the concept of the individual as primary and the second from definitions of autonomy as always already relational. Unlike the personal, intimacy requires openness to others" (997)

15 A poetic moment built by words for whoever will enter suggests – as does my discussion, in my second chapter, of a similar readerly space in Rich's "An Atlas of the Difficult World" – Allen Grossman's argument about "the laws of the instrument of representation as the principle of life" (117) in Walt Whitman's "Whoever You Are Holding Me Now in Hand." For Grossman, Whitman's poem is a "revision of the fundamental logic of representation" (116): "*In effect, the story of the love of the person who is known by reason of representation (because he or she appears) will be already written as the history of representation itself. Why? Because the story of love always has the same structure as the representations which manifest the lover, so that the healing of the story of love consists of the overcoming of the structure of representation*" (117). Brand's poem reaches here for a reader as a "*companion*" who "*utters the laws of his own making*" (117).

16 Elaine Scarry describes a long tradition of understanding beauty as a beckoning: "Not Homer alone but Plato, Aquinas, Plotinus, Pseudo-Dionysius, Dante, and many others repeatedly describe beauty as a 'greeting.' At the moment one comes into the presence of something beautiful, it greets you. It lifts away from the neutral background as though coming forward to welcome you – as though the object were designed to 'fit' your perception. In its etymology, 'welcome' means that one comes with the well-wishes or consent of the person or thing already standing on that ground. It is as

though the welcoming thing has entered into, and consented to, your being in its midst. Your arrival seems contractual, not just something you want, but something the world you are joining wants" (25–6). She also suggests this beckoning is imperishable: "Something beautiful fills the mind yet invites the search for something beyond itself, something larger or something of the same scale with which it needs to be brought into relation" (29).

17 Bakhtin speaks of the poet and I of the speaker. The speaker indicates herself as the author of the text we read (the inventory/poem), so this distinction does not seem to me to be an issue. Moreover, though Bakhtin speaks of the union in one individual of the artist and the person, we can, I think, consider this same union of person and art-receiver.

18 I don't mean an impossible always-attention to everything. Rather, I am suggesting that a relationship to the world and other people limited to its flaws and their suffering cannot be the highest form of attention to which to aspire. Rectifying injustice depends on a fuller idea of what a person is than simply one who is vulnerable to suffering. While no one can be entirely open all of the time, it seems imperative to me that the ways and times in which one is open to another's happiness, or the beauty of art or experience of the world, or the profundity of another person's complexity, or the mundane details of daily life be included in considerations of ethical attention and relationship.

CHAPTER FIVE

1 The history Heaney explores is the diversity of the cultural past tied to the geographic location. As Henry Hart writes, Heaney's poetry sits often "at the midpoint between Irish and English literary traditions, Catholic and Protestant camps, Mediterranean and Norse mythologies" (393).

2 Meira Cook lists the multiple forms included in *Country of My Skull* (np).

3 *Wikipedia*'s entry on mimicry suggests the meaning behind Brand's "convergent mimesis": "Mimicry may involve morphology, behaviour, and other properties. In any case, the signal always functions to deceive the receiver by preventing it from correctly identifying the mimic. In evolutionary terms, this phenomenon is a form of co-evolution usually involving an evolutionary arms race. It should not be confused with convergent evolution, which occurs when species come to resemble one another independently by adapting to similar lifestyles." Thus, this mimesis is not even the coming together of adapting communities, but a contest for individual survival. Since

Brand could not expect the majority of her readers to be experts in this field, I use *Wikipedia* as the source readers are most likely to turn to for background knowledge when reading these lines.

4 The film is, however, socially engaged. Uhde provides the political context for *Kostnice*:

> Švankmajer filmed this extraordinary exhibit as a black-and-white
> 10-minute short soon after Czechoslovakia was invaded by the
> Soviet-led Warsaw Pact in August 1968. After a few brief months
> of the Prague Spring, the collective aspiration that the Communist
> regime might finally be liberalised and acquire a "human face" was
> shattered. The post-invasion regime, installed in the fall of 1969,
> became known especially for its repression of culture. (np)

Though "the film was commissioned as a 'cultural documentary,' a form popular with the authorities and considered relatively safe politically" (np), the original soundtrack – "banal, pedestrian, Party-line comments of the tour guide [which] deliberately counterpointed with the riot of skeletal imagery" (np) – was rejected as "ideologically unacceptable and the film-maker was forced to replace the commentary; he chose piano music with a female vocalist singing (in Czech) the surrealist poem by Jacques Prévert, 'Pour faire le portrait d'un oiseau' ('To Paint the Portrait of a Bird')" (np).

5 This pun works in English as it does in the original French.

6 Social and political activist Marlene Green died in 2002. Brand writes that, "beginning with her founding of the Black Education Project in the late 60s, Green's work became a lightning rod for black activism. Her organization was the nexus from which organizing emanated – advocacy and protests against racism in schools, in policing, in the workplace and in civic life" (np).

Bibliography

Ahmed, Sara. *The Cultural Politics of Emotion*. Edinburgh: Edinburgh UP, 2004. Print.

Altieri, Charles. *The Particulars of Rapture: An Aesthetics of the Affects*. Ithaca: Cornell UP, 2003. Print.

Amstutz, Mark R. "Intractable Politics without Truth or Forgiveness: The Case of Northern Ireland." *The Healing of Nations: The Promise and Limits of Political Forgiveness*. Toronto: Rowman and Littlefield, 2005. 164–86. Print.

Anderson, Benedict. *Imagined Communities: Reflections on the Origin and Spread of Nationalism*. London: Verso, 2006. Print.

Antoine-Dunne, Jean. "Look, We Movin Now." *The Routledge Companion to Anglophone Caribbean Literature*. Ed. Michael A. Bucknor and Alison Donnell. New York: Routledge, 2011. 591–8. Print.

"Artichoke." *Oxford English Dictionary*. Oxford: Oxford UP, 2000. Web. 22 Jan. 2013.

"Attend." *Oxford English Dictionary*. Oxford: Oxford UP, 2000. Web. 9 Aug. 2013.

"Attendance." *Oxford English Dictionary*. Oxford: Oxford UP, 2000. Web. 15 Jan. 2012.

"Awry." *Oxford English Dictionary*. Oxford: Oxford UP, 2000. Web. 15 Jan. 2012.

Back, Rachel Tzvia. *On Ruins & Return: The Buffalo Poems (1999–2005)*. Exeter, UK: Shearsman, 2007. Print.

Bakhtin, Mikhail. "Art and Answerability." *Art and Answerability: Early Philosophical Essays by M.M. Bakhtin*. Ed. Michael Holquist and Vadim Liapunov, trans. Austin, TX: U of Texas P., 1990. 1–3. Print.

Balakian, Peter. *Black Dog of Fate: A Memoir*. New York: BasicBooks, 1997. Print.

– "Carolyn Forché and the Poetry of Witness: Another View." *Agni* 40 (1994): 186–93. JSTOR. Web. 2 Oct. 2015.

– "Falling into a Rug: Some Notes on Imagination and the Artifact." *Peter Balakian*. Web. 12 Aug. 2013.

– *June-tree: New and Selected Poems, 1974–2000*. New York: Perennial, 2001. Print.

Balzac, Honoré de. *Colonel Chabert*. Trans. Carol Cosman. New York: New Directions, 1997.

Bedrosian, Margaret. *The Magical Pine Ring: Culture and the Imagination in Armenian-American Literature*. Detroit, MI: Wayne State UP, 1991.

Berger, James. *After the End: Representations of Post-Apocalypse*. Minneapolis, MN: U of Minnesota P, 1999. Print.

Berger, Peter L. *Facing Up to Modernity: Excursions in Society, Politics, and Religion*. New York: Basic Books, 1977. Print.

Berlant, Lauren, ed. "Compassion (and Withholding)." *Compassion: The Culture and Politics of an Emotion*. New York: Routledge, 2004. 1–14. Print.

– "Intimacy: A Special Issue." *Critical Inquiry* 24.2 (1998): 281–8. *JSTOR*. Web. 24 Mar. 2013.

Bernabei, Franca. "Shaking Up the Subject in *Ossuaries*: Dionne Brand's Lyrical Anti-Lyric." In Sanders and Smyth 204–20.

Bery, Ashok. *Cultural Translation and Postcolonial Poetry*. New York: Palgrave, 2007. Print.

Bishop, Elizabeth. "In the Waiting Room." *Poems*. New York: Farrar, Straus and Giroux, 2011. 179–81. Print.

– "The Map." *Poems*. New York: Farrar, Straus and Giroux, 2011. 5. Print.

Bora, Renu. "Outing Texture." *Novel Gazing: Queer Readings in Fiction*. Ed. Eve Kosofsky Sedgwick. Durham: Duke UP, 1997. 94–127. Print.

Brand, Dionne. *A Map to the Door of No Return*. New York: Vintage, 2002. Print.

– "Dionne Brand on Struggle and Community, Possibility and Poetry." Interview by Pauline Butling. *Poets Talk*. Ed. Pauline Butling and Susan Rudy. Edmonton: U of Alberta P, 2005. 63–87. Print.

– *Inventory*. Toronto: McClelland and Stewart, 2006. Print.

– "Marlene Green: 1940–2002." *NOW* 22.10 (2002): np. Web. 29 Mar. 2013.

– *Ossuaries*. Toronto: McClelland and Stewart, 2010. Print.

– "'To Promote Statements That Don't Have an End': In Conversation with Dionne Brand." Interview with E. Martin Nolan. *The Puritan* 11 (2010): np. Web. 4 Sept. 2015.

"Brooding." *Oxford English Dictionary*. Oxford: Oxford UP, 2000. Web. 10 Jan. 2013.

Brydon, Diana. "Dionne Brand's Global Intimacies: Practising Affective Citizenship." *University of Toronto Quarterly* 76.3 (2007): 990–1006. *Project Muse*. Web. 9 Jan. 2012.

"Burning." *Oxford English Dictionary*. Oxford: Oxford UP, 2000. Web. 31 Mar. 2013.

Canovan, Margaret. *Nationhood and Political Theory*. Northampton, MA: Edward Elgar, 1996. Print.

Caruth, Cathy. *Literature in the Ashes of History*. Baltimore, MD: John Hopkins, 2013. Print.

– *Unclaimed Experience: Trauma, Narrative, and History*. Baltimore, MD: John Hopkins, 1996. Print.

Chipasula, Frank M. "Double Song." *Ariel* 12. 3 (1981): np. Web. 20 Nov. 2016.

– "Manifesto on Ars Poetica." *The African Book Review*. 27 Nov. 2014. Web. 25 Nov. 2016.

Chirambo, Reuben Makayiko. "'A Monument to a Tyrant,' or Reconstructed Nationalist Memories of the Father and Founder of the Malawi Nation, Dr. H.K. Banda." *Africa Today* 56.4 (2010): 2–21. *JSTOR*. Web. 2 Oct. 2015.

– "Dissident Writing: Home and Exile in Frank Chipasula's *Whispers in the Wings*." *Marang* 19 (2009): 1–21. Web. 3 Oct. 2015.

Cimarosti, Roberta. "Metaphor and Metonymy in Derek Walcott's Poetry." *Annali Di Ca' Foscari* 35.1–2 (1996): 131–53. Web. 26 Sept. 2015.

Clark, Gary. "History and Ecology: The Poetry of Les Murray and Gary Snyder." *Isle: Interdisciplinary Studies in Literature and Environment*. 10.1 (2003): 27–53. *Oxford Journals*. Web. 25 Jul. 2015.

Clark, Miriam Marty. "Human Rights and the Work of Lyric in Adrienne Rich." *The Cambridge Quarterly* 38.1 (2009): 45–65. *Project Muse*. Web. 6 Jul. 2015.

"Come back." *Oxford English Dictionary*. Oxford: Oxford UP, 2000. Web. 9 Sept. 2015.

"Commemoration." *Oxford English Dictionary*. Oxford: Oxford UP, 2000. Web. 31 Mar. 2013.

"Compassion." *Oxford English Dictionary*. Oxford: Oxford UP, 2000. Web. 9 Jan. 2013.

"Confession." *Oxford English Dictionary*. Oxford: Oxford UP, 2000. Web. 12 Jun. 2015.

"Consideration." *Oxford English Dictionary*. Oxford: Oxford UP, 2000. Web. 15 Jan. 2012.

Cook, Meira. "Metaphors for Suffering: Antjie Krog's *Country of My Skull*." *Mosaic* 34.3 (2001): 73–89. *ProQuest*. Web. 31 Mar. 2013.

Corcoran, Neil. *Poetry and Responsibility*. Liverpool: Liverpool UP, 2014. Print.

Crane, Hart. *The Complete Poems of Hart Crane*. Ed. Marc Simon. New York: Liveright, 2001. Print.

Cuda, Anthony J. "The Use of Memory: Seamus Heaney, T.S. Eliot, and the Unpublished Epigraph to 'North.'" *Journal of Modern Literature* 28.4 (2005): 152–75. *JSTOR*. Web. 28 Aug. 2015.

Davidson, Harriet. "Poetry, Witness, Feminism." In Vogler and Douglass 153–72.

"Dedication." *Oxford English Dictionary*. Oxford: Oxford UP, 2000. Web. 26 July 2012.

Donnelly, Brian. "'The Digging Skeleton after Baudelaire', Seamus Heaney." *Irish University Review: a Journal of Irish Studies* 39.2 (2009): 246–54. *Academic OneFile*. Web. 17 Sept. 2015.

Dorfman, Ariel. *Death and the Maiden*. New York: Penguin, 1991.

Douglas, Mary. "Foreword." In Mauss vii–xviii.

Eagleton, Mary. "Adrienne Rich, Location and the Body." *Journal of Gender Studies*. 9.3 (2000): 299–312. MLA *International Bibliography*. Web. 6 July 2015.

Edelman, Lee. "The Geography of Gender: Elizabeth Bishop's 'In the Waiting Room.'" *Contemporary Literature*. 26.2 (1985): 179–96. *JSTOR*. Web. 26 July 2012.

"Empathy." *Oxford English Dictionary*. Oxford: Oxford UP, 2000. Web. 9 June 2011.

Erkkila, Betsy, and Jay Grossman, eds. *Breaking Bounds: Whitman and American Cultural Studies*. New York: Oxford UP, 1996. Print.

Fabre, Cara. "From Cultural Transformation to Systemic Resistance through Dionne Brand's *thirsty* and *Inventory*." In Sanders and Smyth 101–23.

"Fathom." *Oxford English Dictionary*. Oxford: Oxford UP, 2000. Web. 30 July 2015.

Felman, Shoshana, and Dori Laub. *Testimony: Crises of Witnessing in Literature, Psychoanalysis, and History*. New York: Routledge, 1992. Print.

"Folds." *Oxford English Dictionary*. Oxford: Oxford UP, 2000. Web. 18 Mar. 2013.

Forché, Carolyn, ed. *Against Forgetting: Twentieth-Century Poetry of Witness*. New York: Norton, 1993. Print.

– "The Poetry of Witness." *The Writer in Politics*. Ed. William H. Gass and Lorin Cuoco. Carbondale: Southern Illinois UP, 1996. 135–61. Print.

Forster, Sophia. "'inventory is useless now but just to say': The Politics of Ambivalence in Dionne Brand's *Land to Light On*." *Studies in Canadian Literature* 27.2 (2002): 160–82. *ProQuest*. Web. 30 July 2015.

"Furnish." *Oxford English Dictionary*. Oxford: Oxford UP, 2000. Web. 10 Jan. 2013.

Gaffney, Carmel, ed. *Counterbalancing Light: Essays on the Poetry of Les Murray*. Armidale, NSW: Kardoorair, 1997. Print.

Garman, Anthea. "Global Resonance, Local Amplification: Antjie Krog on a World Stage." *Social Dynamics* 36.1 (2010): 187–200. *Scholars Portal*. Web. Aug. 21 2015.

Garvie, Maureen. "Remaking the Bent Box." *Whig-Standard* 13 Apr. 1991: 1. *ProQuest*. Web. 2 Oct. 2015.

Gibbs, James. "Singing in the Dark Rain." *Index on Censorship*. 17 (1988): 18–22. Print.

Giles, Paul. *Hart Crane: The Contexts of "The Bridge."* Cambridge: Cambridge UP, 1986. Print.

"Girasol." *Oxford English Dictionary*. Oxford: Oxford UP, 2000. Web. 22 Jan. 2013.

"Grace." *Oxford English Dictionary*. Oxford: Oxford UP, 2000. Web. 10 Jan. 2013.

Grossman, Allen. "Whitman's 'Whoever You Are Holding Me Now in Hand': Remarks on the Endlessly Repeated Rediscovery of the Incommensurability of the Person." *Breaking Bounds: Whitman and American Cultural Studies*. Ed. Betsy Erkkila and Jay Grossman. New York: Oxford UP, 1996. 112–22. Print.

Gubar, Susan. *Poetry after Auschwitz: Remembering What One Never Knew*. Indianapolis: Indiana UP, 2003. Print.

Gwiazda, Piotr. "'Nothing Else Left to Read': Poetry and Audience in Adrienne Rich's 'An Atlas of the Difficult World.'" *Journal of Modern Literature* 28.2 (2005): 165–88. *JSTOR*. Web. 7 June 2015.

Harjo, Joy. *A Map to the Next World: Poems and Tales*. New York: Norton,
   2000. Print.

– "A Map to the Next World" and "Grace." *Poetry Foundation*. Web. 22 Nov.
   2016.

– *The Spiral of Memory: Interviews*. Ed. Laura Coltelli. Ann Arbor, MI: U of
   Michigan P, 1996. Print.

Harjo, Joy, and Gloria Bird, eds. *Reinventing the Enemy's Language:
   Contemporary Native Women's Writings of North America*. New York:
   Norton, 1997. Print.

Harjo, Joy, and Tanaya Winder, eds. *Soul Talk, Song Language: Conversations
   with Joy Harjo*. Middletown, CT: Wesleyan UP, 2011. Print.

Hart, Henry. "History, Myth, and Apocalypse in Seamus Heaney's 'North.'"
   Contemporary Literature 30.3 (1989): 387–411. JSTOR. Web. 10 Mar. 2013.

Heaney, Seamus. "A Basket of Chestnuts." *Seeing Things*. London: Faber and
   Faber, 1991. Print.

– "A Basket of Chestnuts." *Seeing Things*. New York: Farrar, Straus and
   Giroux, 1993. Print.

– "Belfast." *Preoccupations: Selected Prose 1968–1978*. Boston: Faber and
   Faber, 1980. 28–37. Print.

– "Bone Dreams." *Opened Ground: Selected Poems 1966–1996*. New York:
   Farrar, Straus and Giroux, 1998. Print.

– "The Digging Skeleton *After Baudelaire*." *North*. London: Faber and Faber,
   1975. Print.

– "The Sense of Place." *Preoccupations: Selected Prose 1968–1978*. Boston:
   Faber and Faber, 1980. 131–149. Print.

Hedley, Jane. *I Made You to Find Me: The Coming of Age of the Woman Poet
   and the Politics of Poetic Address*. Columbus, OH: Ohio State UP, 2009. Print.

Henneberg, Sylvia. "The Self-Categorization, Self-Canonization, and Self-
   Periodization of Adrienne Rich." *Challenging Boundaries: Gender and
   Periodization*. Ed. Joyce W. Warren and Margaret Dickie. Athens, GA: U of
   Georgia P, 2000. 267–83. Print.

"Humane." *Oxford English Dictionary*. Oxford: Oxford UP, 2000. Web. 15
   Oct. 2015.

Hungerford, Amy. "Memorizing Memory." *Yale Journal of Criticism* 14.1
   (2001): 67–92. *Project Muse*. Web. 25 June 2015.

Hussain, Azfar. "Joy Harjo and Her Poetics as Praxis: A 'Postcolonial' Political

Economy of the Body, Land, Labor, and Language." *Wicazo Sa Review* 15.2 (2000): 27–61. *Project Muse*. Web. 9 July 2015.

"Index." *Oxford English Dictionary*. Oxford: Oxford UP, 2000. Web. 5 July 2012.

Izenberg, Oren. "We Are Reading: Collective Intentions across Poems." *Modern Philology* 105.1 (2007): 91–112. *JSTOR*. Web. 10 Jan. 2013.

Jacobs, Joshua S. "'An Atlas of the Difficult World': Adrienne Rich's Countermonument." *Contemporary Literature* 42.4 (2001): 727–49. *JSTOR*. Web. 7 July 2015.

– "Mapping after the Holocaust: The 'Atlases' of Adrienne Rich and Gerhard Richter." *Mosaic* 32.4 (1999): 111–27. *ProQuest*. Web. 7 July 2015.

Jakobson, Roman, and Krystyna Pomorska. *Dialogues*. Trans. Christian Hubert. Cambridge, MA: Massachusetts Institute of Technology, 1983. Print.

Jakobson, Roman and Morris Halle. *Fundamentals of Language*. The Hague: Mouton, 1956.

Kalaidjian, Walter. *The Edge of Modernism: American Poetry and the Traumatic Past*. Baltimore: John Hopkins UP, 2006. Print.

Kamboureli, Smaro. *On the Edge of Genre: The Contemporary Canadian Long Poem*. Toronto: U of Toronto P, 1991. Print.

Kay, Magdalena. *In Gratitude for All the Gifts: Seamus Heaney and Eastern Europe*. Toronto: U of Toronto P, 2012. Print.

Keen, Suzanne. *Empathy and the Novel*. Oxford: Oxford UP, 2007. Print.

Kostnice. Dir. Jan Švankmajer. Krátký Film Praha, 2009. Film.

Krog, Antjie. *Country of My Skull*. New York: Three Rivers, 1998. Print.

– trans. "Country of Grief and Grace." *Poetry International Web*. Web. 22 Nov. 2016.

LaCapra, Dominick. "Lanzmann's 'Shoah': 'Here There Is No Why.'" *Critical Inquiry* 23.2 (1997): 231–69. *JSTOR*. Web. 25 June 2015.

– *Writing History, Writing Trauma*. Baltimore: Johns Hopkins UP, 2001. Print.

Laclau, Ernesto. *The Rhetorical Foundations of Society*. New York: Verso, 2014.

Leer, Martin. "Gravity and Grace: Towards a Meta-Physics of Embodiment in the Poetry of Les Murray." In Gaffney 137–58.

Leys, Ruth. *Trauma: A Genealogy*. Chicago: U of Chicago P, 2000.

Lock, Charles. "*Fredy Neptune*: Metonymy and the Incarnate Preposition."

Australian Literary Studies 20.2 (2001): 122–41. *Academic Search Complete.* Web. 14 Aug. 2015.

Loizeaux, Elizabeth Bergmann. "Women Looking: The Feminist Ekphrasis of Marianne Moore and Adrienne Rich." Cranbury, NJ: Rosemont, 2009. 121–44. Print.

Lousley, Cheryl. "Witness to the Body Count: Planetary Ethics in Dionne Brand's *Inventory.*" *Canadian Poetry* 63 (2008): 37–58. Print.

Macdonald, Tanis. "Bone Memory in Dionne Brand's *Ossuaries.*" *The Memory Effect: The Remediation of Memory in Literature and Film.* Eds. Russell J.A. Kilbourn and Eleanor Ty. Waterloo, ON: Wilfrid Laurier, 2013. 93–106. Print.

Mapanje, Jack. *Skipping without Ropes.* Newcastle upon Tyne: Bloodaxe, 1998. Print.

Maracle, Lee. *Bent Box.* Penticton, BC: Theytus Books, 2000. Print.

– "An Interview with Lee Maracle." Interview by Chantal Fiola. *Transnationalism, Activism, Art.* Ed. Kit Dobson and Áine McGlynn. Toronto: U of Toronto P, 2013. 162–70. Print.

Matthews, Steven. *Les Murray.* Manchester: Manchester UP, 2001. Print.

Mauss, Marcel. *The Gift: The Form and Reason for Exchange in Archaic Societies.* Trans. W.D. Halls. London, UK: Routledge, 1990. Print.

McGowan, Joseph. "Heaney, Caedmon, Beowulf." *New Hibernia Review* 6.2 (2002): 25–42. *Project Muse.* Web. 11 July 2011.

Merriman, Emily Taylor. "'The spider's genius': Verse Technique as Liberating Force in Adrienne Rich's Poetry." *"Catch if you can your country's moment": Recovery and Regeneration in the Poetry of Adrienne Rich.* Ed. William S. Waddell. Newcastle upon Tyne, UK: Cambridge Scholars, 2007. 6–26. Print.

Meyer, Sara. "'Another Attempt at Mastering Infinity': Elizabeth Bishop's Art of Map-Making." *Divisions of the Heart: Elizabeth Bishop and the Art of Memory and Place.* Ed. Gwendolym Davies, Sandra Barry, and Peter Sanger. Kentville, NS: Gaspereau, 2001. 237–48. Print.

Miller, David. "The Nation-State: A Modest Defense." *Political Restructuring in Europe.* Ed. C. Brown. New York: Routledge, 1994. Print.

"Mimicry." *Wikipedia.* Web. 15 Sept. 2015.

Mitchell, Renae L. "A Trans-Atlantic Vandal: Omeros and the Ekphrastic Counter-monument." *Callaloo* 38.1 (2015): 150–66. *Project Muse.* Web. 26 Sept. 2015.

Mitchell, W.J.T. *Picture Theory: Essays on Verbal and Visual Representation.* Chicago: U of Chicago P, 1994. Print.

"Moraine." *Oxford English Dictionary*. Oxford: Oxford UP, 2000. Web. 9 Sept. 2015.

Mossin, Andrew. "Against Witness as Such." *Jacket* 35 (2008): np. Web. 11 Oct. 2015.

Murphy, Sara. "Mourning and Metonymy: Bearing Witness between Women and Generations." *Hypatia* 19.4 (2004): 142–66. *Project Muse*. Web. 31 July 2012.

Murray, Les. "Letters to the Winner." *Australian Poetry Library*. Web. 25 Nov. 2016.

– "Les Murray, The Art of Poetry No. 89." Interview by Dennis O'Driscoll. *The Paris Review*. 173 (2005): np. Web. 12 Aug. 2015.

Muscogee (Creek) Nation. Muscogee Creek Nation, 2008. Web. 5 Jan. 2012. http://www.mcn-nsn.gov/culturehistory/.

Nelson, Penelope. "Irony, Identity and Les Murray's Poetic Voices." In Gaffney 170–83.

Nixon, Angelique V. "Poem and Tale as Double Helix in Joy Harjo's *A Map to the Next World*." *Sail* 18.1 (2006): 1–21. *Literature Online*. Web. 10 July 2015.

Nussbaum, Martha C. *Poetic Justice: The Literary Imagination and Public Life*. Boston: Beacon, 1995. Print.

– *Upheavals of Thought: The Intelligence of Emotions*. Cambridge: Cambridge UP, 2001. Print.

Oliver, Kelly. *Witnessing: Beyond Recognition*. Minneapolis, MN: U of Minnesota P, 2001. Print.

"Ordnance." *Oxford English Dictionary*. Oxford: Oxford UP, 2000. Web. 10 Jan. 2013.

"Ossuary." *Oxford English Dictionary*. Oxford: Oxford UP, 2000. Web. 29 Mar. 2013.

Pederson, Joshua. "Speak, Trauma: Toward a Revised Understanding of Literary Trauma Theory." *Narrative* 22.3 (2014): 333–53. *Project Muse*. Web. 4 July 2015.

The Phoenix Project. Associated Medical Services. Web. 4 Oct. 2015. http://www.ams-inc.on.ca/bringing-compassion-to-healthcare/phoenix-fellows-grantees/.

Pickard, Zachariah. *Elizabeth Bishop's Poetics of Description*. Montreal and Kingston: McGill-Queen's UP, 2009.

Prévert, Jacques. "Pour faire le portrait d'un oiseau." Trans. Jacqueline Michaud. (2007). *Calque*. Web. 31 Mar. 2013.

Quema, Anne. "Dionne Brand's Ossuaries: Songs of Necropolitics." *Canadian Literature* 222 (2014): 52. *Canadian Periodicals Index Quarterly*. Web. 17 Sept. 2015.

Radstone, Susannah. "Trauma Theory: Context, Politics, Ethics." *Paragraph* 30.1 (2007): 9–29. *Project Muse*. Web. 25 June 2015.

Renan, Ernest. "What Is a Nation?" *Becoming National: A Reader*. Ed. Geoff Eley and Ronald Grigor Suny. New York: Oxford UP, 1996. 42–55. Print.

"Revise." *Oxford English Dictionary*. Oxford: Oxford UP, 2000. Web. 22 Jan. 2013.

"Rhetorical Situations." *Online Writing Lab*. Purdue University. Web. 3 Aug. 2015.

Rich, Adrienne. *An Atlas of the Difficult World: Poems 1988–1991*. New York: Norton, 1991. Print.

– *Blood, Bread, and Poetry: Selected Prose 1979–1985*. New York: Norton, 1986. Print.

– "Someone Is Writing a Poem." *What Is Found There: Notebooks on Poetry and Politics*. New York: Norton, 1993. 83–9. Print.

Riley, Jeanette E. "The 'Words Are Maps': Traveling the Poetry of Adrienne Rich." *"Catch if you can your country's moment": Recovery and Regeneration in the Poetry of Adrienne Rich*. Ed. William S. Waddell. Newcastle upon Tyne, UK: Cambridge Scholars, 2007. 121–40. Print.

Ryan, Terre. *This Ecstatic Nation: The American Landscape and the Aesthetics of Patriotism*. Boston: U of Massachusetts P, 2011. Print.

Sanders, Leslie C., ed. "Introduction." *Fierce Departures: The Poetry of Dionne Brand*. Waterloo, ON: Wilfrid Laurier UP, 2009. ix–xvi. Print.

Sanders, Leslie C., and Heather Smyth. "Critical Perspectives on Dionne Brand." *MaComère* 14.1–2 (2013–14). Print.

– "'Nothing Soothing': Critical Perspectives on the Work of Dionne Brand." In Sanders and Smyth 3–11.

Scarry, Elaine. *On Beauty and Being Just*. Princeton: Princeton UP, 1999. Print.

– *The Body in Pain*. New York: Oxford, 1985. Print.

Sedgwick, Eve Kosofsky. "Reality and Realization." *The Weather in Proust*. Ed. Jonathan Goldberg. Durham, NC: Duke UP, 2011. 206–15. Print.

– *Touching Feeling: Affect, Pedagogy, Performativity*. Durham, NC: Duke UP, 2003. Print.

Sedlec Ossuary. Web. 13 Apr. 2013. sedlecossuary.com.

Shreiber, Maeera. "'Where Are We Moored?': Adrienne Rich, Women's Mourning, and the Limits of Lament." *Dwelling in Possibility: Women Poets and Critics on Poetry*. Ed. Yopie Prins and Maeera Shreiber. Ithaca: Cornell UP, 1997. 301–17. Print.

"Sympathy." *Oxford English Dictionary*. Oxford: Oxford UP, 2000. Web. 9 June 2011.

Templeton, Alice. *The Dream and the Dialogue: Adrienne Rich's Feminist Poetics*. Knoxville: U of Tennessee P, 1994.

Topper, Ryan. "Review: *Literature in the Ashes of History*." *Parallax* 21:1 (2015): np. *Scholars Portal*. Web. 16 Oct. 2015.

"Tour." *Oxford English Dictionary*. Oxford: Oxford UP, 2000. Web. 2 Sept. 2014.

Uhde, Jan. "The Bare Bones of Horror." *Kinoeye: New Perspectives on European Film*. 2.1 (2002): np. Web. 26 Mar. 2013.

Vellino, Brenda Carr. "Beyond the Trauma Aesthetic: The Cultural Work of Human Rights Witness Poetries." *The Routledge Companion to Literature and Human Rights*. Eds. Sophia A. McClennen and Alexandra Schultheis Moore. New York: Routledge, 2016. 148–58. Print.

– "'History's Pulse Measured with Another Hand': Precarity Archives and Translocal Citizen Witness in Dionne Brand's *Inventory*." *University of Toronto Quarterly* 82.2 (2013): 242–60. *Project Muse*. Web. 30 July 2015.

Vendler, Helen. *Poems, Poets, Poetry: An Introduction and an Anthology*. Boston: Bedford, 1996. Print.

Vogler, Thomas A. "Poetic Witness: Writing the Real." In Vogler and Douglass 173–205.

Vogler, Thomas A., and Ana Douglass, eds. *Witness and Memory: The Discourse of Trauma*. New York: Routledge, 2003. Print.

Walcott, Derek. "Derek Walcott, The Art of Poetry No. 37." Interview with Edward Hirsch. *Paris Review* 101 (1986): np. Web. 26 Sept. 2015.

– "Ruins of a Great House." *The Poetry Archive*. np. Web. 11 Nov. 2016.

– Warner, Michael. "Whitman Drunk." In Erkkila and Grossman 30–43.

Warrior, Robert. "Your Skin Is the Map: The Theoretical Challenge of Joy Harjo's Erotic Poetics." *Reasoning Together*. Ed. Craig S. Womack, Daniel Heath Justice, and Cristopher B. Teuton. Norman, OK: U of Oklahoma P, 2008. Print.

Waters, William. *Poetry's Touch: On Lyric Address*. Ithaca, NY: Cornell UP, 2003. Print.

Watkins, Paul. "Listening to a Listening: The Disruptive Jazz Poetics of Dionne Brand's *Ossuaries* (a call towards freedom)." In Sanders and Smyth 124–51.

Whitman, Walt. "Crossing Brooklyn Ferry." *Poets.org*. Academy of American Poets. Web. 25 July 2015.

– "To a Stranger." *The Portable Walt Whitman*. Ed. Michael Warner. New York: Penguin, 2004. 21. Print.

– "Whoever You Are Holding Me Now in Hand." Warner 213.

"Witness." *Oxford English Dictionary*. Oxford: Oxford UP, 2000. Web. 18 Jan. 2012.

Womack, Craig S. *Red on Red: Native American Literary Separatism*. Minnesota: U of Minnesota P, 1999. Print.

Young, James E. *At Memory's Edge: After-Images of the Holocaust in Contemporary Art and Architecture*. New Haven, CT: Yale UP, 2002.

Zimmerman, Lee. "The Weirdest Scale on Earth: Elizabeth Bishop and Containment." *American Imago* 61.4 (2004): 495–518. *Project Muse*. Web. 26 July 2012.

Index